Operation Demetrius and its aftermath

A new history of the use of internment without trial in Northern Ireland, 1971–75

Martin J. McCleery

Manchester University Press

Published by Manchester University Press
Altrincham Street, Manchester M1 7JA, UK
www.manchesteruniversitypress.co.uk

British Library Cataloguing-in-Publication Data is available

ISBN 978 0 7190 9630 3 hardback
ISBN 978 1 5261 5026 4 paperback

First published by Manchester University Press in hardback 2015

This edition published 2020

Typeset by Out of House Publishing

From the past for the future, Dessie
and Maidhe Jade

Contents

Preface

One Saturday afternoon in the summer of 1972 two young boys sang the anti-internment ballad 'The Men Behind the Wire' for their father and a group of his workmates on their way home from Bangor. I was one of those young boys, and, unsurprisingly, I never realised how long the recollection of this unremarkable event would stay with me. My overriding memory of that day was leaving the van with my pockets bulging with the loose change I had received for our rendition of the song. As I grew older and learnt more about my family's past, I discovered that my great-grandfather, my grandfather and all his brothers and, indeed, my father had all served in the British Army. My Protestant grandfather married my Catholic grandmother, and, consequently, my father and all his siblings were brought up in the Catholic faith. However, there was no way that my family could have been remotely considered a republican family before 1971. So it always intrigued me how I had ended up singing a republican song for my father and his colleagues that Saturday afternoon. As a consequence, I developed a fascination with the internment period. Indeed, it was around this time also that my eldest brother, Dessie, as a young teenager, was to join the youth wing of the Official Irish Republican Army; he was murdered years later in a republican feud. Fast forward almost forty years, and it just seemed the obvious choice for me to research some aspect of internment for my Ph.D. My expectation was that the use of the measure during this period had already been covered by the existing literature. However, as I began to explore the period, I gradually became more and more convinced that the use of internment had not been given any proper investigation. Indeed, the only books that gave internment significant consideration were John McGuffin's two contemporary anti-establishment monographs, *Internment* and *The Guineapigs*, and Thomas Hennessey's more recent *The Evolution of the Troubles*, which dedicates one chapter to internment. Thus, the central premise of my thesis and subsequently this book became the contention that a re-examination of internment was not only desirable but essential to any story of the development of the early Troubles. Despite the amount of research I have carried out while writing this book, I am acutely aware that I have not had access to many files regarding the use of internment. As a result, this re-examination of the measure should not be considered as the definitive history of its use but very much as a basis for further investigation.

Many people have helped me along the way – too many to mention. I would like to thank all my fellow students and staff in the School of History, the Institute of Irish Studies and the School of Politics, International Studies and Philosophy at Queen's University Belfast, who have made my academic journey thus far so enjoyable. Special mention goes to my Ph.D. examiners, Professor Paul Bew and Dr Niall Ó Dochartaigh, whose constructive criticisms added much to my research. I am forever thankful to my Ph.D. supervisor, Dr Margaret O'Callaghan, whose depth of knowledge never ceased to amaze me. I could not have asked for a better supervisor; her guidance was invaluable. Of course, I would like to thank all my family and friends for their patience and understanding. Two ladies in particular have helped me so much in different ways. My loving mother, Isobel, has been an inspiration to me all my life, and my partner, Lorraine, has given freely of her time throughout this project. It is true to say that the completion of this book would not have been possible without them both.

Foreword

Martin McCleery's *Operation Demetrius and its Aftermath* is a thoughtful, well-researched study of a major episode in Northern Irish history. It focuses on a bloodstained and awful period in the politics of the North, and on the use there of internment without trial during the early 1970s. The book offers a nuanced and fascinating reappraisal of an issue that is too often read too simply, and it adds regional detail in particularly valuable fashion.

Against the tragic deterioration of Northern Ireland into political violence at the start of the 1970s, the United Kingdom and Northern Ireland governments both, reasonably enough, focused attention on how to rectify a terrible security situation.

The head of the British Army in Northern Ireland and also of the Royal Ulster Constabulary argued against recourse to internment; by contrast, the Northern Ireland Prime Minister, Brian Faulkner, favoured its use. Internment had been used with some effectiveness in previous periods of Northern Ireland's past and now again, on 9 August 1971, it was deployed.

Those initially lifted were all from the nationalist community, and the one-sidedness of this 1971 implementation represented one of the endeavour's major problems. Many people in nationalist communities had already come to see the UK state in the North as hostile to their interests. The one-sidedness of the 9 August swoop confirmed this in many people's eyes.

It was not that the arrests were indiscriminate, nor that the intelligence on which they were based was uniformly wrong. But many who were lifted were people without paramilitary involvement, and many who were justifiably named on the original arrest list evaded capture. In those senses, the intelligence as deployed was insufficiently accurate: some names were simply the wrong ones; and some of the right names referred to people on whom up-to-the-minute intelligence clearly did not exist satisfactorily, because the authorities did not know where they were when they tried to arrest them.

Of course, as McCleery rightly makes clear, internment was not merely about taking terrorists off the streets; its aims also involved reassurance of the majority unionist community that the state was effectively dealing with the emergent crisis in Northern Ireland. Far too many analyses of Northern Irish politics discuss UK dealings with Irish republicans without recognising this crucial point: that reassurance to the majority community was itself a way of limiting terrorist violence, given that loyalist attacks tended to increase when loyalist communities felt that the state was unable or unwilling to contain Irish republican militancy.

Whatever its intention, and whatever the benefits of arresting those people who had indeed been involved in republican paramilitarism, there is no question that internment increased nationalist disaffection from the state, that it intensified support for IRA resistance, and that it deepened polarisation in the North. Faulkner maintained the view that the policy had been a success; few, on reading Dr McCleery's detailed book, would agree with him. McCleery fairly points out that the IRA 'had been conducting a provocative and murderous campaign against Stormont and the British prior to August 1971'; but he also makes clear that 'the way in which internment was introduced dramatically increased support for the IRA'. Internment was part of a series of ill-judged and counter-productive state responses, of course; but it emerges from this intriguing study as a major part. Internment alone did not generate long-term IRA violence; but it did help to intensify and sustain that brutal campaign from 1971 onwards.

One of the strengths of this book, as hinted earlier, is the author's attention to regional developments. He examines the effects of internment beyond Belfast and Derry/Londonderry and so brings out some of the complexity, contingency and local dynamics that lie at the heart of any proper understanding of the Northern Ireland Troubles. One important argument here is McCleery's suggestion that internment was the first measure applied by the state *across* Northern Ireland in a way read as repressive and anti-nationalist during these years. The 1970 Falls Curfew in Belfast, or Bloody Sunday in Derry in 1972, obviously carried echoes in places other than their actual location; 1971 internment spread more widely, and it intensified disaffection at a greater number of directly experienced local points of friction. The legacies of that process helped to produce an enduring conflict in Northern Ireland; Martin McCleery's book makes a valuable contribution to our understanding of that terrible era.

Richard English, author of
Armed Struggle: The History of the IRA
Belfast 2019

Abbreviations

CCDC	Central Citizens' Defence Committee
CESA	Catholic Ex-Servicemen Association
CGS	Chief of the General Staff
CRA	Civil Rights Association
DO	Detention Order
DUP	Democratic Unionist Party
FCC	Fermanagh County Council
FCRA	Fermanagh Civil Rights Association
GAA	Gaelic Athletic Association
GOCNI	General Officer Commanding Northern Ireland
ICO	Interim Custody Order
IRA	Irish Republican Army
JIC	Joint Intelligence Committee
LAW	Loyalist Association of Workers
MHA	Minister of Home Affairs
MOD	Ministry of Defence
NCRA	Newry Civil Rights Association
NICRA	Northern Ireland Civil Rights Association
NILP	Northern Ireland Labour Party
NRM	Northern Resistance Movement
NUC	Newry Urban Council
OC	Officer Commanding
OIRA	Official Irish Republican Army
PD	People's Democracy
PIRA	Provisional Irish Republican Army
RUC	Royal Ulster Constabulary
RUCSB	Royal Ulster Constabulary Special Branch
SD	sensory deprivation
SDLP	Social Democratic and Labour Party
SOS	Secretary of State
UDA	Ulster Defence Association

UDR   Ulster Defence Regiment
UKREPNI   United Kingdom Representative for Northern Ireland
ULC   Ulster Loyalist Council
UUP   Ulster Unionist Party
UWC   Ulster Workers Council
WUUC   West Ulster Unionist Council

1

Introduction

This book focuses on the use of internment without trial in Northern Ireland in the early 1970s. It argues that internment has not been given proper academic attention and needs reappraisal. Central to this analysis are the initial years of internment, and subsequent events, which are necessary in any attempt to reanalyse why the Troubles escalated in the manner they did. Three main areas will be considered:

1. the high politics surrounding the introduction of the measure and an assessment of the intelligence available for the initial arrest operation;
2. an examination of the repercussions of the use of internment up to 1975;
3. the development of the dynamics of the conflict, outside of Belfast and Derry, between 1970 and 1972.

Chapter 2 reassesses the intelligence situation in regard to internment. The roles of the British and Stormont governments will also be clarified. This research throws a new light on the political significance of the introduction of internment. The attitudes of the Stormont and Westminster governments regarding the measure are examined. The role of the Dublin government is only mentioned in passing, as it is beyond the constraints of this book. William Beattie Smith contends that this period saw the British government pursue a policy towards Northern Ireland which appeared to give primacy to a security solution over a political settlement.[1] It is not clear if this was actually the case. However, it is obvious that around this time the Westminster government had adopted a policy towards Northern Ireland that contained a much greater security emphasis and that internment was a manifestation of this change of emphasis. This chapter will examine a number of questions. What were the respective positions of the Stormont and Westminster administrations in relation to internment? What was the true nature of the initial arrest operation? What was the level of intelligence on both republican and loyalist paramilitaries?

Many commentators have discussed internment, but it has not been considered in sufficient detail, and key aspects of its importance have been glossed over. Chapter 3 will provide a more comprehensive account of the use of internment that covers most of the repercussions associated with the measure. This will involve a reappraisal of both the long-term and short-term effects of internment, some of which have not been previously identified. This chapter will explore a number of areas. How did the use of repressive measures by a liberal state impact on the targeted community? What were the major effects of internment in the wider context? How did internment change the Irish Republican Army (IRA), especially the Provisional Irish Republican Army (PIRA)? What was the main long-term legacy of the use of internment for the conflict?

This book provides a detailed account of internment and looks at various under-researched aspects, specifically the situation outside of Belfast and Derry in Chapters 4 and 5. In researching the areas outside of the two main cities, a detailed study of four provincial towns will be undertaken: Lurgan (Co. Armagh), Newry (Co. Down), Dungannon (Co. Tyrone) and Enniskillen (Co. Fermanagh). Many republicans, and indeed some historians, claim that the PIRA had already become a significant guerrilla movement before the introduction of internment.[2] This may well be true regarding the position of the PIRA in Belfast and, to a lesser extent, Derry; however, this was not the case in other areas. What is true is that there was undoubtedly an upsurge in PIRA activity across Northern Ireland after the introduction of the measure. The figures show an increase of 600 per cent in people killed by the PIRA, outside of Belfast and Derry, in the year immediately after the introduction of internment.[3]

Niall Ó Dochartaigh maintains regarding the position of the PIRA that:

> despite widespread hostility to the army, alienation from the state and aspiration to a united Ireland, few people in Derry supported an IRA offensive and the Provisionals were still a relatively small and marginalised splinter group. Even by the spring of 1971, the Provisionals were by no means a major political force in Derry.[4]

Similarly, in this study, it will be established that it was not until *after* the introduction of internment that the PIRA began to conduct significant urban guerrilla warfare across the *whole* of Northern Ireland. Allied to this point is the fact that the dynamics of the conflict did not become uniform across the entire country until the same period. In essence, a minute reconstruction of the evolution of the Troubles outside of the two main urban centres will be provided. The two main questions investigated are:

• What was the nature of the political and security situation in the four towns before the introduction of internment?
• What was the nature of the political and security situation in the four towns after the introduction of internment?

There have been many books that have examined the Troubles, although these wider-ranging works obviously have a different focus and do not give a detailed account of internment. Many of the above questions have not been properly examined, and these are the principal areas that will be addressed in this book.

Background

It was in December 1969 that the IRA split into two factions; Sinn Féin was to endure a similar break shortly afterwards. The breakaway group became known as the PIRA while the remaining group was called the Official Irish Republican Army (OIRA). The PIRA were also known as the Provos, while the OIRA became known as the Stickies, a nickname that was a reference to the adhesive nature of the Easter Lily which the OIRA wore to commemorate dead republicans.

The split had essentially occurred over how the movement was to be defined. Under the leadership of Cathal Goulding, directed from Dublin, the organisation had become increasingly left-wing. According to Gerry Adams, Goulding made a landmark speech, at Bodenstown in June 1967, attacking the physical-force tradition and favouring socialist policies.[5] This was a drift that many in republican circles resented, especially among the Northern membership. At a secret meeting in Belfast in August 1969, Belfast IRA men met to discuss their disillusionment with the direction the movement was taking. At this meeting were some of the key figures in the future Provisional movement: Billy McKee, John Kelly and his brother Billy, Joe Cahill, Leo Martin, Seamus Twomey, Gerry Adams, Dáithí Ó Conaill and Jimmy Drumm.[6] These men were to form the nucleus of the new rejectionist movement leadership along with Ruairí Ó Brádaigh and Seán Mac Stíofáin, the Provisionals' chief of staff from 1969 to 1972.[7] The Provisionals were traditional in outlook and saw the organisation's primary role as a military one; they rejected participating in the democratic parliaments of Stormont, Westminster and Leinster House.

In January 1970, the Army Council of the PIRA met to decide military policy. They decided that their most urgent priority was defence from loyalists and the British Army.[8] Crucially, the Army Council also decided that when the movement was strong enough they would launch an 'all-out offensive against the British occupation system'.[9] The British Army had been brought into Northern Ireland because the Royal Ulster Constabulary (RUC) could not cope with the violence that occurred during the civil-rights crisis. Initially they had been welcomed by the Catholic community. As one paratrooper stated, 'always tea and coffee from the Catholics … We felt like knights in shining armour, like Sir Galahad.'[10] This was all to change, and increasingly the Army was seen as the enemy of the nationalist community and the upholder of the unionist government that discriminated against Catholics.

By the end of January 1970, the PIRA had a Belfast brigade which was structured into battalion and company levels. Billy McKee was Officer Commanding (OC), and Seamus Twomey, who had been interned during the Second World War, was his adjutant.[11] Two other prominent figures were Jimmy Steele and Proinsias MacAirt, another internee of the 1940s, who were both responsible for the setting up of the *Republican News*.[12] The republican newspaper was to become very important to the republican movement in its propaganda war during the Troubles. For the PIRA, the conflict that was to unfold was to be seen in simplistic terms, and the responsibility for it lay with the British partition of Ireland. As Seán Mac Stíofáin explained, 'England could not hold any part of Ireland except by military force.' The British Army was not conscripted, and therefore he could have no sympathy for the ordinary British soldier, even if he were killed.[13] This view appears too simplistic and does not take into account that many young men may have joined the Army out of economic necessity. Volunteer Brendan Hughes also recalled,

> The only objective I ever heard in the early days was to get the Brits out of Ireland. I remember sitting in Proinsias McAirt's house, which was the hub of republican activity at the time, and I recall Billy McKee saying that this is our opportunity now with the Brits on the streets, this is what we wanted, open confrontation with the army.[14]

Hughes, also known as 'The Dark', was ultimately to fall out with the Provisional movement in the 1990s over its decision to call a ceasefire and enter the constitutional process. He felt that he had been betrayed by the movement he had served: 'It was like getting a hundred people to push this boat out; a boat that is stuck in the sand … and then the boat sails off, leaving the hundred people behind.'[15]

Initially, the PIRA did not confront the Army in open combat; instead, they became involved in the continuing street violence which, originating from the civil-rights marches and counter-demonstrations, had become more localised sectarian confrontations.[16] Throughout early 1970, disturbances continued in Belfast. On 17 May, the rioting appeared, to the authorities, to be pre-planned and organised, as did the disturbance on the previous weekend, and in both cases the confrontation was between Catholics and the Army exclusively.[17] However, it does not seem that the agitators had the wholehearted support of the local community, as one priest stated:

> Some people are convinced that the disturbances on Sunday and yesterday morning were organised by a small group of militant people who were determined to get rid of the military … One man told me that as far as he was concerned the soldiers were a well-disciplined force and he could find nothing wrong with them. There are people in this area who apparently do not want normal conditions to prevail and are out to create trouble at all costs.[18]

The continuing street violence, along with the Chief Constable Sir Arthur Young's efforts to reform the RUC, brought the Army and Catholics into more confrontations. Under Young's guidance, the Hunt Committee's recommendations were being implemented. A further report, published in February 1970, restructured the RUC along the lines of police forces in Great Britain.[19] Young wanted to turn the RUC into a normal everyday police force which would be supported by the general public. This, of course, meant that it would become less involved in controlling street violence, which, in turn, meant more street confrontations for the Army. This could only lead to further animosity between the Army and nationalists.

As the confrontations were escalating between the Army and nationalists, Major James Chichester-Clark, the Prime Minister of Northern Ireland, was having plenty of problems of his own trying to contain hard-line unionists from within and outside of the UUP. He had been elected on 1 May 1969, replacing Terence O'Neill. In his election address, he made it clear that his two main objectives would be 'peace and the removal of tension'. He also declared that there would be no going back on the reform programme, including the commitment to 'one man one vote'.[20]

Chichester-Clark was to face the same problems as his predecessor in trying to appease hard-liners within unionism who were against reform and at the same time satisfying British demands for change. O'Neill continually made reference to British opinion, which needed to be understood in the context of the changing relationship between Stormont and Westminster. From the mid-1960s on, there was a perception among unionists that the British government was willing to intervene on behalf of nationalists in Northern Ireland affairs, which could possibly lead to direct rule.[21] Tensions over the reform of local government early in 1970 produced a fierce reaction from grass-roots unionists, especially in the west of the province. A widening gap was developing between a modernising government, keen to be seen in a favourable light in Britain, and ordinary unionists, who considered their government to be too compliant to Westminster wishes.[22] These tensions were exposed when Harold Wilson called an election in the summer of 1970.[23] The Revd Ian Paisley attacked Chichester-Clark's security policies:

> We are living in serious days and in the midst of a tremendous battle. I am making a call tonight; let's have the B-Specials back again. When a country is in danger, fellow Protestants, what do you do? You strengthen its defences. What did this government do? They tore down our defences, the first line of which was the RUC and an armed RUC. They took away the guns from the police.[24]

Paisley claimed during the election that a pact had been made with the Ulster Unionists not to field Protestant Unionist candidates in a number of constituencies, a claim rejected by Chichester-Clark. Whatever the case, the election was to prove successful for Paisley, and he won North Antrim; he had struck a blow against the Ulster Unionists.[25] A few months earlier, Paisley had also won the Bannside by-election for Stormont. Both victories were hugely symbolic triumphs for the brand of populist unionism or loyalism which Paisley promoted. He articulated with more conviction the defensive mentality of 'no surrender'.[26]

The situation deteriorated further during the lead-up to the 12 July demonstrations of 1970. In June during the 'Mini-Twelfth' celebrations, in Belfast, the PIRA shot five Protestants dead. This engagement was centred on St Matthew's Church in the Short Strand and has become part of republican folklore, the republican narrative being that the PIRA had emerged victorious in their defence of the area from a Protestant mob hell-bent on destruction. This version is, of course, contested by Protestants, who maintain that they were fired on first.[27] The rank-and-file unionists blamed what they perceived to be the soft approach being adopted by the security forces.[28] The sequel to the June violence came in the shape of the Falls Road Curfew over the weekend of 3–5 July. The curfew and search of the area started just after 10 p.m. on the Friday night and lasted until 9 a.m. on Sunday morning. During the operation, 100 firearms, 100 home-made bombs, 250 pounds of explosives and 21,000 rounds of ammunition were uncovered.[29] The curfew has been seen in republican circles as a defining moment in the history of the Troubles. Gerry Adams believes that it was a 'turning point for many

Catholics in their attitude to the British government and its forces'.[30] Indeed, William Whitelaw, future Secretary of State (SOS), believed that after the curfew 'the image of the army ... shifted towards that of the old enemy" aligning itself with unionism to oppose the beleaguered minority'.[31] By August 1970, the intelligence services were considering what plans needed to be made if internment was to be introduced.[32]

The violence escalated early in 1971 following severe rioting in Ballymurphy and Ardoyne. Then, on 6 February, the PIRA murdered Gunner Robert Curtis, who is recorded in *Lost Lives* as the first British soldier to die violently during the Troubles.[33] However, before Curtis's murder, twenty-one British soldiers had lost their lives, mainly through accidents, in Northern Ireland. These deaths included Sergeant John Platt, who was killed as a result of a road traffic accident on 3 February, apparently after an IRA ambush.[34] The murder of Curtis was followed by the brutal murder of three Scottish soldiers. At this time, PIRA activities were definitely increasing, and these killings were part of this increase in activity. These murders undoubtedly worsened the deteriorating situation, and, two days later, 4,000 shipyard workers marched to UUP headquarters to demand the internment of IRA leaders.[35] The murders of these three young Scottish soldiers will be discussed further in Chapter 3.

Under severe pressure, Chichester-Clark went to London to demand tougher security measures; he met Reginald Maudling, Edward Heath and Lord Carrington on 16 March. He demanded massive troop reinforcements but was offered only 1,300 extra soldiers. In face of such meagre support from Westminster and unbearable opposition at home, Chichester-Clark had no option, and within days he had resigned.[36] Interestingly, at the same time, 'the Emergency Provisions Bill was taken from the files and amended to provide for a "Secretary for Northern Ireland"'.[37]

Constitutional nationalist politics in 1970 were to undergo a dramatic change with the emergence of the Social Democratic and Labour Party (SDLP). The party's inaugural press conference was held on 21 August 1970 in Belfast with John Hume, Ivan Cooper, Paddy O'Hanlon, Austin Currie and Paddy Devlin, with Gerry Fitt as leader – plus a Republican Labour senator, Patrick Wilson, in attendance. As Peter McLoughlin outlines, the party was committed from the start to provide a strong opposition to unionism and to seek a reunification of the country – but only with the consent of the majority in Northern Ireland.[38] Throughout 1970 and 1971, the SDLP became increasingly disillusioned with the unionist government. Although reforms such as the Hunt Report were being activated, it seemed to the party that attitudes had changed little.

The SDLP found itself in a complicated position. They were spectators to the reform package, which was doing little to change radically the plight of nationalists. They were unable to introduce legislation because the parliamentary rules and electoral system were not being reformed. More importantly, although reform was taking place, the determination to end institutionalised discrimination against Catholics was not apparent. The main threat to the SDLP's constitutional position came from the PIRA and escalating street violence. Ian McAllister maintains that, as a result, abstentionism was always considered as an option, and the threat of withdrawal from Stormont was used in connection with the use of internment.[39] As the security situation deteriorated, Chichester-Clark attempted to placate his hard-line critics by obtaining stricter security measures. His failure resulted in his resignation and replacement by Brian Faulkner. It fell to Faulkner to try and achieve some kind of Catholic involvement in government, as well as improve the security position.[40] His efforts were also to be constrained by hard-line unionists. Stormont's own research had confirmed that the loss of two recent by-elections 'pointed clearly to a lack of faith in the government's ability to maintain law and order'.[41] Forebodingly, Ronnie Burroughs, United Kingdom Representative for Northern Ireland (UKREPNI), did not hold out much hope for Faulkner's chances of achieving a political settlement:

> In the earnest hope that I am wrong I believe that Faulkner is over-optimistic in believing that he can split the right-wing … Neither the broad mass of the Unionist Party nor the minority have been given anything substantial to cling on to. This is good politics. But I am a little concerned by the initial reactions of the SDLP … Hume in particular smells blood and has been uncompromisingly hostile. If the right-wing and the opposition combine, however unconsciously, to bring Faulkner down his chances of survival are slim.[42]

It wasn't long before Faulkner put forward his proposals for a form of inclusive government. On 22 June, the fiftieth anniversary of the opening of the Northern Ireland parliament – a date which was deliberately chosen – he suggested the setting up of three functional committees covering social services, the environment and industry.[43] These committees were to operate without executive powers, but they would review and consider government policy and provide 'a means of expressing legitimate parliamentary interest in the overall quality of government proposals and performance'. The committees would consist of nine members, each broadly representative of party strength in the House. Additionally, 'the opposition should provide at least two chairmen, the posts being salaried and having real status and importance in the new scheme of parliamentary operation'. As a final enticement, Faulkner hinted that

other constitutional changes, such as the introduction of propor-
tional representation (PR), could be considered in the future. Initially,
the response from the SDLP was reserved, although Paddy Devlin did
believe that the proposal showed 'plenty of imagination';[44] while Gerry
Fitt wanted to test Faulkner's offer of accommodation to the minority
community.[45]

Of course, Faulkner's motives can be called into question here; there
is some doubt as to whether they were genuine or not. It could well have
been that he hoped once he had got the SDLP into the constitutional
framework that they would not be prepared to risk all their gains by
listening to the inevitable calls for a walkout once repressive security
measures were introduced. The proposals seem to have been an attempt
at a balancing act by Faulkner. He hoped to keep constitutional nationalists on board while at the same time satisfying the hard-liners within
unionism with harsher security measures. It is also just possible too that
Faulkner had one eye on the Westminster when he introduced his proposals. With internment in mind he wanted to show the British that he
had already tried the political path but that it had failed.

Whatever the case, for a short period he did seem to have obtained the
cautious support of the SDLP, who were hoping to use the proposals as
a basis for more reform.[46] Any such approval proved to be short-lived.
Street violence continued to escalate, and, in May 1971, Faulkner
announced that 'any soldier seeing any person with a weapon or seeing
any person acting suspiciously may fire either to warn or may fire with
effect, depending on the circumstances and without waiting on orders
from anyone'.[47] Effectively, the army was given permission to shoot anyone they deemed to be a danger. The directive was seen by many nationalists as proof of a new, tougher security policy. Faulkner was playing to
the 'hawks' within unionism and delivering the tougher security measures that they had been demanding. It didn't take long for the new rules
of engagement to effect the SDLP's position. On 8 July, Seamus Cusack
and Desmond Beattie were shot dead, in contested circumstances, during
rioting in Derry. The SDLP issued a statement on 12 July:

> There comes a point where to continue to do so is to appear to condone
> the present system. That point in our view has been reached … The British
> government must face up to the clear consequences of their intervention
> of August 1969 and reveal their determination to produce a political solu-
> tion … If our demand is not met … we will withdraw immediately from
> parliament.[48]

The statement demonstrated the pressure the party was under. Its continued presence in Stormont led the nationalist community to see it as

accepting the actions of the government's security forces.[49] A few short days later, after having obtained no assurances from the British government, the SDLP confirmed their intention to withdraw from Stormont. Certainly, Faulkner could be left in no doubt that the nationalist community and the SDLP would be opposed to any attempt to introduce internment. Despite this, Faulkner was to claim in his memoirs that he had 'received many letters from housewives in places such as Andersontown, in West Belfast, urging him to get the terrorists "off our backs".' He also maintained that he felt at the time that very many Catholics were prepared to tolerate internment in order to break the IRA.[50] Similar sentiments had been expressed by Gerry Fitt, according to Burroughs when he advocated the 'immediate internment of all Provisional IRA men ... He [Fitt] assures me that the Catholic population of the city would on the whole be vastly relieved by the removal of the IRA yoke on their necks.'[51] Burroughs' position of UKREPNI had been introduced by the Wilson government, and his mandate was to see that the reform programme was carried out and there was no backsliding.[52] Faulkner's and Burroughs' claims may have had some substance, especially after the murder of the three Scottish soldiers in February 1971. However, it is certainly debatable whether or not the introduction of the measure had any support from the nationalist community by August. The importance of the timing of the introduction of internment will be examined further in Chapter 3.

In late June, Belfast was becoming increasingly ungovernable, and the Army had virtually lost control. All the blame for the ongoing street violence should not be apportioned solely to nationalists as the rioting and intimidation came from both sides. Indeed, it is claimed that as many as 1,500 Catholics fled over the border in July 1970 as a result of loyalist actions.[53] Outside of Northern Ireland, a new Conservative government was elected, with Heath as Prime Minister. Heath appointed Maudling as Home Secretary, Douglas-Home as Foreign Secretary and Lord Carrington as Defence Secretary.[54] The new government continued the policy of reform of the previous Labour administration. These policies included police reform under the auspices of the Hunt Report of October 1969, the establishment of the Community Relations Commission and its ministry, legislation prohibiting incitement to hatred, the centralisation of housing responsibilities and of local-authority functions.[55] However, the period of just less than two years that saw the Conservatives coming to power and the introduction of direct rule was to be marked by increased violence, the resurgence of the IRA and the growing importance of an effective security policy. As Snedden outlines, the Conservative government had adopted 'a tougher line focused on regaining control over the catholic [sic] working class heartlands'.[56] In addition, the reform package looked increasingly inadequate to halt the slide to large-scale communal violence. The government's frustration was to be articulated by Maudling when he stated that 'the disorder no longer related to legitimate grievances of an oppressed minority'.[57]

As Anthony Craig points out, much political debate, on the introduction of internment, centres on Faulkner and when he became convinced of its necessity. Some of the literature suggests that he had always been convinced of its usefulness;[58] while others depict Faulkner as being gradually persuaded.[59] Craig believes that 'this axiom ignores one crucial point, as the British could have introduced internment alone, something that Stormont could not have done. Indeed London had been planning for such a scenario for just as long as the Northern Ireland government.'[60] So, what were the respective governmental positions over the introduction of internment? With this in mind, the differing positions adopted by Stormont and Westminster over the introduction of internment, and the intelligence surrounding the operation, will now be examined.

Notes

1 William Beattie Smith, *The British State and the Northern Ireland Crisis, 1969–73: From Violence to Power Sharing* (Washington, DC, 2011), pp. 395–96.
2 Thomas Hennessey, *The Evolution of the Troubles, 1970–72* (Dublin, 2007), p. 52.
3 Figures compiled from David McKittrick, Seamus Kelters, Brian Feeney, Chris Thornton and David McVea, *Lost Lives: The Stories of the Men, Women and Children Who Died as a Result of the Northern Ireland Troubles,* 2nd edn (Edinburgh, 2007), pp. 56–245.
4 Niall Ó Dochartaigh, *From Civil Rights to Armalites: Derry and the Birth of the Irish Troubles* (Cork, 1997), p. 239.
5 Gerry Adams, *Before the Dawn: An Autobiography* (Kerry, 2001), p. 82.
6 Richard English, *Armed Struggle: The History of the IRA* (London, 2004), p. 105.
7 English, *Armed Struggle,* p. 111.
8 Hennessey, *Evolution of the Troubles,* p. 7.
9 Seán Mac Stíofáin, *Memoirs of a Revolutionary* (London, 1975), p. 146.
10 Max Arthur, *Northern Ireland Soldiers Talking* (London, 1987), p. 32.
11 Raymond J. Quinn, *A Rebel Voice: A History of Belfast Republicanism, 1925–72* (Belfast, 1999), pp. 155–57.
12 Hennessey, *Evolution of the Troubles,* pp. 7–8.
13 Mac Stíofáin, *Memoirs of a Revolutionary,* p. 167.
14 Quoted in Kevin Bean and Mark Hayes (eds), *Republican Voices* (Monaghan, 2001), p. 50.

15 Ed Moloney, *Voices from the Grave* (London, 2010), p. 274.
16 Henry Patterson and Eric Kaufmann, *Unionism and Orangeism in Northern Ireland since 1945: The Decline of the Loyal Family* (Manchester, 2007), p. 91.
17 Hennessey, *Evolution of the Troubles*, p. 12.
18 *Irish News*, 19 May 1970.
19 *Belfast Telegraph*, 12 February 1970.
20 Patterson and Kaufmann, *Unionism and Orangeism*, p. 89.
21 Catherine O'Donnell, 'Pragmatism versus unity: The Stormont government and the 1966 Easter commemoration' in Mary Daly and Margaret O'Callaghan (eds), *1916 in 1966 Commemorating the Easter Rising* (Dublin, 2007), p. 253.
22 Patterson and Kaufmann, *Unionism and Orangeism*, p. 101.
23 Hennessey, *Evolution of the Troubles,* p. 18.
24 *Belfast Telegraph*, 8 June 1970.
25 Hennessey, *Evolution of the Troubles*, p. 21.
26 Graham Walker, 'The Ulster Unionist Party and the Bannside by-election of 1970', *Irish Political Studies*, 19 (2004): 59–73.
27 Hennessey, *Evolution of the Troubles*, pp. 34–35.
28 Patterson and Kaufmann, *Unionism and Orangeism*, p. 106.
29 Peter Taylor, *Brits: The War against the IRA* (London, 2002), p. 50.
30 Adams, *Before the Dawn*, p. 142.
31 William Whitelaw, *The Whitelaw Memoirs* (London, 1989), p. 129.
32 Office of UKREPNI to P. Leyshaw, J2 Division, 11 August 1970, The National Archives (TNA): Public Record Office (PRO) CJ 4/462.
33 McKittrick et al., *Lost Lives*, p. 64.
34 Ken Wharton, *Bloody Belfast: An Oral History of the British War against the IRA* (Stroud, 2010), p. 8.
35 Paul Bew, *Ireland: The Politics of Enmity, 1789–2006* (Oxford, 2007), p. 502.
36 Patterson and Kaufmann, *Unionism and Orangeism*, p. 125.
37 Alvin Jackson, *Home Rule* (London, 2004), p. 295.
38 Peter John McLoughlin, 'John Hume and the revision of Irish nationalism, 1964–79', Ph.D. thesis, Queen's University Belfast, 2004), p. 48.
39 Ian McAllister, *The Northern Ireland Social Democratic and Labour Party: Political Opposition* (London, 1977), pp. 83–86.
40 McAllister, *The Northern Ireland Social Democratic and Labour Party*, p. 87.
41 Note of a meeting in the Prime Minister's room, Stormont Castle on Wednesday, 22 April 1970, Public Record Office of Northern Ireland (PRONI), CAB/9/G/89/2.
42 UKREP Belfast to UK Comms, 24 March 1971, TNA: PRO, FCO 33/1464.
43 Sir Kenneth Bloomfield, *Stormont in Crisis: A Memoir* (Belfast, 1994), p. 142.
44 Bloomfield, *Stormont in Crisis*, p. 88.

45 Gerard Murray and Jonathan Tonge, *Sinn Fein and the SDLP* (Dublin, 2005), p. 26.
46 McAllister, *The Northern Ireland Social Democratic and Labour Party,* p. 90.
47 McAllister, *The Northern Ireland Social Democratic and Labour Party,* p. 91.
48 *Irish Times,* 12 July 1971.
49 McLoughlin, 'John Hume and the revision of Irish nationalism', p. 65.
50 Brian Faulkner, *Memoirs of a Statesman* (London, 1977), pp. 117–19.
51 Hennessey, *Evolution of the Troubles,* p. 86.
52 Taylor, *Brits,* p. 41.
53 Adams, *Before the Dawn,* p. 142.
54 Hennessey, *Evolution of the Troubles,* p. 28.
55 Michael Cunningham, *British Government Policy in Northern Ireland, 1969–2000* (Manchester, 2001), pp. 6–7.
56 S. E. Snedden (n.d.) 'Defence Research Paper', Ministry of Defence, available online at www.da.mod.uk/defac/colleges/jscsc/jscsc-publications/drp/Lt.Col .Snedded.pdf (accessed 16 July 2012).
57 Cunningham, *British Government Policy in Northern Ireland,* p. 9.
58 See Taylor, *Brits,* p. 61; Jonathan Bardon, *A History of Ulster,* 2nd edn (Belfast, 2001), p. 683.
59 See Bew, *Ireland,* p. 502; David McKittrick and David McVeigh, *Making Sense of the Troubles: The Story of the Conflict in Northern Ireland* (Chicago, Ill., 2002), p. 67.
60 Anthony Craig, *Crisis of Confidence: Anglo-Irish Relations in the Early Troubles* (Dublin, 2010), pp. 95–96.

2

High politics, intelligence and the introduction of internment

The decision to implement

In 1963, the South African Minister of Justice, B. J. Vorster, speaking in the South African Parliament, offered to exchange the Bill he was presenting for one clause of the Northern Ireland Special Powers Act.[1] One of these clauses authorised the power to introduce internment without trial. The British themselves had used internment in a number of former colonies such as Kenya when during the Mau Mau uprising:

> Under the emergency laws, suspects could be detained without trial on the basis of a Delegated Detention Order ... These sparse documents set down the detainees name, pass number, and location of origin, with a brief comment on the reason for the order. Nothing more was needed to condemn a man to incarceration for two years, or more. Suspicion that a man had taken an oath, or even that he was thought to be in sympathy with the aims of Mau Mau, was sufficient for detention without trial.[2]

In 2012, a number of survivors from the detention camps in Kenya won a court case against the British government over their detention and torture. This has led to thousands of files from the colonial period being opened which the British government had kept secret. Interestingly, among those detained during the Mau Mau insurgency was Barack Obama's grandfather. During the case, the British government admitted that many Kenyans were tortured during the uprising. Coincidently, one of the judges who sat on the Advisory Committee on Internment in Northern Ireland in 1971 was 'Mr. Justice Dalton, a former Kenyan judge who fulfilled the same duty in the Kenyan uprising'.[3]

Internment had been available in both the South and North since 1921. The Civil Authorities (Special Powers) Acts (Northern Ireland) 1922–43, Regulation 12, gave the Minister for Home Affairs power to issue an internment order against a person 'suspected of acting or having acted or being about to act in a manner prejudicial to the preservation of the peace and the maintenance of order in Northern Ireland'.[4] This was obviously a very draconian measure.

When, in April 1971, Faulkner met with Heath, both parties agreed that the most pressing matter was internal security. Faulkner pledged that he would not agree to any proposal for the use of internment powers unless advised by the Army and the RUC that it would bring IRA terrorism to an end. The General Officer Commanding (GOC) and the Chief Constable had indicated that they were against internment, although the Royal Ulster Constabulary Special Branch (RUCSB) was marginally in favour.[5] In fact, prior to the introduction of internment, the Army's position was that the IRA could be defeated, within a certain timescale, without the use of the measure.[6] Moreover, Sir Harry Tuzo, General Officer Commanding Northern Ireland (GOCNI), and Sir Michael Carver, Chief of the General Staff (CGS), were both opposed to the measure.[7] This period was to be marked by a more aggressive policy from the Army. The role of intelligence was to be essential, and 'no-go' areas were not to be tolerated.[8] On the surface, the period from March to June was relatively quiet with only a handful of fatalities; however, July was to see an upsurge in IRA activity. At the same time, Stormont had been considering various tactics to counter the IRA, one suggestion being a poster campaign that showed pictures of maimed children who had been injured during the violence.[9] The IRA had, of course, supplied Stormont with plenty of ammunition for any proposed propaganda campaign; republican paramilitaries had been responsible for many murders and bombings since the start of the Troubles.

For Faulkner, the final straw came on 17 July when Northern Ireland witnessed its most expensive explosion yet, as the PIRA bombed the *Daily Mirror* newspaper offices just outside Belfast. Faulkner took the decision to operate internment.[10] Before its introduction, General Tuzo proposed the arrest of known IRA leaders, taking them away for questioning for forty-eight hours and searching their homes, an operation known as Linklater. However, internment was still looming large on the horizon.[11] According to Field Marshal Carver, Linklater made the army look ineffective, 'almost ridiculous'.[12] Surely Linklater must also have acted as a warning to republicans that internment was a distinct possibility.

The question was not would Faulkner ask for internment but how long it would be before he requested it. It was not long before the answer came. On 28 July, Faulkner telephoned Maudling to inform him that every one of his cabinet colleagues now believed that the time for internment had come.[13] It had been introduced on three occasions previously by the Stormont administration, 1922–24, 1938–45 and 1956–61. The use of internment during the IRA border campaign, in the late 1950s, proved to be particularly effective, especially when the government of the Republic of Ireland introduced the measure in 1957.

However, this dual introduction of internment did not occur in 1971. Furthermore, following the deployment of British troops in Northern Ireland in 1969, it became impossible to introduce internment without the help of the British Army; as a consequence, Stormont had to obtain the consent of the British government. In a meeting in Downing Street on 5 August 1971, with the backing of the Chief Constable, Faulkner asked for internment – although the Army still believed that internment was not essential. Heath informed Faulkner that internment could not be contemplated without some kind of 'balancing action'. He also pointed out that if it did not work then the only option left open would be direct rule. This option had been contemplated by the British for quite some time. Its necessity would be dictated by a marked upsurge in violence, or by Faulkner's resignation, which, they believed, could only produce a more hard-line unionist administration. In either of these two circumstances, Westminster felt that it would have to take control of security matters. As Heath admitted:

> The more or less inevitable successor to Faulkner would be a hard-line and right wing government led by Ian Paisley. I could not allow this to happen and made it clear to Faulkner, that if significant progress was not made in the next year or so, we would have to introduce direct rule of the province ... He was aware from the day he took office, that his premiership was Stormont's last chance.[14]

The Army's analysis of the political situation was probably close to the reality. 'Time, however is not on the side of Stormont. The political nerve of the government is limited and that of its party supporters yet more so.'[15] It was eventually agreed to introduce internment along with a six-month ban on parades, and there was to be no granting of new gun-club licences.[16]

Operation Demetrius

On 9 August 1971, the arrests of suspects got under way. This was despite the supposed reluctance of the British Army and the reservations of Westminster that internment might not work.[17] Interestingly, on the draft message which was to inform the Taoiseach, in the Irish Republic, of the introduction of internment, a sentence had been crossed out. It read 'Protestant as well as Catholic and IRA extremists will be liable to internment.'[18] The policy of internment was to unite most Northern nationalists in their opposition to the authorities like never before.

Of course, the Army had been involved in incidents such as the Falls Road Curfew. However, this was the first repressive operation during the Troubles involving the Army and implemented across the whole of Northern Ireland. After the introduction of internment, Faulkner explained, 'I have taken this step solely for the protection of life and the security of property. We are quite simply at war with the terrorists and in a state of war many sacrifices have to be made.'[19] A government statement outlined how the situation had deteriorated: 'there were 16 explosions in January, between 30 and 40 in each of the months of March and April, between 40 and 50 in May and June, 94 in July and 23 in the first eight days of August.'[20] One underestimated aspect of the bombing campaign was the attacks on infrastructure, which took place in the latter half of 1971. There were at least thirteen successful attacks on the main electricity distribution system of Northern Ireland. These attacks had brought Stormont close to declaring 'a state of emergency'.[21] It was also estimated that there had been 'no less than 972 single shots and twenty-eight bursts of gunfire' in the week before internment was introduced.[22] Obviously Faulkner's government had been facing an increased onslaught from the IRA on all fronts.

Operation Demetrius, the Army's code name for the operation, commenced at 4 a.m. Some commentators refer to the whole period of internment in Northern Ireland, 1971–75, as Operation Demetrius, while this study uses the term solely for the initial arrest operation on 9 August. The reason for the choice of name is not clear, although a film of the 1950s, *Demetrius and the Gladiators,* features as its main character Demetrius, who is arrested for assaulting a Roman soldier. Ultimately he is released and told to tell the Christians that they have nothing to fear if they do not attack the Empire again. These are two messages that the authorities may have wanted to convey. Those who attacked the security forces would be caught, and the Catholic community had nothing to fear if they did not attack, or aid those who would attack, the state. Internees were held at Crumlin Road Prison in Belfast, in camps at Long Kesh and Magilligan and, for a time, on board the *Maidstone* prison ship moored in Belfast Lough, simply because the space was not available within the existing prison system.[23] Indeed, as early as December 1970, the Northern Ireland government had asked the UKREPNI 'whether emergency contingency plans could be put in hand to make HMS Maidstone, anchored in Belfast Lough, available as a place of detention for internees'. At the same time, the British were studying the 'question of internment further'.[24]

The use of internment has been described by Paddy Hillyard as 'an example of unfettered ministerial discretion and highlighted the political nature of the struggle. The state's involvement in suppressing political opposition was clear an unequivocal.'[25] Indeed, the internees at Long Kesh and Magilligan were held in huts and cages, 'were allowed to wear their own clothes and permitted a large degree of freedom within the cage. They were also granted the same rights as prisoners on remand, having more visits, letters and parcels than convicted persons.'[26] This granting of de-facto political status for internees was to have profound consequences in the future history of the Troubles.

The operation went ahead despite the concerns of the British government that international opinion would not be favourable and that internment would be in contravention of the European Convention on Human Rights. On 9 August, Faulkner informed his cabinet that when he told Heath that internment should be introduced, concerns had been expressed that

> [t]he introduction of internment would involve the UK in derogation of the European Convention on Human Rights and that the matter was of obvious concern to the UK government but they nevertheless accepted the need for the course proposed as a means of achieving the restoration of law and order.[27]

Indeed, on 20 August 1971, the British government informed the Secretary General of the Council of Europe of its derogation from the European Convention on Human Rights as a result of the introduction of internment.[28] As early as August 1970, the office of the UKREPNI had been approached by the Director of Intelligence in Northern Ireland who made inquiries about contingency planning for the use of internment. Further to this, the UKREPNI office made inquiries from the Home Office about the accuracy of arrest lists.[29] It is apparent that the Home Office did not want to get involved in the selection of detainees and was quite aware of the pitfalls of any such involvement:

> I don't think the Home Office could allow itself to be concerned in the selection of people to be interned. The object of any such exercise would presumably be to see that the Northern Ireland authorities do not 'run wild' but the maintenance of order in Northern Ireland is the responsibility of the Northern Ireland government and I don't see that we would be able to interfere with their use of the special powers. We would at the same time risk being identified as co-operators with the Northern Ireland Government in the execution of these powers and we could thus lose all semblance of neutrality in the eyes of whichever section of the community felt itself oppressed at that particular time.[30]

It is clear that the arrest figures for Operation Demetrius deserve closer scrutiny. The original arrest list actually contained 520 names, and, according to John McGuffin, the list consisted of 130 IRA men, 350 IRA sympathisers, fifty ex-internees and some political opponents of the government.[31] Of the 520 individuals on the list, 178 evaded arrest and 342 were arrested, with 116 being released within forty-eight hours. There were approximately 100 individuals held for longer than forty-eight hours who had no paramilitary involvement. This certainly does not make the operation appear as indiscriminate as it has been portrayed in some quarters. Interestingly, the expectation had been, less than a month before the operation commenced, to arrest in the initial swoop between 20 and 40 per cent of a list of between 325 and 375 suspects.[32] This equates to approximately 150 individuals, well under one-third of the numbers supplied for the arrest operation. Why would there be such a discrepancy in the figures? The authorities may have decided to go for all the names on the July list, but even this does not account for the 520 names on the August list. Among those arrested were retired republicans, trade unionists and civil-rights campaigners, a drunken man picked up at a bus stop and several people held on mistaken identity. The inclusion of civil-rights campaigners is perhaps not so surprising given that operational instructions circulated on 8 August stated that '[b]oth factions of the IRA, NICRA and People's Democracy (PD) have contingency plans for a campaign of violence and civ [sic] disobedience if internment should take place'. It appears that civil-rights campaigners were being treated just the same as militant republicans. The list had been clearly augmented to include opponents of Stormont who were not involved with the IRA. Additionally, soldiers were told that if 'suspects cannot be identified by mil [sic], all males over 18 yrs at the selected address are to be arrested'.[33] This can only have added to the indiscriminate nature of the arrest operation. As a consequence, people were arrested, like Edward Campbell from the Springfield Road, along with a friend, when soldiers had raided a house he was in, 'looking for someone called Fox but when told that nobody of that name lived there, they decided that "You'll do"'.[34]

It seems fair to assume that most of those who evaded arrest were PIRA members, especially as the PIRA had excellent intelligence and knew several days beforehand that the raid was about to take place. As Tommy Gorman, an ex-PIRA member, remembers,

> I was expecting internment as an IRA volunteer. I had been on the run for several months. We wanted to get behind the public reaction to it, to utilise it and to exploit it. Only Catholics were being interned, despite what was happening on the other side. It was obvious to us what was going on.[35]

Joe Cahill also confirms that the PIRA had excellent intelligence and, furthermore, that they actually had a source inside Stormont who informed them that internment was imminent; as a result, 'senior IRA members were instructed in late July not to sleep at home'.[36] It seems the fact that the PIRA may have had prior warning of internment had not been taken into account by the authorities. Only a week after the initial internment swoop, the British estimated that there were 2,000 IRA still at large.[37]

So, if we take the 178 individuals who evaded arrest and add to this over fifty individuals who had been arrested who were either members of or people who helped the PIRA,[38] then it appears accurate to estimate that approximately 200 individuals on the original arrest list were either PIRA members or supporters. This contradicts the standard narrative that the original arrest operation was based on poor intelligence. Furthermore, if we add the number of individuals released within forty-eight hours to the number of PIRA members and associates arrested, we get a total of somewhere around 170, which means that roughly 50 per cent of the men detained in Operation Demetrius were either associated with the PIRA or released almost immediately; this does not take into account how many of the remaining detainees were members of the OIRA. This also does not make the initial arrest operation appear as indiscriminate as has been portrayed.

Nevertheless, several of those on the arrest lists turned out to be dead.[39] This may be a reflection of the standard of intelligence on political opponents as much as the quality of intelligence on republican paramilitaries. Moreover, the British found that the internment orders submitted after the initial arrest operation

> contained only the briefest of grounds for internment and were not accompanied by supporting evidence. Each order gave the reason for internment, which ranged from stating that the person concerned was a known member of the IRA, to stating that he was believed to be a member of the IRA.

In fact, the Home Office informed Faulkner:

> [t]hat there should be grounds on the face of each order which Mr. Faulkner signed to justify internment. It was not sufficient that there might be evidence elsewhere. It was also desirable that there should be no reference on the order to grounds not connected to terrorism such as allegations that the person concerned had stirred up anti-Northern Ireland government feeling. Mr. Woodfield had indicated to officials that a UK minister would not be prepared to act on the basis of the information which he had seen. It was admitted that the exercise had not been very well prepared. It appeared that only 10 to 20 of the people at present detained would be released when Internment Orders were made.[40]

So, while the reliability of the internment orders being issued was being questioned, this does not mean that the initial arrest lists were totally flawed. The accuracy of the intelligence provided for the arrest lists did not seem entirely unreliable; it does appear that the authorities had good intelligence on a number of suspects. The original arrest lists for Counties Armagh, Down and Tyrone did contain the personal details of a number of prominent republicans. The information provided included name, address and date of birth, occupation and, in some cases, vehicle make, model and registration.[41] As admitted by the Home Office, '[w]hatever unknown IRA sympathisers there may be, there is reliable intelligence about the disposition, if not specific activities, of a number of dangerous men'.[42]

The inconsistency of the intelligence was further reflected by the British analysis of the arrests. They found that 'a disturbing picture emerges from our own inquiries. Among those detained, there is, without doubt, a "hardcore" perhaps 80 strong of IRA activists. This includes some very dangerous men. But the total appears to include many cases of men whose republican connections amount to no more than inactive sympathy.'[43] This appears to be consistent with an arrest list which has some good intelligence on main IRA operators but has been augmented with opponents of the government who do not necessarily actively support the IRA.

In September 1971, it seems the authorities felt the need to clarify who should be detained, the advice being that only those who were members of the IRA since 1969 should be arrested and that those individuals who were members of the civil-rights movement or People's Democracy (PD) or, indeed, any other political organisation should not be detained provided that they were not also IRA members.[44] The Stormont government was also showing some concern about the effects of the apparent 'blanket arrest' on the nationalist community. But the unpredictable nature of the arrests continued. For instance, in the same month, an ex-RAF man had his four stepsons arrested, even though only two had been on the original arrest warrants.[45]

Indeed, the British had been pushing for the names of those who had been arrested to be publicised so they could 'refute assertions on the one hand that the operation had failed because nobody of importance had been taken in, and on the other hand that we have been unnecessarily arresting large numbers of innocent civil rights leaders'. It also seems that the RUCSB was refusing to provide any such list because it would 'put their sources at risk'.[46] As late as November 1971, the Ministry of Defence (MOD) had still not received a list of those who had been detained or interned; despite the fact that 1,356 people had been arrested under the Special Powers Act by this stage.[47] The concern over the reasons for detaining certain suspects was perhaps fuelled by the case of John Murphy, a detainee about whom Frank Taylor MP had asked the Home Secretary. The British found the reasons for his detention to be 'a little disturbing in that they give some support to the view that a number of those on the list were there mainly because of general left-wing attitudes and membership of left-wing organisations'. The following question was also asked:

> Do you think there is any possibility that Special Branch have seen internment as a splendid opportunity to pull in characters whom they would like to get their hands on for reasons not too closely connected with IRA activity, so that they can question them before releasing them; and if so are there likely to be any embarrassing repercussions?[48]

It was clear that some of the nationalists arrested had little or no political involvement, as admitted by some of those who administered the internment system. Whitelaw acknowledged:

> Now if you say that I put some in who shouldn't have been in, yes I think that is certainly right … I have the greatest doubts looking back whether internment was ever right. I question whether internment is right unless you have really good intelligence and I think that is the mistake that was made initially.[49]

Whitelaw realised that internment was 'a serious decision which can be justified only if it succeeds in reducing violence' and which must 'ensure … only the really dangerous terrorists are quickly taken out of circulation'.[50]

In total, between 9 August 1971 and 14 February 1972, 2,447 people were detained, with 934 later being released.[51] Field Marshal Carver believed 'that the poor intelligence received could be blamed on the short notice given for the operation but also there was a suspicion that Faulkner encouraged the RUC to recommend a large arrest operation for the sake of its political impact on the Protestant community'.[52] This is contested by Faulkner, who recalled, 'the army and police proposed a wide sweep involving the arrest of over 500, in order to strike a crippling blow at the terrorist organisation'.[53] However, it must be remembered that the RUCSB prepared the arrest lists at the behest of Stormont.

United front

In the immediate aftermath of the introduction of internment, both the British and Unionist governments did seem to have underestimated its impact. Heath initially congratulated General Tuzo on the successful internment operation and the job that the Army was doing in 'restoring order to the streets'.[54] This is not to say that both administrations were not aware of the dangers of the operation. A Westminster review of government strategy had warned in September 1971 that 'Northern Ireland is the joker in the pack: it is not an exaggeration to say it could be the UK's Vietnam. A new initiative is imperative, well before 1974–5.'[55]

Heath, Maudling, Carrington, Douglas-Home and Faulkner attended a meeting at Chequers on Thursday, 19 August 1971. This meeting gives us a insight into the thinking of both administrations immediately after the introduction of internment. Carrington talked of the Army concentrating on border areas once peace had been restored. Heath believed that representations should be made to the government in the South for better cooperation from their security forces.[56] This must have been an unlikely prospect. Faulkner stated that the really serious bombing attacks had dramatically decreased since internment.

The position of the British government regarding the introduction of internment was probably outlined best by Maudling: 'if it worked, it would avoid the necessity of introducing direct rule, but if direct rule could not be avoided, it would be preferable for internment to already be in place as a result of a Stormont decision.'[57] Smith maintains that by August 1971 the British government had moved from a policy of reform to coercion essentially in an effort to sustain the Stormont administration.[58] It may be debatable whether or not reform had been abandoned totally, but what is quite clear is that a greater emphasis on security measures took place at this time, a change that was evident from the meeting at Chequers.[59] Heath was pressing for a second 'lift' to take place as soon as possible. He asked that all available manpower be put into interrogation and follow-up operations. Maudling pointed out that no English detectives could be used in the interrogations. This was because the Police Federation had been given an undertaking that none of its members would be involved in operations in Northern Ireland that involved the Special Powers Act. The federation was obviously worried about the use of such powers.

Heath expressed concerns that there was a need to counteract the propaganda that was being mounted against internment, especially the allegations of army brutality. He criticised the newspaper coverage of the arrests, which he felt were being stimulated by some of Jack Lynch's statements. He stated that it was also possible that the measure might attract more criticism from the Labour Party and even some sections of the Conservative Party, as party-conference season was fast approaching. There followed a discussion on the merits of the appeal procedures and the possibility of recruiting a Catholic member of the Advisory Committee. All the ministers felt that if this was not possible then some kind of independent voice was needed to reassure public opinion.

In addition to some kind of independent scrutiny of the arrests, it was felt that good counter-propaganda should be used. Heath admitted that many Catholics honestly believed that the majority of the internees had no direct involvement in terrorist activity, the case of a seventy-year-old man being often cited. He proposed that the Army should make known what information they had about such individuals. The discussion turned to the conditions of the internees. Heath emphasised that much could be made of this topic by the public. Carrington assured him that, although conditions on the *Maidstone* were not ideal, the new camp at Long Kesh was well above the standard of the average army camp. He stated that the 'new facility should be able to cater for 150 detainees by 8 September'. He added that it was inevitable the new facilities be inspected by some independent international organisation, preferably the International Red Cross. He was quite adamant that Amnesty International should not be used, as none of the UK ministers held it in high esteem. He also said that he did not envisage that further troop reinforcements would be needed. Indeed, he was hopeful that troop numbers could be reduced if things quietened down.

The discussion on political problems continued. Heath stated that in regard to political opinion in Great Britain, emphasis should be put on the reforms that had already been carried out in Northern Ireland. He felt that if this were properly presented, 'the man in the street' would support the action that the government had taken. However, he did admit that the general public wanted to see the return of the SDLP to Stormont and the fears of the minority removed. Heath felt that the British public oversimplified the situation, but some moves needed to be made as there had been some unreasonable demands. There had been a clamour for tri-partite talks. This was a suggestion which the British government ruled out completely. However, Heath did realise that it would be necessary to meet with Lynch, and Faulkner also accepted this.

Heath said that he would have a number of objectives when meeting with Lynch. He would press for tougher border security and tighter court proceedings and would persuade him of the need for internment in the South, although he felt that this was only a realistic prospect if the government in the South believed that it were being directly threatened by the IRA, which had been its fear the previous December. The discussion turned to possible political initiatives. The SDLP was criticised for walking out of Stormont. Faulkner and the ministers maintained that any moves to give the minority a greater say in the affairs of Northern

Ireland must be within the framework of majority rule. Suggestions such as coalition government were out of the question.

The British ministers praised Faulkner's earlier proposals to the opposition and admitted that they were thinking along the same lines. They believed that their role was very much as a catalyst in the process of reconciliation and reform. They also believed that this was the role that the British public wanted to see them play. Heath did admit that opinion across the world wanted to see the different parties talking. He stated that he did hold the SDLP culpable for some of their actions but that there was a need to isolate the more extreme elements. Maudling believed that he should be involved in any discussions with the opposition. Assurances were given to Faulkner that the authority of the government of Northern Ireland would not be undermined and open-ended talks were not possible. Heath emphasised that the constitutional position of Northern Ireland could not be threatened by terrorist violence, abstentionism or a campaign of civil disobedience. At the same time, the minority must be reassured that the pace of reform would continue. Douglas-Home reiterated that nothing should be done which could be interpreted as a step towards direct rule as this was a course of action which the British government was not prepared to entertain. From the discussions it seems clear that, as Cillian McGrattan states, '[t]he British cabinet was broadly supportive of Faulkner's stance on security and political reform in the immediate aftermath of internment'.[60] It is also evident that although political moves had not been abandoned, both administrations were attaching a greater importance to security measures.

Defending internment

Faulkner received many protestations from all walks of society in Northern Ireland regarding internment. In October 1971, Senator James Lennon, representing the joint opposition of both houses, wrote to Faulkner, informing him that they had passed a resolution that unanimously condemned the Advisory Committee on Internment. They further stated that,

> to expect internees to appear without a lawyer was to expect the impossible ... even more obnoxious to expect internees to provide a written submission without knowledge of the allegations against them (even if they had a lawyer) was unjust to the internees and an insult to the legal profession.[61]

Faulkner replied that the Advisory Committee was carrying out a difficult task in a professional manner and that it was not a court of appeal.[62] The legal mechanics of internment detailed that the Minister of Home Affairs issued internment orders which he could refer to an advisory committee, although he was free to reject or accept that committee's advice.[63] Brian Faulkner, by 1971, had combined both the post of Prime Minister and Minister of Home Affairs for Northern Ireland.

After the imposition of direct rule in 1972, this system was modified by the British government to include a 'quasi-judicial element'.[64] Under the new legislation, the Secretary for State could order the 'interim custody' of a 'suspected terrorist' for up to twenty-eight days.[65] The detention was then examined by a commissioner. However, the defendant could be excluded from the hearing, evidence inadmissible in a criminal court could be heard, and witnesses to the defendant's 'crimes' (usually RUC officers) gave their evidence from behind a screen. The system was further modified in 1975 with the SOS issuing detention orders after receiving a report from a committee of advisers.[66]

The different procedures for administering internment, or detention as it was termed after the imposition of direct rule, can be quite confusing. To simplify the different systems, it is useful to break them up into three periods. From August 1971 until March 1972, the Minister of Home Affairs (MHA) or the SOS issued Interim Custody Orders (ICOs) for the arrest of suspects; after interrogation, these suspects appeared in front of an advisory committee that made a recommendation for internment or release, which the MHA/SOS could either accept or reject. This system was administered by Faulkner up to March 1972 and very briefly by Whitelaw as SOS until the commission process was introduced. The commission system was introduced in March 1972 and ran to 1975. Under this procedure, the SOS issued an ICO for a suspect's arrest. After interrogation, the Chief Constable decided to either release or, more often than not, send the detainee to appear in front of a commission. The commission then decided whether or not to issue a detention order (DO). This system was presided over by three SOSs: Whitelaw from 1972 to 1973, Francis Pym from 1973 to 1974 and Merlyn Rees from 1974 to 1975. Finally the system was modified further in 1975, when internment was being phased out, to give control back to the SOS. The SOS issued the ICO, which was then considered by a panel of advisers that gave advice to the SOS, who decided whether or not to issue a DO.

However, as the Gardiner Report later acknowledged, 'the procedures are unsatisfactory, or even farcical'.[67] Some of the charges levied against the defendant, under these systems, can only be regarded as unsound. One detainee was accused of being involved in multiple murders and bombings inside a couple of weeks, which even the RUCSB man who arrested him knew was impossible.[68] An individual who was brought before the commissioner was suspected of being responsible for robbing a post office in 1943, while another defendant was accused of 650 explosions in a six-month period.[69]

The nature of the commission hearing can be assessed when we examine a transcript of one of the hearings. In June 1973, Kenneth Gibson appeared in front of the commissioners. Gibson was Chairman of the Ormeau Ulster Unionist Party (UUP) until 1971 when he joined the Democratic Unionist Party (DUP). He attended the Revd Ian Paisley's church, and Paisley shared a platform with him 'at the dedication of the new banner Gibson had painted as master of the Lee's Temperance Orange lodge'. During the hearing, the police witness appeared behind a screen, and the informant did not even appear at the hearing.[70] Gibson was represented at the hearing by Desmond Boal, a prominent barrister. Boal was once an Ulster Unionist MP who later became the first Chairman of the DUP.[71] At the hearing, the grounds for Gibson's arrest were read out to him: 'that you in and before 1972 were an officer in the Ulster Volunteer Force'. The first witness against him was an RUC officer, who gave his evidence from behind a screen, and was questioned by the prosecutor (Counsel):

COUNSEL: Is the remainder of what you have to say as a result of information?

OFFICER A: It is.

COUNSEL: Can that be disclosed in your view – of course, it will await the final decision of the learned commissioner – without the risk to the safety of a person or persons?

OFFICER A: There would be a risk, I feel, if it was disclosed openly.

COMMISSIONER: Well Mr. Boal I'm afraid the usual routine would seem to apply.

BOAL: I don't accept that routine and I formally protest.

COMMISSIONER: I exclude the respondent and his representatives under paragraph 17.

[The tribunal then sits in camera with only the Commissioner, Counsel and Officer A present. Then Boal and Gibson are readmitted.]

COMMISSIONER: The substance of the matters dealt with in your absence don't relate at all to the ground. It related to the source, and all that I can tell you, the most I can disclose, is that there was one informer, that he was paid and that the witness had found him to be reliable. I regret that I can't allow any other questions about the source.

BOAL: In that case there is no useful function I can perform by way of cross examination.

COMMISSIONER: I fear so.

COUNSEL: Did you get information from this informer about Kenneth Gibson?

OFFICER A: Yes.

COUNSEL: At that date, and if so what?

OFFICER A: That Kenneth Gibson is second in command of the East Belfast Ulster Volunteer Force.

[*However, Boal does try to ask some questions about how often the informer was paid which the commissioner rules out of order. Boal continues the line of questioning.*]

BOAL: All right. Do you pay him apart from getting information from him?

COMMISSIONER: This again, I must rule out. Sorry.

BOAL: Do you pay him according to the importance of the information?

COMMISSIONER: I rule that question out.

BOAL: Use my professional ingenuity as I may, I can't really, within that structure, ask any more questions.

COMMISSIONER: I know it's an impossible situation.

Boal sums up his assessment of the case against Gibson by saying, 'So that all you're doing, really, is you're retailing to this tribunal, a bit of tittle-tattle that you heard from somebody that you don't know very well and who has sometimes been proved, to your knowledge to be wrong.'[72]

At the end of the hearing, Gibson was interned by the commission – a decision he appealed, but his appeal was turned down. He was eventually released in December 1973 after being held without trial for eleven months. The nature of this tribunal does not appear to be uncommon for these types of hearings. Indeed, Japanese and German detainees in Hawaii, following the attack on Pearl Harbor in the Second World War, were only allowed a twenty-minute hearing at which they were not allowed to have a lawyer or to question government witnesses.[73]

Meanwhile, perhaps surprisingly, Faulkner received a letter from the Police Authority of Northern Ireland shortly after the introduction of internment. The Authority deplored the necessity of the use of the measure and expected its use to be impartial. It also asked Faulkner to consider that the Advisory Body that was to be set up should have executive powers. This was obviously an attempt to ensure the independence of the committee from any political influence from Stormont on its decisions. The letter concluded by asking that all detainees who appeared in front of the committee be provided with free legal aid and a solicitor with counsel.[74] The Law Society of Northern Ireland also expressed its concerns at a Special General Meeting in February 1972, the details of which were passed on to Harold Black, Permanent Secretary to the Cabinet, by a lawyer who happened to work at Stormont. The society deplored the existence of the Special Powers Act and called for its immediate repeal.

They called for all police officers who broke the law to be prosecuted. The Law Society condemned the use of arrest and interrogation procedures, especially with regard to children and young people. They also expressed concerns regarding the treatment of its members by the security services. Of particular concern were the facilities for lawyers at internment camps and the fact that members of the security services were reading their confidential files.[75] Objections to the introduction of internment came from another surprising quarter, the Revd Ian Paisley. In what can be described as a piece of political opportunism, Paisley stated, 'He [Faulkner] should charge these men [the internees] with their crimes, bring them to the court of law, and show what evidence he has.'[76] Paisley also asked, 'Does the minister accept the basic principle of British justice – that a man is innocent until proven guilty? If his department has any evidence why has he refused to bring these subversives to the courts?'[77] Paisley's comments convey the precarious position that Faulkner found himself in over internment; even fierce opponents of republicans could attack him over the issue by portraying the measure as an attack on civil liberties.

In a Stormont debate Faulkner vehemently defended the use of internment. He stated that since the introduction of the measure many arrests had been made and that the net was tightening further. He also believed that the arrests had proven useful in the area of intelligence and more was known about the IRA than had been known. Faulkner refuted allegations that innocent men had been arrested. He stated:

> It is alleged that there are those interned who have no connection at all with the IRA. I do not know on what evidence those who claim to know this base their statements. But I am confident that the Advisory Committee set up to consider representations from internees will do their work thoroughly and that if anyone has not been as deeply indicated in the IRA campaign as the initial evidence suggested or can establish that his release would entail no danger to others this will come to light and so enable the decision on internment to be reviewed.[78]

However, even when a detainee was to satisfy the Advisory Committee that they presented no danger, these individuals were expected to give an undertaking stating that 'I swear by almighty god that, for the remainder of my life, I will not join nor assist any illegal organisation, nor engage in any violence, nor counsel nor encourage others to do so.'[79] The Advisory Committee itself admitted that by March 1973 only four or five internees had been released without giving this undertaking.[80] After direct rule, the British replaced the Advisory Body with a commission, although its fairness can also be questioned. A meeting took place in June 1973 between Lord Carver and Frank Cooper (Permanent Under-Secretary for Northern Ireland). Cooper reassured Carver that the commission was fair but then went on to state, '[t]hey [the authorities] had succeeded in only putting to the commission those cases which they felt would be turned down; 180 of the 200 men put before the commissioners had had their detention confirmed.'[81] In other words, the authorities were seeking to only put before the commission those people they felt would have their cases turned down.

Faulkner reiterated his belief that he had the full support of Westminster, and some critics of internment had been taken in by IRA propaganda on the issue. He compared the situation in Northern Ireland to that of Londoners during the Second World War: 'Amidst the London blitz people put up signs which said "business as usual". That is the spirit of Ulster today.'[82]

In October 1971, the internment camp at Long Kesh was visited by a group of Westminster MPs. Stormont had done its homework on the visiting party and had received information on all of its members. An internal memo gave details on each MP. William F. Deeds (Conservative), leader of the delegation, was described as 'an extremely influential MP close to Ted Heath ... very sympathetic to the problems of Northern Ireland.' Lieutenant Colonel Colin Mitchell (Conservative) was regarded as 'needing no introduction. Even more right-wing than the *Daily Telegraph* and would certainly be in favour of very tough military action.' Norman St John-Stevas was '[w]ell-known, and although he is in favour of a united Ireland in the long-term his comments on the Northern Ireland situation are usually fair. He is, of course, a Catholic.' Merlyn Rees, future SOS for Northern Ireland, was assumed to be '[t]he most influential of the Labour group and an extremely sensible character', whereas Kevin McNamara (Labour) was 'well known and needed no introduction. Has recently been described as a "lunatic".'[83]

After internment was introduced, Faulkner also received many letters of complaint from Britain and across the globe. Concern was expressed by countries as far apart as the USA, Australia, New Zealand, France, Romania, Sweden and even Uganda.[84] A measure of the opposition to internment can be seen from the fact that the anti-internment song 'Men Behind the Wire' spent six weeks in the Irish charts in 1972, to be replaced by Paul McCartney's 'Give Ireland Back to the Irish'.[85] Faulkner could have been left in no doubt of the widespread condemnation that the measure was receiving.

However, Faulkner remained resolute, rejecting the suggestion made by Harold Wilson in March 1971 that those detainees who could not be brought before the courts should be released. Faulkner maintained that these individuals were the most dangerous men. He insisted that all those interned were members of the IRA. He believed it would be quite impossible to provide normal court procedures because of the intimidation of witnesses and to alter court procedures would cause greater consternation. In his view, internment had the advantage that it could be ended once the emergency was over, leaving the court procedures untainted.[86] He also rejected out of hand the suggestion that internment was aimed solely at the Catholic community:

> Internment is not aimed at repressing the Catholic community ... We utterly deplore the necessity of it, but we are convinced that it is absolutely necessary ... But the allegation that the operation was deliberately and maliciously one-sided is totally without foundation. The instructions given to the security forces were and still are that all dangerous men on whom they had reliable information which marked them out as definitely implicated in terrorist operations should be arrested. This is a matter which had nothing to do with politics or religion. It is a straightforward matter of public order and safety.[87]

Faulkner always maintained that internment had been successful. In February 1972 he stated that 'the effectiveness of the IRA had been greatly reduced in spite of the continued bombings and shootings.' According to him, the two main organisations were under pressure, with 700 to 800 of their members arrested, which had undermined their morale and had led to loss of key personnel. Moreover, he said that '[s]ome units had ceased to exist in Belfast and some areas had been completely cleared of IRA, with other areas under increasing pressure.' Faulkner asserted that the Belfast IRA leadership had been severely weakened. Determined to defend the use of internment, Faulkner stated that there were two answers to those who believed that internment had not worked. He reiterated his belief that the security forces had the IRA on the run. He continued with an attack on the wider nationalist community, stating that 'it is unfortunately true that those who have most to fear from the IRA are least articulate in pointing to the comparative freedom from intimidation which they are now beginning to enjoy.' Despite his earlier protestations that internment had been successful, he added that

> [i]nsofar as internment has not yet succeeded, this is due in no small measure to the fact that there are many people outside the IRA who do not want it to work. They include those who while ostensibly deploring the methods of the IRA have little desire to see the IRA put out of action until some at least of the organisations [sic] aims have been achieved.

So, Faulkner was adamant that more needed to be done by the wider nationalist community to curtail the IRA.[88] How much of a realistic prospect this was is certainly open to question given the 'siege mentality' that existed within that community after the introduction of internment.

In the same memo, Faulkner also denied that there had been a substantial increase in IRA recruitment since internment and insisted that recent arrests indicated that most of those taking part in terrorist activity had been recruited before its introduction. Faulkner was also determined that no internees should be released to procure a political settlement that in turn might help defeat the IRA. He reaffirmed his belief that all the internees were involved in terrorism and that none of them could be regarded as purely politically minded. He asserted that, as a result, these individuals, if released, would be likely to return to carrying out acts of violence and helping both factions of the IRA repair the damage that had been inflicted on them by the introduction of internment. Faulkner believed that released internees would target RUCSB members who had arrested and interrogated them. He maintained that the IRA would also see such releases as a success which the police and general public would see similarly and that, as a result, the IRA would be able to dictate future terms in any negotiations. He stated that '[i]f there were any releases the IRA would intensify its campaign and those individuals on the run would be likely to return to Northern Ireland ... it must be remembered that intelligence had been gained from the arrests.' Faulkner did concede that internment was the main cause of Catholic alienation and that it had increased support for the IRA, even from people who would normally have no truck with violence. However, he did not see what advantages could be gained from 'letting gunmen loose to re-impose their will on areas from which they had been expelled.' Faulkner also believed that talks could not take place with a fully armed, undefeated IRA, which the constitutionalist nationalists had no control over, in the background. He added that the defeat of the IRA would not be a painless exercise, and, as such, the need for internment would need to be explained more effectively. He proposed to give as much publicity as possible in defending the policy and correcting the propaganda that had been directed against internment. He hinted that it might also be possible to include proposals for the ending of internment once the IRA's campaign had ceased. Additionally, there would be an improvement in the internees' conditions including better welfare and rehabilitation facilities. Regulations regarding existing procedures, which were considered to be arbitrary, were soon to be removed. Also, legislation was being considered that would put the Special Powers Acts into suspension once the present emergency was over.

Faulkner's insistence that all those detained were members of the IRA seems hard to justify in light of some of his correspondence. In the same month that he had vehemently defended internment, February 1972, he received a handwritten internal note signed Ken (most probably Ken Bloomfield, a top civil servant) requesting information about an internee called Patrick Joseph Martin. The author states that friends of his approached him regarding Martin who worked for them and who they knew well. The note outlines Patrick Joseph Martin's fear of appearing in front of the Advisory Committee and requests when his case would be heard. In the note, Ken describes this internee as 'a plausible rascal' who has very serious charges against him. At the bottom of the note, in different handwriting than the author's, it is written 'Auxillary [sic] IRA, E company, 1st Battalion, deeply involved.' The note had obviously been passed to someone for investigation and had been returned to Faulkner with the intelligence on Martin supplied. This is certainly not the sort of individual that you would expect to be released by Faulkner. Another internal memo reported on Martin's status. In March 1972 he was being held on the *Maidstone* where the Advisory Committee did not sit, but, according to the memo, his case was due to come up 'fairly soon'. The final memo in this series of correspondence, dated 14 March 1972, simply stated that Martin had been released unconditionally.[89] It must be noted that Faulkner himself signed every DO individually and personally reviewed the evidence in each case; this he did, according to his memoirs, under self-imposed 'quite stringent conditions for the evidence required … and only if I was satisfied with the quality of evidence was the order made'.[90] The likelihood of a 'heavily involved' IRA man being released by Faulkner must surely have been very slim.

The natural conclusion, therefore, is that Faulkner must have known that the intelligence in at least this case was flawed. It seems possible that Faulkner knew this because the initial arrest lists had been augmented to include individuals who had opposed the Northern Ireland government but who were not members of the IRA. As a bonus, the operation would frighten nationalists so that they would not give support to the IRA, just as the Romans had hoped that Demetrius's experience would send a message to the Christians. Another plus for introducing such an operation is that it was likely to yield much valued intelligence. The intelligence was needed because, although the security forces knew the main operators within both sections of the IRA, they did not have a complete picture. Of course the operation would also serve to quell demands from hard-line unionists for action and intimidate the nationalist community in the hope of reducing support for the IRA. As Faulkner knew that this was the type of operation that had been undertaken then he almost certainly knew also that there was little danger in releasing Patrick Martin, as maybe he wasn't as heavily involved as had been suggested.

Furthermore, many unionists did have perceptions that a substantial section of the Catholic community supported the IRA, perceptions that were given credence by the statements of some nationalists, as can be seen from a Stormont press release in March 1971 following the murder of two RUC men. The statement attacked comments made by Kevin Agnew, leader of the Northern Ireland Civil Rights Association (NICRA). Agnew had apparently called for the 'planters to be sent back home' and stated that 'there would be no peace until the Union Jack goes'.[91] The Protestant perception of the deteriorating security situation is obvious from Robert Ramsey's analysis of the period leading up to August 1971:

> Their [The IRA's] attacks were more cruel and frequent and they appeared to be able to bomb at will. Ulster citizens in every town were having to go about their daily business in fear of their lives and to walk past the smouldering ruins of shops and offices in the main streets. Many towns were hit several times. Every news bulletin was a litany of murder and mayhem. Normal social life was frozen in many areas and, worst of all, nothing seemed to be able to be done about the deteriorating state of affairs. Public disquiet was perceptibly changing into a mood of outrage and we began to worry about how long the government could contain this anger and prevent the outbreak of civil disorder.[92]

In other words, the IRA's campaign had driven the Stormont administration to the point where it could see no alternative but to introduce internment. If it did not there was a possibility of civil disorder from within the unionist community. It was quite possible that failure to act would result in Faulkner's resignation because of the demands of hard-line unionism for sterner security measures. Faulkner also expressed sheer frustration at 'how unpleasant it was to see at liberty day after day not merely apologists for but the ultimate directors of a campaign of terrorism that daily erodes moral standards and diminishes the quality of life'.[93]

An insight into some of the political thinking at Stormont surrounding the decision to implement internment can be gathered from an internal memo from Robin Baillie, Minister of Commerce, to Faulkner less than two weeks after its implementation:

> At present we are in a position of some political strength. Paisley's power and credibility have been greatly shaken in the last two weeks ... The government stature with its supporters has been greatly enhanced by Heaths' rebuke to Lynch and the backing which he has given us. On the propaganda front our standing is better than for some time. The situation is not permanent and cannot be taken for granted ... But security is only one aspect of the situation now facing us in our political fight for survival.[94]

The significance of this statement is given extra importance by the fact that Baillie was regarded as a moderate within the UUP. Baillie clearly indicates the political advantage that has been gained, over Paisley and the hard-line unionists, by the introduction of internment. These concerns were evident as early as November 1970 when Faulkner's cabinet felt that 'recent events made it increasingly difficult for the government to convince its supporters that it was effectively handling the law and order problems'.[95] This is in direct contradiction to Faulkner's assertions that the decision to introduce internment was for security reasons alone. Baillie does also consider what political initiatives are available, and he suggests that he can see no other way forward than to include the minority in the government 'as of right not in a coalition'. He also warns of the dangers of such a move and the possible Protestant backlash, asking, 'What would be the Protestant backlash? Can you trust the minority leaders on past form? Would you be able to have a stable government with people with such diverse views?'[96] This backlash was also prominent in the thoughts of politicians at Westminster. As Maudling recalled, 'The point simply was that a Protestant backlash was the great danger we all feared.'[97]

Faulkner continued to defend the use of internment and claimed that it had only been introduced after months of provocation by the IRA. He also castigated the government in the South for its criticism, stating that, 'Mr. Lynch had publicly threatened to bring in internment … on the basis of a rumour.' Therefore, he argued, if the South had faced anything like the level of violence in the North then surely Lynch would have 'long since opened the already prepared Curragh internment camp'.[98]

We have seen how the main commanders in the British Army were opposed to internment prior to its introduction, but, once the operation was launched, some of the same commanders were steadfast in defence of the measure. General Tuzo believed that it had been carried out in an efficient manner and that the security forces were in a very difficult position. As a result, they had 'the smallest reason to place any trust in the people arrested or those likely to rally to them given half a chance'. This seems to be an effort to excuse the arrest of individuals who should have not been arrested. He also maintained that 'internment had proved to be a considerable success and was their best available weapon in the fight against the IRA'.[99]

Tuzo also addressed the question of interrogation techniques. He maintained that, whatever people thought of internment, intelligence-gathering was an essential part of the measure. He also maintained that the intelligence gained from the interrogation methods used was 'vital to the conduct of future operations and the good results obtained so far fully justify the continuation of interrogation in depth'. However, Tuzo did concede that the 'other side had already won a propaganda victory'. He also made a number of suggestions of how any inquiry into the interrogation techniques used should be conducted. He wanted it held behind closed doors and the only evidence made available about the techniques to be medical reports of the detainees before and after interrogation. He also argued that the Army needed to be represented by a high-level legal adviser.[100] The use of the interrogation techniques in Northern Ireland developed from their use in the colonies and is an issue that will be examined in Chapter 3.

There have been many protestations from key British political figures – at the time and since – that they were not in favour of the introduction of internment. Sir Robert Andrew, Private Secretary to Lord Carrington at the time of internment, was in no doubt that it was political pressure from Faulkner and Stormont that persuaded a reluctant British government and army to act in the draconian way it did:

> I think most people in Whitehall who were involved had grave doubts about it. Possibly if the British government had been in direct control, as we were of course a little bit later on, it wouldn't have happened. The biggest problem was what to do with these people once you've arrested them. By definition, you haven't got evidence that would stand up in a court of law so you can't bring them to trial. You either have to keep them inside indefinitely, which would be the subject of much criticism, or eventually you have to let them go as they had to do in the end. So I think the policy was a failure.[101]

Heath and Maudling were also apparently sceptical about the policy.[102] Heath, in his autobiography, however, refuted the allegation that internment was forced on the British by Faulkner. He stated that the Cabinet Committee on Northern Ireland had discussed the possibility of internment as early as 15 March 1971, before Chichester-Clark resigned.[103] Indeed, the possibility of introducing internment had been considered as early as February by Westminster. Admittedly, the cabinet agreed that any such decision would need to be taken with great caution. The cabinet also agreed that any such operation could only prove effective if 'the terrorist leaders could be identified and arrested'. There was also an understanding that internment would be 'liable to exacerbate the situation'.[104] Nevertheless, it is apparent that the British were committed to internment once it had been introduced. The discussions at the Chequers meeting clearly show the commitment of both governments to the workings of internment. Indeed, they were considering ways of improving the systems of detention and countering attacks on internment.

How had the British ended up in this position? Undoubtedly they had wanted to introduce internment in the hope that it would succeed and in the process save Faulkner's tenure. Equally, they also wanted it to succeed in the hope that it would curtail the activities of the IRA who were murdering British soldiers. The Army had initially been welcomed to Northern Ireland in 1969 as saviours by the Catholic community. However, even then, at least one cabinet minister saw the potential dangers of such a development:

> Cabinet must now discuss the constitutional consequences of the involvement of British troops. I don't think we can get them out of Northern Ireland at all easily now they have gone into Belfast … I fear that once Catholics and Protestants get used to our presence they will hate us more than they hate each other.[105]

These thoughts were to prove prophetic – at least in the case of the Catholic community, especially after the introduction of internment. The British had come with good intentions but, by necessity, had found themselves working with the existing unionist authorities. This had brought them increasingly into direct conflict with nationalists. They crossed their own Rubicon when the IRA began to shoot members of the British Army. As James Callaghan maintained, after the murder of the first British soldier in February 1971, 'This was the weekend on which the Provisionals declared war on the British Army', and they had also 'by this time seriously changed their tactics and were proceeding to wage all-out war on the British Army'.[106] Callaghan also told republican supporters on a visit to Belfast, 'If you stop shooting at British soldiers there would be no need to use the Special Powers Act.'[107]

Intelligence on loyalists

It seems clear that both governments could not have expected all of the serious repercussions that were about to unfold following Operation Demetrius. These repercussions were not to be helped by the nature of the initial arrest operation.

The standard narrative regarding the introduction of internment is that it was a mistake, based on poor intelligence, which led to an increase in support for the IRA, the implication being that this was the reason why innocent nationalists were arrested and some subsequently interned and also why no loyalists were interned until 1973.[108] Alternatively, republicans, and many nationalists, maintain that internment was an indiscriminate attack on the nationalist community. Which version of events stands up to scrutiny? A number of questions need to be asked. Was the introduction of internment an indiscriminate attack on the nationalist community? What was the quality of intelligence on republican paramilitaries? This chapter has shown that the introduction of internment was not an indiscriminate attack on the nationalist community. It has also demonstrated that there was a reasonable level of intelligence on republican paramilitaries. We also need to consider whether or not there was intelligence available on loyalist paramilitaries.

It is obvious that the initial arrests targeted only nationalists. Despite this, Faulkner insisted that there was no case to detain loyalists. Furthermore, he stated that 'the Attorney General had informed him that the police had been unable to furnish him with any information suggesting that a subversive organisation existed in the Protestant community'.[109] However, between May and August 1970, the RUCSB provided three reports to the Stormont cabinet, of which Faulkner was a member, that considered the implications of introducing internment.[110] The RUCSB outlined the number of loyalists to be detained. This lists included 145 republicans, sixty-two extreme loyalists and fifteen anarchists. They advised that, in their view, internment was not necessary at this time. They warned that its introduction could result in destruction of property and murders, with Protestants likely to respond. It could also result in a return to the streets on a large and widespread scale by all elements under the civil-rights umbrella. They advised that the position should be kept under review. With this in mind, contingency planning had been undertaken by RUCSB, and detention lists had been compiled.

The number of republicans anticipated to be arrested does appear fairly accurate in relation to the actual membership figures of the IRA at this time. These lists were compiled around the time of the Falls Road Curfew, when many people in Belfast joined the IRA. At the time, the PIRA in Belfast had sixty to seventy members in each company. However, of these, only half a dozen or so individuals from each company were actively involved in operations, and most of these men were known to Special Branch.[111] As one Special Branch officer stated, 'We knew what their structure was and who the leaders were in most areas ... we wouldn't have known the individual members of the units.'[112] Working on these figures, it does seem that the RUCSB report was reasonably accurate, with roughly fifty active PIRA members in Belfast. The remaining names could have been made up of IRA members from outside Belfast. So, the RUCSB did have a reasonable level of intelligence on many PIRA members, though admittedly not all – the point being that a targeted arrest operation could have proved more successful. Some in the British establishment also believed that internment could have been used as it was 'in the colonies, with only a few suspects removed at any one time'.[113]

Stormont was further advised in the reports on the potential dynamics of introducing internment. The RUCSB recommended that the power of introducing internment be kept in reserve as the situation had not deteriorated to the extent that the 'existence of the state is in such peril that to resort to them can be no longer avoided'. The advice given was that conditions were not favourable for the use of such a measure, and a number of considerations were listed by the RUCSB. According to the report, since the onset of the civil-rights era, internment had been regarded by the nationalist community as the most emotional issue of all. Furthermore, the introduction of internment could not be defended on moral grounds, considering national and international opinion.

According to the RUCSB, 'republicans, opposition politicians, the civil rights movement and the Catholic Church have now an expertise and a capability in the propaganda field which could not be effectively matched'. The memo further warned that unilateral action against republicans would be indefensible. There was no distinction between republicans and Protestant extremists. Here we see the Special Branch clearly informing the Stormont administration that loyalists would need to be arrested in any internment swoop; they were obviously involved in subversive activity also. Their advice made it clear that the position was not the same as had occurred in Northern Ireland during the border campaign when internment had worked:

> Unlike 1956 ... when the IRA made a declaration of war and the minority did not respond to their call; we now have a conditioned, indoctrinated, vociferous and articulate minority which is highly volatile, together with a similarly inflamed large body of militant Protestants. What was clearly a paper decision then, is not the same decision we are considering taking now. What we are saying is – not now, but yes should we be pushed to the brink of civil war and there is clearly no alternative if we are to save the Province.[114]

The RUCSB also detailed gelignite explosions, attributed to loyalists attempting to make the situation worse. The increase in violence on both sides was considered. The Special Branch concluded that Protestant reaction to the introduction of internment should also be considered, as it was obvious that many loyalists would be candidates for arrest. The concluding advice was again that the time was not right for use of the measure. So the advice in the three papers had clearly indicated the need to arrest individuals from both loyalist and republican groupings.

Additionally, the consequences of the introduction of internment had been highlighted and the probability of a Protestant backlash considered.

Although this was a year before the introduction of internment, it does seem unlikely, given the increase in republican violence leading up to August 1971, that loyalist activity had ceased to exist. Indeed, loyalist paramilitaries were responsible for twenty-two deaths in 1971.[115] Furthermore, the RUCSB analysis in 1970 was also backed up by a report on operations in late 1971. This report detailed the IRA as the principal threat to security, but it also identified a secondary threat in the 'activities of diffuse groups of Protestant extremists loosely known as the UVF [Ulster Volunteer Force]'. The report warned that 'violent action by the UVF is not to be discounted', and it also identified 'hooligan' elements attached to both republican and loyalist paramilitaries.[116]

It seems clear that the RUC and Stormont had information on subversive illegal activity by Protestants in 1970. It also appears obvious that Faulkner must have known of the potential threat posed by loyalists in 1971. Even Faulkner's principle private secretary believed that loyalists should have been interned.[117] This prompts the question, why was it then that no loyalists were interned in the first internment swoops? Faulkner responded to the criticism of the operation, that 'one or two Protestants were among those arrested for suspected IRA activities'.[118] Indeed, a few Protestants had been arrested, including John McGuffin (future author of *Internment* and *The Guineapigs*) and Major Bunting's son, Ronald, but they were both opponents of Stormont. This does seem to miss the point though that no loyalists had been arrested during the initial internment swoops. It was not until 1973 that the first loyalist was interned.

The idea that only the Stormont administration ignored intelligence on loyalist paramilitaries can be discounted when we look at the situation after the introduction of direct rule. The British were quite aware of the dangers of loyalist paramilitaries, even on the ground, as one member of the Parachute Regiment admitted in 1971: 'We knew there were stacks of weapons on the Shankill, we knew about the UVF, we knew all about the Protestant bad boys.'[119] Whitelaw held talks with the Ulster Defence Association (UDA) in which he pointed out that 'Protestant violence could only be to the advantage of the IRA, since it enabled them to represent themselves as the protectors of the Roman Catholic population.'[120] Interestingly, it is clear from internal documents that the British pursued a policy of not arresting Protestant suspects with a view to them being subjected to internment. Whitelaw himself was briefed on the policy by a memo from the GOC's representative, which stated that:

[t]his policy does not therefore provide for the arrest of Protestants or other non-Provisional terrorists except with the object of bringing a criminal charge. Protestants are not, as the policy stands, arrested with a view to their being made subject of Interim Custody Orders (ICOs) and brought before the commissioners … Ministers have judged that the time is not at the moment ripe for an extension of the arrest policy in respect of Protestants.[121]

This was a clear policy statement that loyalists were not to be subjects of ICOs and consequently should not be interned at this time. The reasoning behind such a policy was also outlined. It was thought that since not all Protestant paramilitary organisations, with the exception of the UVF, were illegal, it was hard to draw up precise criteria for who should be arrested and also that these loyalists posed no threat to the state. This policy was adopted despite the murders of innocent Catholics which were being carried out. The Chief Constable reported in September 1972 that there had been forty-eight murders since 1 July, twenty-six of Roman Catholics and twenty-two of Protestants, where political or sectarian motives might be involved.[122] Furthermore, Whitelaw was informed by Cardinal William Conway, at a meeting in December 1972, that on average four Catholics were being murdered a week in 1972 and that there had been no official recognition of this campaign. In fact, a total of 107 Catholics with no paramilitary connections were murdered by loyalists between the introduction of internment and the end of 1972. After the meeting, Whitelaw said that he would see what he could do about getting the 'Protestant backlash publicised'.[123] A further indication that the British knew of the dangers of loyalist paramilitaries came in August 1972 when Whitelaw made it known that he wanted it conveyed to the UDA that 'he could not tolerate any further military activity on their part'.[124]

Obviously the British had not been involved in compiling the original arrest lists and therefore cannot be blamed for the initial one-sidedness of the operation. Furthermore, it may have been that they feared that if they began to intern loyalists that this could only make a bad situation worse. Counterfactually, it seems Whitelaw was beginning to realise at the same time that something would have to be done about loyalist paramilitaries. As he stated in November 1972,

[f]rom some points of view the Protestant extremist factions now presented a more serious threat than the IRA particularly as regards their gross intimidation of Roman Catholics in isolated areas. Their raids across the border also constituted an increasingly serious problem, since they made it more difficult for us to bring pressure on Lynch to take stronger action against the IRA operating against Northern Ireland from the Republic of

Ireland. Moreover authorities in the Republic would be fully entitled to fire on raiding parties, to arrest or charge any raiders whom they might catch and to seek extradition of the identified raiders who returned to Northern Ireland. For all these reasons it might soon be necessary to detain some of the leading Protestant extremists and to bring them before the new tribunals.[125]

This was three months before the first loyalist was interned, an event that occurred on 5 February 1973 because of alleged involvement in the murder of two Catholics. In this three-month period, a total of thirty-seven innocent Catholics were killed by loyalist paramilitaries; their victims included two women, six boys (two aged fourteen) and a fourteen-year-old girl. However, the fear of a Protestant backlash still held the British back from interning loyalists. They believed that even though the situation was bad, that it could get much worse, rejecting suggestions that the possible Protestant backlash was a myth and warning of grave consequences from the loyalist community.[126]

Moreover, British government records of the period consistently demonstrate a determination not to intern Protestants. As early as August 1971 it was assumed that the security forces had enough on their hands dealing with nationalists without trying to detain loyalists. The British did not want to face 'mob resistance' from the Protestant community. They also did not want to leave themselves open to the allegation that Westminster was forcing Stormont to detain Protestants 'without good cause but simply for political reasons'.[127] When Maudling, Home Secretary, met Dr Patrick Hillery, Irish Minister of External Affairs, on 11 August 1971, he informed him that

> [a]ll of those arrested under the internment operation were people who the security forces believed to be active in terrorism … As terrorism was conducted by the IRA it followed that the people arrested would be suspected of IRA activities few of whom would be Protestants. If Protestants were engaged in terrorism they too would be dealt with; so far there was no information to confirm that Protestants had been sniping.[128]

In 1972, Maudling stated that '[t]he potential Protestant backlash is not a myth. It is based on the fear and prejudice of many thousands of tough and determined men. I would not seek to disguise from my colleagues the simple fact that any action we may take may produce grave consequences.'[129] However, the loyalists were becoming an increasingly serious threat. The breakdown of terrorist acts had been estimated by the British to be 95 per cent committed by the IRA and 5 per cent attributed to loyalists and other individuals.[130] In July 1972, General Tuzo had informed Whitelaw that

[t]he major threat from the UDA is that their militant action will lead to widespread intersectarian [sic] conflict and eventually civil war although serious military action against the IRA should prevent the latter. Nevertheless, assuming that civil war is averted and an anti-IRA campaign begun in earnest, the UDA could be a constant source of irritation and worry to the security forces. Their strength is now approximately 25,000 with 12,000 in Belfast ... They may indulge in indiscriminate shooting into Catholic areas ... It will be even more necessary to acquiesce in unarmed UDA patrolling and barricading in Protestant areas ... Indeed it is arguable that Protestant areas could almost be entirely secured by a combination of UDA, Orange Volunteers and RUC. It may even be necessary to turn a blind eye to UDA arms when confined to their own areas.[131]

The British were careful not to advertise their arrest policy for Protestants. Prior to Heath's meeting with Jack Lynch in October 1972, he had been briefed to tell Lynch that '[t]he police draw no distinction between Catholics and Protestants in the investigation of security offences and the prosecution of such offences'. Heath was further supplied with figures on arrests of Protestants and arms and explosives finds. He was told that four members of the UVF had been sentenced to six years for armed robbery and that sixteen members of the UDA had been arrested on firearms charges. Since Operation Motorman, up until 12 October 1972, eighty-five Protestants had been arrested on security offences. Fifty were on bail, and seventeen had been released without charge; there had been no convictions. In total, there had also been seventy-nine arms, 12,762 rounds of ammunition and over 1,000 pounds of explosives recovered from loyalists in the same period. Further information was given to Heath on the riots that occurred over 11/12 October in Belfast: sixty-five people had been arrested in the Shankill area with six being charged. Heath was also briefed on the trouble in Belfast from 16–18 October 1972, which had involved forty shooting incidents in which the security forces had been shot at by loyalists. The brief concluded that '[t]he growth of Protestant violence represents a very serious change in the security situation ... The shooting and other attacks on the Army in the Protestant areas of Belfast on Monday and Tuesday night had nothing to do with the IRA or with incidents engineered by them'.[132] In detailing the number of attacks carried out by loyalists and arrests made, the authorities were trying to show that they were acting against loyalists. This, however, rather undermines their policy of not interning loyalists.

The British reiterated their belief that Protestants should not be interned in December 1972, insisting that only two classes of persons should be arrested. These included 'those against whom there is a likely criminal charge, irrespective of whether they are Catholic or Protestant' and 'Provisional officers, and volunteers who are an exceptionally serious threat to security, irrespective of the likelihood of criminal charges'. It was made quite clear that 'Protestant terrorists' were not to be arrested with the view to serving an ICO. The Army's civil adviser outlined that this subject had been discussed with ministers who did not feel that the time was right to start signing ICOs for loyalists. The RUC was examining ways in which loyalists might be served with ICOs, but it was felt that this was very problematic, the main obstacle being that 'the arrest of prominent leaders might have disastrous repercussions'. The question of the timing of serving such orders was also a very important concern because 'to start sending Protestants to the tribunals would be a very significant new departure'.[133]

The fact that the internment of Protestants was a politically charged issue was also highlighted even after loyalists had begun to be interned. In late 1973, the Northern Ireland Office sought to clarify the situation with regard to Protestants and internment:

> I thought I would write to you to clear up any misunderstanding which there may be about the arrest of Protestants. The practice of pre-auditing some ICO applications of Protestants arose at a time when evidence against them was hard to come by, and because it was important to consider the political implications of arresting certain prominent figures; but it has never been the case that no Protestant could be arrested for an ICO without prior authority from the NIO. There will however still be a small number of cases where arrest might have political implications and on which we should consult the Secretary of State first – just as we would for certain top IRA men.[134]

This reluctance of the British government to introduce the internment of loyalists may have made some political sense, but it did not take into account the effect of such a policy on the nationalist community. There can be no doubt that the PIRA was their main target during this period, and this made sense as they were the main group who were murdering security-force personnel. However, the policy can only be described as myopic; with ongoing and sustained loyalist violence, if the policy was to be pursued, then loyalists needed to be detained much earlier than was the case.

Overview

It is obvious that Faulkner could be in no doubt about the depth of feeling regarding the way internment had been introduced. However, Faulkner remained steadfast in his defence of internment and the

Advisory Committee. In truth, Baillie's comments to Faulkner seem to provide us with much of the reasoning behind the decision to introduce the measure. Faulkner's claim that internment had been introduced purely for security reasons seems somewhat dubious. The pressure he was under from hard-line unionists for tougher security measures clearly had an impact in his decision. Indeed, the influence of hard-line unionism reached as far as Westminster. As Jim Callaghan outlined, 'neither Faulkner nor the British government were ready to consider the kind of political proposals that would have improved the prospects of Catholic co-operation, because of the fear of adverse Protestant reaction'.[135]

Internment had been introduced with limited intelligence, and, as a consequence, the initial arrest lists were augmented with names of people who were political opponents of Stormont. At the very least, the correspondence regarding Patrick Martin leads us to question Faulkner's position regarding the introduction of internment. It seems very likely that Faulkner knew that innocent people had been interned. The British government admitted that many innocent people had been arrested even if unionists did not. However, both governments seemed to underestimate the sense of repression that the nationalist community felt.

The British were wary of 'propaganda' concerning the arrests and interrogation techniques and suggested a counter-campaign be mounted. They recognised the need for better conditions and that independent inspections of the new facilities would be required. They were conscious of public opinion in Northern Ireland and farther afield. Despite all of this they were not prepared to entertain discussing internal Northern Ireland matters with the government of the Republic initially, a move which could perhaps have allayed some nationalist fears but which would have undoubtedly antagonised unionists. At the same time, they did realise the need to try and isolate the extremists and get the SDLP back into the constitutional process, as well as proceeding with reform. Any form of coalition government was out of the question, as was the imposition of direct rule. However, they had realised before the introduction of internment that if it failed then this would be the only outcome left open to them.

It seems apparent that both governments had been planning for internment for some time. Indeed, the Northern Ireland cabinet, including Faulkner, had sought the introduction of internment in August 1969. The failure of the operation and the subsequent radicalisation of the nationalist community led to some in the British administration claiming that internment had been forced upon them. This does not seem to be what the evidence indicates. As Craig states, 'The British, by the end of July 1971, had decided they would allow internment ... Its motive was not therefore to genuinely kill off the IRA but, rather pessimistically, to have internment in place before Direct Rule was imposed.'[136] They had given a greater emphasis to the use of security measures in the hope of sustaining Stormont and also in an effort to combat the IRA who were killing members of the security forces.

So which narrative of the introduction of internment is true? Was it a mistake based on poor intelligence? Or was it an indiscriminate attack on the nationalist population? The truth is that both narratives, while having some element of truth, need to be qualified; a more nuanced interpretation of events is required. It is important to note that the IRA (particularly the PIRA) had been conducting a provocative and murderous campaign against Stormont and the British prior to August 1971. It is also true that Faulkner knew that his administration was Stormont's last chance before direct rule was implemented. It is obvious that both the Stormont administration, before the introduction of direct rule, and the British government, after its introduction, had intelligence on loyalist paramilitaries which was not acted on. The main reason loyalists were not detained was because of the fear of a backlash from the Protestant majority. This policy may have made some sense, as it was republicans who were murdering members of the security forces. In another respect, however, the policy can be considered as misguided as it did not take into account the effect the policy would have on the nationalist community. It seems likely that the initial arrest operation had been undertaken to placate hard-line unionism, intimidate nationalists and provide intelligence. The fact that over a third of those detained in the original arrest operation were released within two days demonstrates that intelligence-gathering was a major part of the exercise. Their release is a clear indication that people loosely associated with republican paramilitaries were being arrested, questioned and then released. It seems unlikely that Faulkner would not have appreciated the pitfalls of an indiscriminate arrest operation. However, the augmentation of the arrest lists, coupled with the Army's instructions to arrest anyone over the age of eighteen if they could not find their intended targets at their addresses only served to exacerbate the problem, especially as many PIRA members had been forewarned and were 'on the run'. Many innocent individuals were detained, and some were interned; therefore, the arrest operation appeared indiscriminate. This increased the nationalist community's sense of victimisation at the hands of the authorities, which in turn must have led to the increase in support and membership of the IRA. Neither can it be said that the authorities had no intelligence on republican paramilitaries. It seems apparent that they did have information on the 'main players'. Perhaps, as suggested by some, a more targeted operation may have proved more useful for the authorities.[137]

Finally, technically, the introduction of internment did not need the consent of both governments; however, in reality, Stormont and Westminster needed each other's support if the operation was to succeed. According to Craig, Westminster was able to implement 'internment alone, above and beyond Stormont's wishes', this must have been an unlikely scenario.[138] It is true to say that the British could have introduced internment by themselves, something that Stormont could not have done. Despite this, it was desirable to undertake the operation as a joint venture in the hope of defeating the IRA. Operation Demetrius was actively supported by both governments. The nature of the initial arrests and subsequent treatment of detainees, along with a policy of not interning loyalists until 1973, undermined this strategy and sowed the seeds for an escalation of the Troubles.[139] In the months that followed, Northern Ireland was plunged into a period of unprecedented violence. The repercussions of this policy decision will now be explored.

Notes

1 Adrian Guelke, 'Political comparisons: from Johannesburg to Jerusalem', in M. Cox, A. Guelke and F. Stephen (eds), *A Farewell to Arms? Beyond the Good Friday Agreement*, 2nd edn (Manchester, 2006), p. 372.

2 David Anderson, *Histories of the Hanged* (London, 2005), p. 203.

3 Members Brief Ulster Research Department, UUC, on Internment, 5 October 1971, Linenhall Library Political Collection (LLPC), P6861.

4 The Civil Authorities Act Northern Ireland 1922–43, Regulation 12.

5 Hennessey, *Evolution of the Troubles*, p. 94.

6 Note of a meeting at 10 Downing Street, 5 August 1971, PRONI, CAB/9/B/83/6.

7 Michael Carver, *Out of Step: The Memoirs of Field Marshal Lord Carver* (London, 1989), p. 407.

8 Hennessey, *Evolution of the Troubles*, p. 95.

9 'Publicity and psychological warfare against terrorists.' Paper presented by the Joint Security Committee … law and order, 11 June 1971, PRONI, HA/32/5/6.

10 Hennessey, *Evolution of the Troubles*, p. 111.

11 Hennessey, *Evolution of the Troubles*, p. 113.

12 Carver, *Out of Step*, p. 406.

13 Hennessey, *Evolution of the Troubles*, p. 120.

14 Edward Heath, *The Course of My Life: My Autobiography* (London, 1998), pp. 426–27.

15 Confidential operations instructions, 8 August 1971, TNA: PRO, WO/296/71.

16 Note of a meeting at 10 Downing Street, 5 August 1971; PRONI, CAB/9/B/83/6.
17 Kieran McEvoy, *Paramilitary Imprisonment in Northern Ireland* (Oxford, 2001), p. 210.
18 Hennessey, *Evolution of the Troubles*, p. 129.
19 Timothy Shanahan, *The PIRA and the Morality of Terrorism* (Edinburgh, 2009), p. 95.
20 Patterson and Kaufmann, *Unionism and Orangeism*, p. 132.
21 Tony Craig, 'Sabotage! The origins, development and impact of the IRA's infrastructural bombing campaigns 1939–97', *Intelligence and National Security,* 25 (3) (2010): 309–26.
22 Members Brief, Unionist Research Department UUC, 5 October 1971, LLPC, P6861.
23 John McGuffin, *Internment* (Tralee, 1973), p. 97.
24 P. J. Woodfield (NI Department) to Sir Philip Allen, Attached note on internment, 11 February 1971, TNA: PRO, CJ/4/462.
25 Paddy Hillyard, 'The normalisation of Special Powers: from Northern Ireland to Britain', in Philip Scraton (ed.), *Law, Order, and the Authoritarian State* (Milton Keynes, 1987), p. 284.
26 Laurence McKeown, *Out of Time: Irish Republican Prisoners, Long Kesh, 1972–2000* (Belfast, 2001), p. 13.
27 Cabinet conclusions of meeting held at Stormont, 9 August 1971, PRONI, CAB/4/1607/14.
28 Brice Dickson, *The European Convention on Human Rights and the Conflict in Northern Ireland* (Oxford, 2012), p. 64.
29 Office of the UKREPNI to Home Office, 11 August 1970, TNA: PRO CJ/4/462.
30 J2 Division Home Office analysis of Civil Emergencies (Special Powers) Acts, 18 August 1970, TNA: PRO CJ/4/462.
31 John McGuffin, *The Guineapigs* (Harmondsworth, 1974), p. 45.
32 Note of a meeting held in Room 406, Home Office, Whitehall on 15 July 1971, PRONI, HA/32/2/54.
33 Confidential operation instructions, HQ 19, 8 August 1971, TNA: PRO WO/296/71.
34 Ciaran De Baroid, *Ballymurphy and the Irish War,* 2nd edn (London, 2000), p. 73.
35 Quoted in Bean and Hayes, *Republican Voices*, p. 39.
36 Brendan Anderson, *Joe Cahill: A Life in the IRA* (Dublin, 2002), p. 223.
37 Kelvin White (Western European department) to Sir S. Crawford Private Secretary, TNA: PRO FCO 33/1464.
38 Mac Stíofáin, *Memoirs of a Revolutionary*, p. 184.
39 Patrick Bishop and Eamon Mallie, *The Provisional IRA* (London, 1987), p. 186.
40 Note of a meeting at the Home Office, 13 September 1971, TNA: PRO DEFE/24/1215.

41 Confidential operation instructions from HQ 19, 8 August 1971, TNA: PRO WO/296/71.
42 Memo on internment from SOS for the Home Department to SOS for Defence, 12 March 1971, TNA: PRO DEFE/24/1214.
43 Secret Perimeter, n.d., TNA: PRO CJ/4/57.
44 Letter from Government Security Unit (NI) to D. Johnston, then Assistant Chief Constable of the RUC, 18 August 1971, PRONI, HA/32/2/54.
45 Letter from P. Stonnell to Home Office, 21 September 1971, PRONI, CAB/9/B/83/9A.
46 Letter from A. P. Hockaday (MOD) to P. J. Woodfield (HO), 20 August 1971, TNA: PRO CJ/4/56.
47 Letter from J. F. Halliday to J. T. A Howard-Drake, 11 November 1971, TNA: PRO CJ/4/56; memo from Ministry of Home Affairs, Belfast, to J. Nicholson (HO) London, 13 December 1971, TNA: PRO CJ/4/57.
48 J. A. T. Howard-Drake to H. F. T. Smith (Office of UKREPNI), 26 August 1971, TNA: PRO CJ/4/56.
49 R. Spjut, 'Internment and detention without trial in Northern Ireland (1971–75)', *Modern Law Review*, 49 (1986): 712–39.
50 Whitelaw, *Memoirs*, p. 78.
51 Spjut, 'Internment and detention'.
52 Carver, *Memoirs*, p. 409.
53 Faulkner, *Memoirs*, p. 119.
54 Prime Minister to Lieutenant General Tuzo, 12 August 1971, TNA: PRO PREM/15/478.
55 Review of government strategy, 30 September 1971, TNA: PRO CAB/129/158/24.
56 Cabinet conclusions of meeting held at Chequers, 19 August 1971, PRONI, CAB/4/1607/19.
57 Smith, *The British State and the Northern Ireland Crisis*, p. 128.
58 Smith, *The British State and the Northern Ireland Crisis*, p. 133.
59 Cabinet conclusions of meeting held at Chequers, 19 August 1971, PRONI, CAB/4/1607/19.
60 Cillian McGrattan, *The Politics of Entrenchment* (London, 2010), p. 48.
61 Letter from Senator James Lennon to Faulkner, 1 October 1971, PRONI, CAB/9/B/83/7.
62 Letter from Faulkner to Senator James Lennon, 27 October 1971, PRONI, CAB/9/B/83/7.
63 Civil Authorities Act (NI), Reg. 12 (3).
64 *Hansard*, 17 April 1973, vol. 855, col. 280.
65 Detention procedures under the Detention of Terrorists (NI) Order 1972, TNA: PRO CJ/4/1333.
66 Detention procedures under the Northern Ireland (Emergency Provisions) (Amendment) Act 1975, TNA: PRO CJ/4/1333.
67 [Gardiner Report], *Northern Ireland committee to consider, in context of civil liberties and human rights, Measures to deal with terrorism in Northern Ireland*. Cmnd, 5847 (London, HMSO, 1975: 44).

68 Interview with Jim Auld, 21 July 2010. Auld was arrested at 3.30 a.m. on 9 August 1971, the first person to be arrested in Operation Demetrius. He appeared in front of the Advisory Body when Harry Taylor RUC (SB) presented the evidence against him from behind a screen. Both men addressed each other by their Christian names during the hearing. Taylor and Auld laughed as Taylor outlined the accusations against Auld. Auld was also one of the original twelve men subjected to the controversial SD treatment during interrogation.
69 *Irish News*, 5 July 2010.
70 *Sunday Times*, 23 December 1973.
71 'Desmond Boal biography' (n.d.) *Cain*, available online at www.cain.ulstr .ac.uk/othelem/people/biography/bpeople.htm (accessed on 2 June 2011).
72 *Sunday Times*, 23 December 1973.
73 James L. Dickerson, *Inside America's Concentration Camps: Two Centuries of Internment and Torture* (Chicago, Ill., 2010), p. 48.
74 Letter from Police Authority to Faulkner, 21 August 1971, PRONI, CAB/9/B/83/7.
75 Letter from Law Society of Northern Ireland to all members, 2 February 1972, passed to Harold Black by lawyer who worked at Stormont, PRONI, CAB/9/B/83/6.
76 *Protestant Telegraph*, 2 October 1971.
77 *Northern Ireland House of Commons Debates*, 12 October 1971, vol. 82, col. 1183.
78 Commons debate on law and order motion, 13 October 1971, PRONI, CAB/9/B/83/6.
79 Internal Stormont memo from G. B. Newe, 17 February 1972, PRONI, CAB/9/B/83/7.
80 Meeting of the Advisory Committee, 9 March 1972, PRONI, HA/32/2/54.
81 Meeting between CGS and Permanent Under-Secretary NIO, 14 June 1973, TNA: PRO, DEFE/25/283.
82 Commons debate on law and order, 13 October 1971, PRONI, CAB/9/B/83/6.
83 Notes on Westminster MPs visiting internment centres (n.d.), PRONI, CAB 9/B/83/6.
84 Note on foreign reactions to situation in Northern Ireland (n.d.), TNA: PRO, FCO 33/1475.
85 Craig, *Crisis of Confidence*, p. 106.
86 Letter from Faulkner to Wilson, 7 March 1972, PRONI, CAB/9/B/83/6.
87 Press release from Faulkner, 24 August 1971, PRONI, CAB/ 9/B/312/4.
88 Memo by the Prime Minister as Minister of Home Affairs, 18 February 1972, PRONI, CAB/4/1639/5.
89 Detention and internment under the Civil Authorities (Special Powers) Acts, miscellaneous papers, internal memo Ken to Brian, PRONI, CAB/9/B/83/9A.
90 Faulkner, *Memoirs*, p. 123.
91 Stormont press release, 2 March 1971, PRONI, CAB/9/B/312/4.

92 Robert Ramsey, *Ringside Seats: An Insider's View of the Crisis in Northern Ireland* (Dublin, 2009), p. 87.
93 Faulkner, *Memoirs*, p. 149.
94 Memo from Baillie to Faulkner, 23 August 1971, PRONI, CAB/9/B/83/6.
95 Conclusions of a meeting of the cabinet, 30 November 1970, PRONI, CAB/4/1558/4.
96 Memo from Baillie to Faulkner, 23 August 1971, PRONI, CAB/9/B/83/6.
97 Reginald Maudling, *Memoirs* (London, 1978), p. 184.
98 Extracts from a speech made by Prime Minister to Annual Conference of the Confederation of Ulster Societies, 11 September 1971, PRONI, CAB 9/B/83/6.
99 Note of a meeting between heads of departments and GOC, Chief Constable and UKREP, 4 October 1971, PRONI, CAB/9/J/83/1.
100 Tuzo to UK Representative NI and Chief Constable, 23 August 1971, PRONI, CAB/9/B/83/6.
101 Taylor, *Brits*, p. 68.
102 English, *Armed Struggle*, p. 141.
103 Heath, *The Course of My Life*, p. 428.
104 Cabinet meeting, 9 February 1971, TNA: PRO CAB/128/49/9.
105 Richard Crossman, *The Diaries of a Cabinet Minister* (London, 1977), p. 620.
106 James Callaghan, *A House Divided: The Dilemma of Northern Ireland* (London, 1973), pp. 153–55.
107 Callaghan, *A House Divided*, p. 160.
108 See M. L. R. Smith, *Fighting for Ireland* (London, 1995), p. 101; English, *Armed Struggle*, pp. 139–40. McKittrick et al., *Lost Lives*, p. 80; Bardon, *A History of Ulster*, p. 682; Ed Moloney, *A Secret History of the IRA* (London, 2002), p. 100.
109 Cabinet conclusions of a meeting held 17 August 1971, PRONI, CAB/4/1609/17.
110 Cabinet conclusions, letter from RUC Special Branch, first paper on detention and internment under Civil Authorities (Special Powers) Acts, 21 May 1970; second paper, 1 July 1970; third paper, 6 August 1970, PRONI, CAB/9B/83/6.
111 Interview with Auld, 21 July 2010.
112 Taylor, *Brits*, p. 64.
113 Caroline Kennedy-Pipe, *The Origins of the Present Troubles in Northern Ireland* (London, 1997), p. 55.
114 Cabinet conclusions, second RUC Paper, PRONI, CAB/9/B/83/6.
115 McKittrick et al., *Lost Lives*, p. 61.
116 Assessment of operations in Northern Ireland, 1 May–1 November 1971, PRONI, HA/32/2/51.
117 Ramsey, *Ringside Seats*, pp. 92–93.
118 Minutes of Cabinet Meeting, 20 August 1971, PRONI, CAB/4/1610/12.
119 Arthur, *Northern Ireland Soldiers Talking*, p. 63.

120 Cabinet meeting, 15 June 1972, TNA: PRO, CAB/128/48.
121 'Arrest policy for Protestants': Memo by Major G. Bulloch, for GOC, for SOS morning meeting, 11 December 1972, PRONI, CAB/9/G/27/6.
122 Conclusions of a meeting … law, order, sectarian murders, 29 August 1972, PRONI, CAB 9/G/27/6/4.
123 Note of a meeting between the SOS, Cardinal Conway and Bishop Philbin, 5 December 1972, PRONI, CAB/9/J/90/10.
124 Conclusions of a meeting… law, order, victims, 1 August 1972, PRONI, CAB/9/G/27/6/4.
125 Cabinet meeting, 2 November 1972, TNA: PRO CAB/128/50/49.
126 Memorandum by SOS for the Home department, 3 March 1972, TNA: PRO CAB/129/162/1.
127 Maudling (UKREPNI) to Howard-Drake, dated August 1971, TNA: PRO CJ/4/56.
128 Note of a meeting between Home Secretary and Dr Hillery, 11 August 1971, TNA: PRO PREM/15/478.
129 Memo from Home Secretary, 2 March 1972, TNA: PRO CAB/129/162(26).
130 Telegram from Douglas-Home to FCO, 15 September 1972, TNA: PRO FCO/87/81.
131 Tuzo to Whitelaw, 'Military operations in the event of a renewed IRA campaign', 9 July 1972, TNA: PRO FCO/87/81.
132 Platt to Roberts, 10 Downing Street, 18 October 1972, TNA: PRO FCO 87/81.
133 J. F. Howe (CIVAD) to CLF 'Arrest Policy', 14 December 1972, TNA: PRO DEFE/24/824.
134 Letter from Frank Cooper (NIO) to James Flanagan (CC RUC), 13 November 1973, TNA: PRO CJ/4/724.
135 Callaghan, *A House Divided*, p. 164.
136 Craig, *Crisis of Confidence*, p. 97.
137 Carver, *Out of Step*, pp. 408–9.
138 Craig, *Crisis of Confidence*, p. 96.
139 See also McCleery, Martin J., 'Debunking the myths of Operation Demetrius: The introduction of internment in Northern Ireland in 1971' *Irish Political Studies* 27 (3) (2012b): 411–30.

3

Legacies of internment

Not a foregone conclusion

There is no doubt that the way in which internment was introduced dramatically increased support for the IRA, especially the PIRA. As the British admitted, as early as November 1971, it had made the 'IRA look for the first time like a mass movement instead of a small body using Catholics as cover'.[1] The PIRA declared 1972 would be their year of victory; however, this was to be far from the truth. Nationalist support for the PIRA did continue to increase, and this increase was due, in no small part, to the mistakes made by the authorities. Paradoxically, this period also saw a number of grave mistakes by both wings of the IRA, which led to a decrease in support for both organisations. Additionally, with the imposition of direct rule, the British made attempts to appear increasingly impartial. This was the time that lay the foundations for a prolonged conflict; it is this period that will now be explored. The introduction of internment, and subsequent events, had many consequences for the conflict, both short- and long-term, some of which have not been previously highlighted. This chapter will provide a more comprehensive analysis of internment, bringing together most of the repercussions associated with the measure. It will examine the use of repression by a liberal state in the context of the early 1970s in Northern Ireland, the effects of internment on the wider community, the impact of the measure in the international arena, how internment changed the IRA and the long-term legacy of the period for the conflict.

How the situation unfolded will be demonstrated by examining a number of key events: the Ballymurphy Killings between 9 and 11 August 1971, in-depth interrogation during the internment operation and the Compton and Parker Reports, the McGurk's Bar bombing, Bloody Sunday, the Widgery Inquiry, the Abercorn Restaurant bombing, direct rule, the PIRA ceasefire, Bloody Friday, Operation Motorman, the Claudy bombing, the Diplock Report and the internment of loyalists.

Before doing so, the killing of three Scottish soldiers in Belfast in March 1971 will be discussed briefly. It will be demonstrated that it was not a foregone conclusion that the introduction of internment would lead to a vast increase in support for republican paramilitaries. It has already been shown that a more balanced and targeted arrest operation could have taken place. Another factor which may have influenced the reaction to internment was the timing of its introduction. For example, if internment had been introduced immediately after a republican paramilitary operation that outraged the nationalist community, then it seems less likely that it would have resulted in a large increase in support for the IRA.

The three soldiers murdered were John McCaig, aged seventeen, his eighteen-year-old brother, Joseph, and Dougald McCaughey, aged twenty-three. McCaughey's brother was also a serving soldier in Belfast at the time. They were the first soldiers to be murdered off-duty; all three were shot in the head on a lonely mountain road. It seems they had been drinking in a bar in Belfast and had been persuaded to leave with their killers. The murders had two immediate consequences: first, all soldiers under the age of eighteen were barred from serving in the North. Second, the murders led to the creation of 'tartan gangs', gangs of young loyalists who supposedly adopted tartan scarves as a uniform in memory of the three soldiers. These gangs were eventually to fall under the control of the UDA. The killings caused outrage across Northern Ireland. Certainly, at the time of the murders of the Scottish soldiers, the PIRA did not have widespread support within the Catholic community. As one Special Branch officer commented,

> [t]he revulsion was unbelievable. People in the republican community weren't ready for that ... In fact that was a real turning point, the point at which the IRA themselves thought that internment would have been introduced. Indeed the thinkers in the movement at that time felt that the government would have got away with it then and there wouldn't have been the difficulties there were when it eventually came in.[2]

There was stinging criticism of the murders from the Central Citizens' Defence Committee (CCDC): 'Strong enough words cannot be found to express the horror and revulsion of decent people at the foul murders of three young soldiers last night. It is frightening to think that their murderers are at large somewhere in Belfast. Such men are godless monsters.' Indeed, initially the PIRA also strongly condemned the murders; moreover, they never admitted responsibility in the *Republican News*. Immediately after the murders, a PIRA spokesman stated, 'We have checked with all our units in Belfast and wish to state that none of them carried out any actions tonight.' The PIRA was at pains to disassociate themselves from the brutal killings, later stating, 'We were as horrified as anyone else at the murders. We do not shoot men in the back.' However, according to rumours at the time, one of those involved in the murders was PIRA member Patrick McAdorey. Clearly, the Provisionals were worried about the impact the murders could have on the support they received from the nationalist community. The murders were condemned by both the SDLP and the Nationalist Party. The nationalist *Irish News* was highly critical, suggesting that 'internment without trial was obviously something to be considered'. In a particularly scathing editorial, it declared,

> No word but barbaric can fitly describe the nature of this senseless killing ... They are the latest example of how truly rotten our society has become. These deaths are enough to make the stomach turn ... Perhaps the very horror of the manner of these deaths may point the way to some approach by which the rupture that divides this distraught society can be healed. If not, we face a stern and painful period of reassessment until the primacy of justice and peace can be asserted over violence and death.[3]

These sentiments seem to suggest that the suspension of normal legal procedures and the imposition of stricter security measures may have been tolerated by the nationalist community, at this time, in order to restore peace. Faulkner's and Burroughs' claims that some nationalists supported internment were highlighted in Chapter 1. Their claims are debatable, but what certainly does seem possible is that if selective intelligence-led internment had been introduced at this point, the surge in support the IRA received in August 1971 might not have occurred. Major General Ford of the British Army was to concede many years later that the military should have 'tooth-combed the lists and gone for the key people. If we'd [sic] done that there wouldn't have been the repercussions that there were.'[4] Once again, the point is that a more balanced and targeted, and perhaps better-timed, operation might have led to less serious repercussions. Admittedly, there could have been a public outcry against the measure, timed and targeted campaigns such as civil disobedience might have still taken place, but perhaps not as many nationalists would have turned to the IRA if the policy had been applied differently. Many nationalists were indeed still suspicious of the Stormont administration, despite the reforms that had taken place. Moreover, as Spjut points out, within the nationalist community 'the re-introduction of internment was identified as another instance of unionist abuse of unfettered ministerial discretion which was directed not narrowly to suppressing violence, but to subjugating the political opposition which was mounted during the civil rights campaign'.[5] This did not mean that a substantial numbers of nationalists supported the IRA. However, it was axiomatic that there would be repercussions from the way internment had been introduced.

So far it has been argued that internment was badly timed, planned and implemented, which led to it being perceived as an indiscriminate attack by most of the nationalist community. Unfortunately, the flawed introduction of internment was not the only mistake the authorities were to make that increased support for the IRA.

Under siege

White and White have identified the dimensions of state repression within a liberal society as formal, 'in that it is sanctioned by state authorities. Internment provides an example of this.' Further, they have identified that states also use informal repression, which is 'undertaken by low-level state agents of their own volition. Bloody Sunday may provide an example of this.' They define state repression as 'the use or threat of coercion by a government against opponents or potential opponents to weaken their resistance to authority'.[6] Bloody Sunday was an obvious example of such repression as it was carried out in full view of the media. The manner of Operation Demetrius can also be considered as a form of this secondary repression. When soldiers are used in an arrest operation, to arrest people they believe have been involved in the murder of their colleagues, it is almost inevitable that violence and brutality will take place. It certainly seems to have taken place in the days that followed the initial arrest operation. Padraig O'Malley vividly describes the morning of the arrests:

> The horrifying circumstances of that morning were never to be forgotten. Whole areas were sealed off, paratroopers smashing doors open and literally dragging men from their homes in front of hysterical wives and terrified children, the brutal knock in the middle of the night ... The army, 'the Brits' had become the enemy.[7]

The heavy-handed way in which the operation was carried out helped to increase support for the IRA in Ireland and abroad. The greatest effects of the Army's brutality were felt by the nationalist community. So it was that many within the nationalist community across Northern Ireland began to identify themselves more closely with the IRA.

It is clear that the Army used brutality during the arrest operation; it is equally clear that such actions aided the republican movement in the propaganda war. In addition, John Whyte maintained in 1990 that the army was operating in support of the civil power, which remained in Protestant hands until the introduction of direct rule in 1972, and the troops therefore slid during 1970–72 into operating openly on behalf of the unionist regime, as witness their part in the Falls Road Curfew of 1970, the introduction of internment in 1971, and Bloody Sunday in January 1972. Many Catholics would feel that, ever since, British policy has been skewed in favour of the Protestants.[8]

The sense that the whole community was under attack from the authorities was widespread. In this period also, women began to play a more prominent role in opposing the state, and, by late 1971, a few women had started to join the PIRA. Women were also largely in charge of the early-warning systems for army raids. These systems included the banging of bin lids to warn people that raids were taking place and the organising of 'hen patrols' to monitor army activity. Women also took the lead in the campaign of civil disobedience. Approximately 30,000 households joined the rent and rates strike, and, because women were the household administrators, they were in the best position to enforce the campaign. To neutralise this action, the government introduced the Payment for Debt Act of 1971, which permitted the government to withhold wages and welfare benefits from the pay cheques of the people on rent and rates strikes.

At this time the Army also started to recruit informers, a tactic which was to be used many times throughout the Troubles. In November 1971, the army began using these techniques pioneered by Frank Kitson during the Mau Mau Uprising in Kenya. The idea was to induce somebody from the other side to work for you. These informants became known as 'Freds' and worked for the security forces for financial reward or freedom from conviction.[9] The large influx of new IRA members, derived from the introduction of internment, must surely have meant that it was easier to plant informants within the republican movement.

Field Marshal Carver has claimed, like many others in the authorities, that 'in spite of the escalation of incidents, progress was made in terms of captures of weapons and ammunition and of arrests – 400 men on the "wanted list" were picked up and 112 "routine arrests" were made in November and December', the implication being that internment was proving a success in terms of the capture of weapons and wanted men. While it may be true that, after the initial arrest operation, intelligence was gradually improving and wanted men were being captured, the increase in arms seizures is also likely to have been partly due to the increase in paramilitary activity. It is universally agreed that the introduction of internment resulted in a major upsurge in IRA activity. It is unsurprising maybe that as a consequence of this increase in activity more weapons were going to be uncovered and more paramilitaries were going to be arrested. In response to the upsurge in paramilitary activity, the number of British Army battalions was increased to from thirteen to sixteen by October 1971.[10]

Ballymurphy

The most obvious example of informal state repression in the immediate aftermath of Operation Demetrius occurred in the Ballymurphy area of Belfast when ten people were shot dead by the Army between 9 and 11 August 1971; another man died of a heart attack after allegedly being subject to a mock execution by soldiers. The killings took place during an operation, carried out partly by the Parachute Regiment, to round up suspected paramilitaries for internment. It is perhaps significant that the Parachute Regiment had also lost the first of its members in the Troubles in May 1971, when Sergeant Michael Willetts was killed when a bomb was thrown into a police station in Belfast. The paratrooper had thrown himself in front of the bomb and, in the process, saved two children from almost certain death. Also injured in the blast were seven police-men, one soldier, five men, four women and three children. The Paras are renowned as a fighting force and a very close band of soldiers. The use of the regiment in such a hostile civilian environment may not have been appropriate and, in hindsight, ultimately proved unwise.

The victims of the Ballymurphy Killings included a Catholic priest and a mother of eight children, Joan Connolly. Joan Connolly was shot while searching the streets for her children during the post-internment riots. Fr Hugh Mullan was shot, in scenes similar to Bloody Sunday, while carrying a white handkerchief, making his way back from attending an injured man. Immediately after his death, Dr William Philbin, Bishop of Down and Connor, stated, 'The circumstances of Father Mullan's death call for the most vigorous investigation in the interests of justice and truth and in the hope of bringing the present dreadful contagion of kill-ing to an end.'[11]

Perhaps one of the reasons why the killings in Ballymurphy did not obtain as much publicity as Bloody Sunday was because they did not happen in the full view of the media. A campaign was started in 1998 by relatives of those killed in Ballymurphy, which called for an independ-ent international investigation examining the circumstances surround-ing all the deaths and for the British government to issue a statement of innocence and an apology.[12] In 2010, the Catholic Church discovered eyewitness accounts of the Ballymurphy shootings which described how the British Army fired unnecessarily when shooting eleven people in the area. The relatives' campaign received a setback in June 2012 when the then Secretary for State for Northern Ireland, Owen Paterson, refused an independent investigation into the deaths because it was believed it would not be in the public interest to do so. However, the families have continued their campaign.

The deaths in Ballymurphy were not the only deaths in the aftermath of Operation Demetrius. Indeed, between 9 and 12 August 1971, twenty-five people were murdered: two women, five teenage boys and eighteen men. The casualties included one PIRA man, three soldiers, five Protestants and sixteen Catholics, with the Army killing nineteen people and the IRA killing five. The PIRA man killed was Patrick McAdorey, who was reputed to have been one of the gunmen who killed the three young Scottish soldiers in March. In a macabre postscript, it seems that '[p]hotographs were taken of military personnel shaking hands with McAdorey's dead body in Lagan Bank mortuary'.[13] The Army was obviously pleased that McAdorey had met his end.

Somewhat ironically, Stormont took out a series of adverts in the press at the time that depicted a soldier on patrol and stating, 'His job is hard enough! Help him and the others in the security forces by keeping off the streets at night.'[14] In what may be considered an unfortunate choice of language, Faulkner stipulated that '[i]nternment is by contrast a *discriminatory* weapon in that its whole purpose is to put the terrorist out of action with the least risk of death and injury to ordinary defenceless people'.[15]

Catching Gaddafi's eye

Shortly after the introduction of internment, Joe Cahill, Chief of Staff of the PIRA, gave a press conference at which he claimed that only thirty IRA men had been detained. The audacity of Cahill's appearance at the press conference has been highlighted many times. However, the conference was to produce an unexpected consequence. Many miles away, the twenty-nine-year-old Libyan leader, Colonel Muammar Gaddafi, was assessing its significance. Indeed, it was around this time that Cahill, who impressed Gaddafi, said that 'Muammar Gaddafi's roving ambassador began making contact, through intermediaries' with him.[16] Almost unbelievably, as late as July 1972, the Royal Navy was still being paid to train the Libyan Navy, despite the fact that Gaddafi had made clear his support of the IRA's campaign against the British.[17] Of course, in the years to come, the supply of arms from Libya was to become a major factor in the PIRA's ability to carry on its campaign. Additionally, there can be no doubt that the introduction of internment and subsequent events focused the attention of the international community on Northern Ireland.

Civil disobedience

The manner in which internment was introduced and its portrayal as an indiscriminate attack on the nationalist community united both constitutional nationalists and republicans in opposition; a civil-disobedience campaign was launched immediately. Both republicans and constitutional nationalists supported the rent and rates strike in protest against internment, and it was estimated that '25,000 tenants and a total of 135,000 people in public housing were on strike with 32 out of 60 councils affected'.[18]

The Catholic Church also became involved in opposition to internment. However, as noted by Gerald McElroy, 'there was an important difference in emphasis between higher and lower clergy. A majority of priests condemned the policy as immoral ... It was in November 1971, that this view was clearly seen to be held by members of the lower clergy.'[19] The majority of priests strongly opposed internment and the alleged harsh treatment of detainees. Sometimes, members of the lower clergy were also involved in actively aiding republicans. In November 1971, two escaped IRA men were caught on the border dressed as priests accompanied by two monks. However, this kind of support for republicans was not widespread among the clergy. Indeed, many in the church agreed with Cardinal Conway when he asked, on 12 September 1971, '[w]ho wanted to bomb a million Protestants into a United Ireland'.[20] Nevertheless, there was definitely a difference of opinion within the Catholic Church over how to register protest over internment; it was almost nine months after the introduction of internment before any member of the Catholic hierarchy visited any of the internees.[21] The Church's opposition to the introduction of internment was reflective of the resentment to the measure that existed in the nationalist community, evidenced by the large anti-internment rallies that were taking place across Northern Ireland.

Unionism/loyalism reacts

The ongoing escalation in confrontation between nationalists and the authorities over internment also contributed to a hardening of attitudes within unionism. In September 1971, the UDA was formed, and October saw the formation of the DUP. The UDA was formed out of a wide range of vigilante and paramilitary groups. Its membership was largely working-class, and, at its peak in 1972, it had a membership of between 40,000 and 50,000 men. The organisation provided an outlet for working-class loyalists to channel their frustrations at the deterioration in the security situation by attending marches and manning barricades. It also had an intensely sectarian element dedicated to attacking Catholics. The DUP was formed by the Revd Ian Paisley and Desmond Boal. Prior to the formation of the DUP, negotiations between Paisley and right-wing members of the UUP proved unsuccessful. The DUP was more right-wing on constitutional issues than the UUP. For many years, it was seen as a manifestation of hard-line unionism that saw the assimilation of Catholics into unionism as undesirable. Just how the unionist community reacted on the streets will become more apparent in Chapters 4 and 5.

The experiment

The mistakes made during the introduction of internment were compounded by the treatment of fourteen men who were subjected to sensory deprivation (SD),[22] which may be considered as a form of formal or informal state repression, depending on whether or not you believe it was officially sanctioned. Indeed, it does seem that the use of the techniques in 1971 was sanctioned by British ministers, in particular Lord Carrington, the then SOS for Defence.[23] What is certain is that the use of SD outraged the nationalist community.

Eunan O'Halpin reveals that the five techniques had been approved by the Joint Intelligence Committee (JIC) in 1965 and reviewed by a senior barrister in 1967, who tightened up the procedures 'to ensure careful medical oversight of detainees'.[24] In April 1971, the RUCSB requested that the intelligence services conduct a course on the techniques for selected personnel. This course was run from 16 to 26 April and was attended by twelve inspectors.[25] It was apparent in July 1971 that the British were very much aware that the proposed use of 'in-depth interrogation' would be controversial and, consequently, were keen to ensure that the operation was undertaken jointly by the RUC and the Army.[26] However, the British military assessment in 1971 was that, 'We must make a big effort in the intelligence field and in particular make use of the technique of interrogation in depth whenever we have a suitable candidate.'[27] The fourteen men who underwent SD in 1971 were Jim Auld, Joe Clarke, Mickey Donnelly, Kevin Hannaway, Paddy Joe McClean, Francis McGuigan, Sean McKenna, Gerry McKerr, Pat McNally, Mickey Montgomery, David Rodgers, William Shannon, Pat Shivers, and Brian Turley. The interrogations were carried out by RUCSB, but it is clear that the Army did have involvement in the interrogation methods used.[28] At first, the RUCSB was sceptical about the effectiveness of the five techniques, but they became convinced that they were more effective and less brutal than their own 'traditional methods'.[29]

Lord Balniel, Minister of State for Defence, stated about the use of the techniques that, '[t]he interrogation was authorised by the Northern Ireland Government with the knowledge and concurrence of Her Majesty's Government'.[30] Furthermore, the government admitted that the first twelve cases 'were not cleared individually with Ministers in Whitehall. Ministerial authority for the general use of interrogation was obtained in the wider context of the decision to introduce internment.' However, the Minister of State did agree on 1 September 1971 for a prisoner called Toner to be subjected to the five techniques, although this never happened as he was released on compassionate grounds.[31]

SD refers to the artificial deprivation of the senses using in fact six main techniques, which include:

1. hooding the prisoner prior to interrogation;
2. the constant use of a sound machine that produces 'white noise', a high-pitched hissing sound;
3. long periods of immobilisation, being forced to lean against a wall, legs wide apart with only fingertips touching the wall;
4. little or no food and drink;
5. being forced to wear loose overalls;
6. being deprived of sleep for days on end (while technically not SD, it accentuates the process).

Techniques 1, 2, 3 and 5 cause visual, auditory, kinaesthetic and tactile deprivation, while the use of 4 and 6 deprive the brain of oxygen and sugar necessary for normal functioning. Furthermore, the use of 1, 4 and 6 may also disturb the normal body metabolism. The effects of the use of SD included the inability to concentrate and disintegration of logical thought patterns leading to severe hallucinations. Hooding causes mental confusion, wall-standing is extremely painful and causes, in addition to fatigue and swollen wrists and ankles, poor circulation of the blood which leads to a reduced supply of oxygen and sugar to the brain. Lack of food and liquids causes the subject's thinking ability and perceptual judgement to be impaired. Lack of exercise and sleep deprivation ensure a progressive disintegration of personality and rational behaviour.[32]

It was not until 1981 that some of the alleged abusers were identified by John McGuffin. Those purported to be involved included Special Branch Chief Michael J. Slevin, who was later awarded an MBE; Inspector Harry Taylor; Inspector S. H. Kyle; Inspector Peter Flanagan from Omagh; Inspector N. Crowe, Armagh; Inspector D. J. Robinson,

Derry; Captain Eric Ronaldson Bryson; Lieutenant Ian Roger Barton; and military doctor, Captain David Plant. The interrogations took place at Ballykelly Airfield in Co. Derry.[33]

In response to the allegations of ill-treatment, the government set up an inquiry under Lord Compton. He delivered his findings in November 1971.[34] According to Compton, wall-standing constituted ill-treatment, hooding was ill-treatment, white noise a form of physical ill-treatment, sleep deprivation was ill-treatment and so was the rationing of food and water. He concluded that there was no evidence at all of major trauma from either medical reports or photographs. However, it should be noted that only one complainant appeared in front of the inquiry. Compton also found that questioning in depth constituted a measure of ill-treatment. In regards to other accusations he found that the forced running of the obstacle course was a measure of unintended hardship, and the helicopter experience was a measure of ill-treatment. The helicopter experience he referred to involved throwing a hooded man from a helicopter, when he had no way of telling what height the aircraft was at, to the ground. Compton somehow believed that military witnesses to the incidents were independent: 'In this regard we give special weight to the evidence of the RAF crewman, who has the status of an independent eye-witness.' He did outline the number of hours each man was made to stand spreadeagle against the wall: Auld, forty-three hours; Clarke, forty hours; McKenna, thirty hours; McClean, twenty-nine hours; Shivers, twenty-three hours; Hannaway, twenty hours; McKerr, fifteen hours; McGuigan, fourteen hours; McNally, thirteen hours; Donnelly and Turley, nine hours each; no mention was made of Montgomery. Jim Auld maintains that he was made to stand spreadeagle for virtually the whole period except for when he was actually being interrogated. The report only served to alienate further the nationalist community, who regarded it as a whitewash.

However, the government remained unrepentant, Maudling stating, 'I think the House, on studying the report, will conclude that the operation, which was one of considerable difficulty and danger, was accomplished in a highly creditable manner … The purpose of this interrogation was to obtain vital information about the terrorist forces and their stocks of arms and explosives.'[35]

The British Army was also keen to keep using the techniques. In December 1971, the effectiveness of the five techniques was reviewed by the Army. It was noted that during the Army's own 'resistance training' that soldiers were made to run for two or three days beforehand in order to fatigue them. It was thought that this made the techniques more effective and was recommended for future use of the techniques with

IRA men.[36] One month after the publication of the Compton Report, the Irish government took a case against the British government before the European Commission on Human Rights over the use of SD:

> After years of deliberations, the commission would find Britain guilty of 'torture' and of 'inhuman or degrading treatment' of some internees. Finally, in 1978, the European Court of Human Rights, upon appeal, dropped the 'torture' finding and retained the 'inhuman and degrading treatment' conclusion.[37]

As previously stated, White and White have identified two types of repression within a liberal state: formal and informal. However, an additional problem connected to these two types of repression, which can further alienate the state from a section of society, occurs when state investigations of alleged abuses are clearly not conducted properly; this involves the institutionalisation of denial of any wrongdoing on behalf of the state. It is obvious that the Compton Report fits into this category, and this kind of institutional denial can only exacerbate the problems already created by either formal or informal repression. Most of the nationalist community regarded Compton as a whitewash and believed that the authorities were excusing the use of these techniques. In turn this could only lead to further alienation from the state and may have even helped persuade some people that there was no chance of ever receiving fair treatment and that the only alternative was to join republican paramilitaries.

The Compton Report was followed by a second report, into the methods used to interrogate internees, in February 1972, conducted by a committee of British Privy Councillors headed by Lord Parker.[38] In the conclusions of the report, the Privy Councillors found themselves unable to agree, so they submitted 'a majority Report signed by Lord Parker ... together with a minority Report signed by Lord Gardiner'. The Parker Report found that the techniques had been developed in a number of colonial situations: Palestine, Malaya, Kenya, Cyprus, British Cameroons, Brunei, British Guinea, Aden, Borneo, Malaysia, the Persian Gulf and Northern Ireland. The accepted use of the techniques in a colonial context was not the same as using them in Northern Ireland. As O'Halpin notes about the techniques, 'When applied to citizens of the United Kingdom detained just 300 miles from Whitehall rather than nameless locals in the remote fastness of a dissolving empire, these provoked a firestorm of criticism.'[39]

Parker, in the majority report, for the most part defended the techniques, while Gardiner criticised their use. Parker did concede that, 'There is a danger that, if the techniques are applied to an undue degree, the detainee will, either consciously or unconsciously, give false information.' However, Parker did conclude that 'Subject to these safeguards we have come to the conclusion that there is no reason to rule out these techniques on moral grounds and that it is possible to operate them in a manner consistent with the highest standards of our society.' The safeguards included that the techniques were only to be used when it was vitally necessary to obtain information, that they were to be applied only as directed, that they were to be approved by a UK minister after seeking legal advice, that a senior police officer was to be present, that a panel of highly skilled interrogators was to be compiled, that a doctor was to be present at all times and, finally, that a complaints procedure put in place.

Furthermore, Parker believed that the use of the techniques had proved useful: 'It is not without significance that the rate at which arms, ammunition and explosives discovered in Northern Ireland by the security forces increased markedly after 9 August, and much greater part of the haul has resulted either directly or indirectly from information obtained by interrogation in depth.' His conclusions that the interrogations had led to successes against the IRA were backed up by Lord Balniel, who stated in the House of Commons that

> 14 men out of 1,500 arrested have been interrogated in depth, and the information which was obtained was of great value and has enabled the security forces to make significant progress in campaigning against the IRA organisation ... This snowball effect has brought a continuous flow of fresh, accurate information about the terrorists, and the process is still going on, because information generates information.[40]

Nevertheless, as has already been stated, this increase in the discovery of arms can equally be equated with the upsurge in paramilitary activity after the introduction of internment.

In his minority report, Lord Gardiner was opposed to the techniques and could not justify their use even against criminals like the 'Kray gang and the Richardson gang, or against any terrorist organisation or in any war against a ruthless enemy'. He was forthright in his condemnation, believing that

> [t]he blame for this sorry story, if blame there be, must lie with those who, many years ago, decided that in emergency conditions in Colonial-type situations we should abandon our legal, well-tried and highly successful wartime interrogation methods and replace them by procedures which were secret, illegal, not morally justifiable and alien to the traditions of what I believe still to be the greatest democracy in the world.

Following the report, the government decided that 'the techniques which the committee examined will not be used in future as an aid to interrogation'.[41] Other forms of ill-treatment during Operation Demetrius were also alleged, such as men being forced to run distances of 50–100 yards over cinders, barbed wire and broken glass, barefoot, while two lines of soldiers smashed at them with clubs and boots.[42]

So what of the victims of the torture? As the government was keen to point out, they received compensation. Joseph Clarke was awarded £12,500 compensation for ill-treatment.[43] Gerry McKerr received £10,000 compensation. Pat Shivers received £15,000 on 13 February 1974 for 'false trespass, false imprisonment, assault and battery, torture and inhuman and degrading treatment or punishment'.[44] Jim Auld received £16,000; McGuigan £11,000; Donnelly £11,500; Hannaway £12,000; McClean £15,250; Rodgers, Shannon, Montgomery, Turley and McNally between £10,000 and £11,500 each. Sean McKenna never received any compensation, as he died in June 1975.[45]

It also seems as though those subjected to SD were, like those interned, a mixture of republicans, republican sympathisers and civil-rights activists. There appears to be two explanations as to why a cross-section of detainees were subjected to SD. Perhaps the authorities were applying SD indiscriminately; alternatively, it must be remembered that SD interrogation was still very much in its infancy and its effectiveness was not yet proven. It does seem plausible that, as with all scientific experiments, there was a need for a control group, which, in this case, consisted of some innocent individuals. In order to make sure that the intelligence provided by the other detainees was not false and given purely to stop interrogation, the authorities tested SD on detainees who they knew were not members of the IRA to see if they gave false statements purely as a result of the interrogation techniques. This in no way excuses the use of SD but does give an alternative explanation for its use on innocent individuals. This reasoning also suggests a level of organisation for the use of SD and is backed up by the assertion of Paddy Joe McClean that 'Whether you are innocent, as I was, or guilty, it makes no difference. They weren't concerned on [sic] whether we were guilty or not – indeed they knew that some of us were completely innocent – they were concerned with our reactions to the extreme stress of Sensory Deprivation.'[46] Essentially, one of the main problems that arises with the use of this type of interrogation technique is how do you determine its effectiveness. It needs to be established whether the technique is effective enough to make the subject tell the truth and that it is not so harsh that it makes the subject falsify statements so as to halt the interrogation.

The authorities were adamant that the interrogations had proved useful. Major General Anthony Farrar-Hockley, Commander Land Forces Northern Ireland, 1970–71, maintained that '[t]he dozen or so people who were taken, and not by any means the most junior ranks in the IRA were described by those who were carrying out interrogations as "singing like canaries".'[47] Heath, despite the fact that nationalists saw the Compton Report as a whitewash, was totally unimpressed by the report:

> It seems to me to be one of the most unbalanced, ill-judged reports I have ever read. It is astonishing that men of such experience should have got themselves so lost in the trees ... they were asked to look at allegations about interrogation, and here they seem to have gone to endless lengths to show that anyone not given 3-star hotel facilities suffered hardship and ill-treatment – nowhere is this set in the context of war against the IRA ... [This report] will infuriate Commanders in the Army, undermine the position of the soldiers and the RUC in Northern Ireland, and produce grave international repercussions for us throughout the world.[48]

By February 1972, the Army was drawing up a future interrogation policy that excluded the 'previous five handling techniques'. The new criteria included proper medical examinations, normal food provision and sleep while not being interrogated for suspects.[49] Despite this and the government's declaration that the techniques would not be used again, other forms of ill-treatment were alleged.

In October and November 1972, two men, Liam Holden and William Parker, alleged that they were subjected to water-boarding. This is of course a well-known torture, used in particular by the French in Algeria and the military regime in Greece. Holden was found guilty of murdering a soldier and was the last man to be sentenced to death in the UK. He had his sentenced commuted to life imprisonment by Whitelaw and was to spend seventeen years in jail. in June 2012 he had his conviction quashed by the court of appeal because of 'non-disclosure issues'.[50]

There were also other allegations of torture, including the use in January 1972 of electric-shock treatment and 'Falanga', the beating of the soles of the feet with heavy rods, at Palace Barracks.[51] Such accusations did not deter the intelligence services, who were still making contingency plans for the use of military interrogators as late as March 1973, while recognising that ministers were opposed to such plans.[52]

There have also been other recent allegations from the families of men killed by the security forces of institutional denial of any wrongdoing by the authorities. Discussions were taking place between the British Army and Stormont on how to prevent soldiers who shot civilians in the early years of the Troubles being tried for murder. Minutes of a meeting between the Attorney General, Sir Basil Kelly, and a British Army representative regarding the shooting of Billy McGreanery in 1971, show that the Army believed that 'the Attorney General is doing all within his power to protect the security forces against criminal proceedings in respect of actions on duty'. The minutes of the meeting also show that the 'Chief Crown Solicitor pledged to notify the army of any RUC recommendations that a soldier be prosecuted before papers were passed to the Attorney General.'[53] McGreanery had been unarmed at the time of his shooting, and his family did later receive compensation for his death.

McGurk's

On 4 December 1971, McGurk's Bar in North Queen Street, Belfast, was bombed, killing fifteen people and injuring thirteen. Almost immediately, the authorities blamed the IRA and suggested that the bomb had been an 'own goal' and had exploded in the bar in transit to somewhere else. At a meeting in the Home Office, in December 1971, Faulkner said that:

> Mr McGurk … had been interviewed by the police in hospital and had said that there were no strangers in the bar on the night of the explosion. The army also discovered that the bomb went off on the ground floor. Both point strongly to the likely-hood [sic] that the bomb was carried by the IRA rather than Protestant extremists. Mr. Faulkner had asked the RUC to find out whether anything was known about the associations of the people who were killed or injured.[54]

Faulkner made the allegations despite the fact that a British explosive expert who 'happened' upon the scene of the massacre recorded the fact that the bomb was planted outside the bar.[55]

A long campaign for the truth of what happened was undertaken by the families of those killed, many of whom believed that the myth of an IRA 'own goal' was espoused by the authorities in order to justify the policy of interning only nationalists. In 2011, the Police Ombudsman released a report on his findings into the bombing. His investigation established that in 1972 and 1973, at least two persons, neither of whom were loyalist, were interned in connection with alleged terrorist activity, including the bombing of McGurk's Bar.[56] The report also established that one of the men in question appeared before the Detention Tribunal in June 1974, and allegations of his involvement in the bombing were on his charge sheet. However, the defence team arranged for an eyewitness to the bombing to attend an identification procedure. This witness stated that the internee was not the person he saw placing a bomb on the doorway of the bar. At his tribunal, the bombing was not mentioned, and the man was released. The report also found that the bombing was committed by loyalists and that 'an investigative bias leading to the failure to examine properly evidence and intelligence attributing the bombing to loyalist paramilitaries undermined both the investigation and any confidence the bereaved families had in obtaining justice'; furthermore, 'inconsistent police briefings, some of which inferred that victims of the bombing were culpable in the atrocity, caused the bereaved families great distress, which has continued for many years.' However, the report also found that '[t]here is insufficient evidence to establish that the investigative bias was collusion on the part of the police.'

It is certain that the version of events promoted by the authorities at the time was untrue. It seems likely that this was done to try and gain a propaganda advantage over the IRA. Clearly a battle for 'hearts and minds' was taking place; with the massive upsurge in republican violence and increased hostility from the nationalist community since the introduction of internment, the authorities may have been trying to discredit the IRA. They probably hoped that if they could blame republicans for the bombing that this would decrease support for their campaign.

The relatives of those murdered are continuing their campaign. Following the release of the report, the Chief Constable of the PSNI, Matt Baggott, rejected some aspects of the report. He suggested that the hurt caused to the families was somehow caused by confusion and not the direct result of a deliberate campaign of disinformation. The families want the Police Ombudsman's report accepted in full.

End of 1971

Towards the end of 1971, republicans began to widen their list of potential targets, and the OIRA murdered Unionist Senator Jack Barnhill. Republican paramilitaries also began to attack members of the Ulster Defence Regiment (UDR) and the RUC when they were off-duty. Paul Dixon maintains that '[t]he murder by the IRA of Catholic members of the security forces and the repressive policy of Stormont – which alienated many in the Catholic community – and perhaps also sectarianism within the force, contributed to a decline in Catholic recruitment to both the UDR and the RUC.'[57] Despite this, even in the immediate aftermath of the introduction of internment, the targeting of security-force personnel was not always a straightforward matter. Interestingly, in August 1971, the PIRA did stop an angry crowd attacking Constable Daniel Barr, an off-duty Catholic policeman, in Derry. The PIRA then kidnapped him and took him across the border, but, in an unexpected move, they released him the next day unharmed.[58]

The PIRA's campaign continued unabated throughout 1971. A week after the McGurk's Bar bombing, a bomb on the Shankill Road killed four people. This bombing was to have an unforeseen consequence as Michael Stone joined the UDA after witnessing the aftermath of the explosion.[59] Stone was to achieve notoriety in the loyalist community as a paramilitary in the years that followed, most infamously when he carried out an attack on mourners at the funeral of a PIRA man in 1988.

By the end of 1971, the IRA in the whole of Belfast was well over 1,000-strong. 'In propaganda terms, too, the republican movement gained increased legitimacy in its claim that, in face of such state terror, the only option left open to the minority was to rise against it, to overthrow British rule in Ireland and to unite the country by force.'[60] Counterfactually, internment was beginning to have an effect on republicans.

Protests against internment also continued, and, on Christmas Day 1971, 1,000 Northern Resistance Movement (NRM) members attempted to march along the M1 to Long Kesh, and following this there were six more illegal marches leading up to Bloody Sunday.[61] A pattern of confrontation between the security forces and nationalist protesters was being established which was to have profound consequences for the evolution of the Troubles. The NRM had been formed to coordinate resistance committees and to organise mass demonstrations; it was supported by the PIRA and PD. 'The NRM differed from NICRA which was controlled by the Official republicans, because one of its central aims was the abolition of Stormont.'[62]

1972

In total there were 1,700 shootings in 1971. In the year to follow, this figure increased to 10,000.[63] The escalation in violence also saw a rise in troop numbers and a hardening of attitudes on both sides. The increasingly sectarian nature of the conflict was exemplified by a UDA bulletin in February 1972, when a letter to the editor asked, 'Why have they [loyalist paramilitaries] not started to hit back in the only way those nationalist bastards understand? That is, ruthless, indiscriminate killing … If I had a flame-thrower I would roast the slimy excreta that pass for human beings.' The UDA replied: 'Without question most Protestants would agree with your sentiments. We do.'[64]

The membership of loyalist paramilitary organisations continued to increase; by mid-1972, the UVF had approximately 2,000 members, and the UDA as many as 20,000 to 30,000 men. In addition, the Ulster Loyalist Council (ULC) was formed, consisting of the UDA, Vanguard and other loyalist associations.

The fact that internment was proving more successful was largely as a result of improved intelligence on republicans, as O'Halpin states: 'The secretary of the JIC found that intelligence had much improved in January 1972 compared to a year earlier although there was still difficulties over sharing intelligence between the police and army.'[65] Additionally, as admitted by some former republicans, 'The big battalions, which had grown, to hundreds of volunteers in 1972, were bound to be leaky.'[66]

Although more actual members of the IRA were being interned, it is also true to say that for those internees who were active republicans, internment proved a useful training ground. They organised themselves in command structures, conducted military drills and educated them-selves. Republican internees also received periodic morale boosts; in January 1972, seven men swam free from the *Maidstone*: 'they swam 500 yards to freedom across the very icy waters of the Musgrave Channel, and hijacked a bus, which was later found in the Markets area of the city. The men cut through a bar protecting a porthole.'[67]

Protests on the outside against internment were also on the increase. The authorities had opened a new internment camp at Magilligan, Co. Derry. The civil-rights movement organised a protest, in January 1972, on the beach near the camp. The response of the Army to the protest was a prelude of what was to come: 'Rubber bullets were fired at point-blank range and soldiers baton-charged a mob which tried to break into the newly opened internment camp. Many people, includ-ing one soldier and several women and children, were injured.'[68] The heavy-handed approach of the Army was perceived by some unionists as being exactly the opposite; they felt that the Army had been too soft. Ian Paisley alleged that the 'army offered 1,000 cups of tea and 1,000 buns to the marchers if they would have a meeting at a certain place'. His allegations were to produce a scornful response from Faulkner who replied, 'The army did not seem very hospitable to the marchers. I seen [sic] them on television.'[69]

Bloody Sunday

Bloody Sunday took place on 30 January 1972 when British paratroop-ers sent in to make arrests at a civil-rights parade in Derry shot dead thirteen civilians. Although it is more precise to describe the march as an anti-internment protest because the civil-rights movement was mori-bund until the introduction of internment. By 1971, the NICRA had achieved most of its major objectives with the exception of the repeal of the Special Powers Act. So, without the introduction of internment, it is very unlikely that there would even have been a protest march on that fatal day. Many authors have dealt extensively with Bloody Sunday. Instead of detailing the events of that day, a comparison of the conclusions of the Widgery and Saville Reports, both of which investigated the killings that occurred, will be undertaken. It has already been identified how the Compton Report was an example of an institutional denial of any wrongdoing. It is also obvious that the Widgery Report in 1972 was another striking example of the same kind of denial. This is demonstrated here by comparing the failings of Widgery findings with those of Lord Saville.

On 31 January, the Lord Chief Justice of England met with the British Prime Minister, Heath, and was informed by him, 'It had to be remembered that we were in Northern Ireland fighting not only a military war but a propaganda war.'[70] It seems as if Heath was trying to warn Widgery about the undesirability of an unfavourable report. However, in the nationalist community there was nothing but a feeling of contempt for the authorities, and this alienation was to be compounded by the findings of Lord Widgery in April 1972. The *Irish News* printed an editorial, commentating on Widgery, which stated that:

> It was seen as making the task of the Secretary of State for Northern Ireland, Mr. William Whitelaw, infinitely more difficult and probably demanding some dramatic move by him-such as the immediate release of all internees – to restore faith in Mr. Heath's initiatives and give renewed impetus to the almost universal desire for peace and justice which has always been there and which manifested itself spontaneously when direct rule was introduced.[71]

Widgery came to conclusions that, like the Compton Report, bewildered the nationalist community. He concluded, 'There would have been no deaths in Londonderry on 30 January if those who organised the illegal march had not thereby created a highly dangerous situation in which a clash between demonstrators and the security forces was almost inevitable.'[72] However, he did concede, 'If the army had persisted in its "low key" attitude and not launched a large scale operation to arrest hooligans the day might have passed off without serious incident.' Despite this, he believed the Army's version of events to be truthful. He asserted, 'When the vehicles and soldiers of Support Company appeared at Rossville Street they came under fire … There is no reason to suppose that the soldiers would have opened fire if they had not been fired upon first.' Furthermore, he concluded, 'Soldiers who identified armed gunmen fired upon them in accordance with the standing orders in the Yellow Card … At one end of the scale some soldiers shared a high degree of responsibility; at the other, notably Glenfada Park, firing bordered on the reckless.' Widgery did not accept that there had been a breakdown in discipline and seems to suggest that the deaths were due to the confusion that existed on the day and the general violent nature of everyday life in Northern Ireland in 1972: 'There was no general breakdown in discipline ... The individual soldier ought not to have to bear the burden of deciding whether to open fire in confusion such as prevailed on 30 January. In the conditions prevailing, in Northern Ireland, this is often inescapable.'

Widgery concluded:

> None of the deceased or wounded is proved to have been shot while handling a firearm or bomb. Some are wholly acquitted of complicity in such action; but there is a strong suspicion that some others had been firing weapons or handling bombs in the course of the afternoon and yet others had been closely supporting them.

However, this assertion was the most contemptible as far as the families of the victims, and the nationalist community, were concerned. Widgery leaves us in no doubt that some of the people killed were involved in paramilitary attacks on the security forces.

The conclusions of Lord Saville almost forty years later are in stark contrast to Widgery. As British Prime Minister David Cameron stated in 2011, 'Saville found that the first shot was fired by the British Army, none of the casualties were armed, no warning was given by the soldiers and many of the soldiers lied.' Cameron went on to apologise for the deaths:

> But the conclusions of the report are absolutely clear. There is no doubt, there is nothing equivocal, there are no ambiguities. What happened on Bloody Sunday was both unjustified and unjustifiable. It was wrong ... The government is ultimately responsible for the conduct of the armed forces and for that, on behalf of the government, and indeed, on behalf of our country. I am deeply sorry.[73]

Indeed, Saville's conclusions highlight the inadequacies of Widgery.[74] He found, 'The immediate responsibility and injuries on Bloody Sunday lies with those members of Support Company whose unjustifiable firing was the cause of those deaths and injuries. The question remains however, as to whether others also bear direct or indirect responsibility for what happened.' Additionally, he found,

> The firing by soldiers of 1 Para on Bloody Sunday caused the deaths of thirteen people and injury to a similar number, none of whom was posing a threat of causing death or serious injury. What happened on Bloody

Sunday strengthened the PIRA, increased nationalist resentment and hostility towards the Army and exacerbated the violent conflict of the years that followed.

Again in direct contradiction to Widgery, he concluded, 'It is our view that the organisers of the civil rights march bear no responsibility for the deaths and injuries on Bloody Sunday.'

However, Saville rejected suggestions that the events of Bloody Sunday had been planned by the state, contending, 'The allegations were based on one of two propositions, either what happened on Bloody Sunday was intended and planned by the authorities, or that it was foreseen by the authorities as likely to happen. We are of the view that neither of these propositions can be sustained.' He also stated that accusations had been made that '[t]he authorities tolerated or encouraged the use of unjustified lethal force; and that this was a contributory cause of what happened on Bloody Sunday. We found no evidence of such toleration or encouragement.' However, 'It was known to ministers that there was to be an action to contain the march.'[75] As a result, one of the key determinations that some of the victims' relatives had been seeking was not met by Saville, namely 'whether the whole operation had been sanctioned at the highest level by the Cabinet in Whitehall, recognising that such an exercise necessarily involved an inevitable and foreseeable risk of serious injury or death to innocent civilians'.[76] Nevertheless, Saville was seen by many of the relatives of the victims of Bloody Sunday as confirmation that their loved ones had been murdered.

Regarding the accusation that a culture existed in the Army that soldiers were safe from prosecution, Saville remained unconvinced: 'We are not in a position to express a view either as to whether or not such a culture existed among soldiers before Bloody Sunday or, if it did, whether it had any influence on those who fired unjustifiably that day.' Saville did exonerate most of the British Army officers on duty that day, including Major General Ford, Brigadier Patrick MacLellan and Major Ted Loden among others. However, he found that Lieutenant Colonel Derek Wilford should not have sent soldiers into the Bogside because he 'had disobeyed orders given by Brig. MacLellan', that 'soldiers would have had no means of identifying rioters' and that

he should have not sent soldiers into an unfamiliar area which he and they regarded as a dangerous area, where the soldiers might come under attack from republican paramilitaries, in circumstances where the soldiers response would run a significant risk that people other than those engaging the soldiers with lethal force would be killed or injured by Army gunfire.

Additionally, 'He knew that his soldiers would accordingly be very much on their guard, ready to respond instantly with gunfire at identified targets, as they were trained to respond.'

The Widgery Report and the Compton Report were obvious examples of institutionalised denial of any wrongdoing. As had happened with the Compton Report, this denial can only have compounded the polarisation between the nationalist community and the state. The comparison between Widgery and Saville demonstrates the major inadequacies of Widgery which were only too obvious to the nationalist community at the time. Undoubtedly, Saville confirms that nationalists were right to believe that Widgery was a whitewash. The further protestations of many in the British establishment that Widgery had conducted a fair and impartial investigation into the events of Bloody Sunday only served to exacerbate the situation even more.

The question of whether or not the actions of the Paras on that day had been sanctioned by the higher echelons of government has not yet been fully answered. So we cannot be sure if any form of formal state repression took place, but what we can be sure of is that informal repression, in the shape of the killings of innocent civilians, was followed by an official denial of any wrongdoing. Undoubtedly, the killings increased support for the IRA as did the position adopted by the authorities in the aftermath of Bloody Sunday. So we can see how the use of formal or informal repression combined with the denial of any wrongdoing helped to create a core republican community that would be able to sustain the conflict until the Hunger Strikes of 1981 when this community was to receive a further boost and as a result contributed to the continuation of the conflict. This analysis will be further explored later in this chapter.

Direct rule approaches

The intensification of the conflict caused by the introduction of internment and the subsequent increase in membership of the IRA continued to draw reactions from unionists, and in February 1972, William Craig formed Vanguard. In March, Vanguard held a large rally in Belfast at which Craig stated that it may become necessary to 'liquidate the enemy'. The IRA campaign continued, but despite this, contacts between the authorities and republicans were also ongoing. In March 1972, Harold Wilson and Merlyn Rees met Joe Cahill and Dáithí Ó Conaill.[77]

A further indication that a continued armed struggle was bound to bring disastrous mistakes came in the shape of an OIRA attack on an army barracks in Aldershot. On 22 February, they planted a bomb in the barracks that killed five women cleaners, a padre and a gardener.

The bombing was followed a couple of months later by the murder of a nineteen-year-old British soldier, Ranger William Best, which sparked a major controversy in Derry with angry protest marches.

On 29 May 1972, the OIRA announced a ceasefire, which was prompted by a combination of the Best murder, the Aldershot bomb and the increasingly sectarian nature of the conflict. The OIRA cease-fire prompted the ending of internment for that movement, and, by early June, seventy-five of its internees had been released. The rest were released by the autumn.[78] Ruairí Ó Brádaigh maintains that the PIRA was happy with the OIRA ceasefire as they believed it cleared the way for them to become the main militant republican group.[79]

The PIRA obviously knew the risks involved in carrying out bomb-ings; nevertheless, they were still determined to undertake such opera-tions. Their determination resulted in them carrying out an attack that proved to be a propaganda disaster and that undoubtedly lost them support. On 4 March 1972, they bombed the Abercorn Restaurant in Belfast. Details of what happened were relayed in Stormont by Faulkner:

> At 4.28 pm an anonymous person called the operator at Telephone House and stated that a bomb, due to go off in five minutes, had been placed in Castle Lane. One minute later, before its whereabouts were known and before security forces could move into the area, a bomb of approximately five pounds exploded on the ground floor of the Abercorn Restaurant. As a result two young women were killed and 136 other people injured. Of those 27 are still in hospital, many of them maimed for life.[80]

The murders of two young women, Anne Francis Owens (twenty-two) and Janet Breen (twenty-one), were particularly gruesome, as were the injuries suffered by those caught up in the blast. The casualties included two sisters: one lost both legs, an arm and an eye while the other lost both legs. Another man lost two legs, a female lost one leg and one arm, and three people lost eyes.[81] The reaction of republicans showed that they were clearly worried about the impact such atrocities could have on their support in the nationalist community. Indeed, the revulsion at the bombing caused tremors through the republican ranks. An editorial in the *Republican News* read:

> To you people who have stood behind us in the last few years and who now find yourselves in doubt following the horrible crime at the Abercorn Restaurant last Saturday. I wish to give you my own personal assurance, as god is my judge, I would not write another word for this or any other Republican paper if I thought or even suspected that the Republican move-ment or any of its branches or units could be guilty of such an atrocity![82]

In the same month as the bombing, the security forces continued to make important arrests, including Gerry Adams, who was reported as being of 'particular value to the security forces'. According to the *Newsletter*, he had been 'the commander of the PIRA Second Battalion based in Ballymurphy for the past year.'[83] Despite these successes, Eamon McCann maintains that:

> [t]he British strategy from mid-1970 until March 1972 was militarily to defeat the IRA and to hope that the Protestant population would be so cheered by this victory that they might readily accept a reformed Stormont. The Catholics, suitably de-moralised by the IRA's defeat, would thankfully accept the reforms and wait quietly for them to have some effect. That is what the Falls Curfew ... and internment were all about. It failed totally. The reason why it failed was that the Catholic guerrilla forces were not defeated.[84]

Direct rule

Of course, Faulkner was aware from the moment he asked for internment that if it failed the only option Westminster felt it would have would be to introduce direct rule. Indeed, Cillian McGrattan contends that 'the evidence suggests that it was the decision [internment] – rather than simply the catastrophe that was Bloody Sunday ... that led directly to the prorogation of Stormont the following March.'[85] By March 1972, Westminster felt that the situation was so bad that it would have to take control of security in Northern Ireland. As Heath stated in his autobiography, 'I feared that we might, for the first time, be on the threshold of complete anarchy.'[86] He made three proposals to Faulkner: that a plebiscite on the border take place, that a start be made on the phasing-out of internment and that control of law and order be transferred to Westminster.[87] Faulkner rejected Heath's proposals and so direct rule was introduced. The British had realised for a long time that the imposition of direct rule might become unavoidable. Heath stated in March 1972, 'I think that governments of both parties ever since 1969 have recognised that this test might come and that we would have to be prepared for it.'[88]

On 28 March 1972, more than 100,000 Protestants marched on Stormont to protest against the imposition of direct rule. Vanguard organised a two-day strike, which was to prove relatively successful, with public transport stopped, power supplies cut off and most major industries closed. A precedent had been set; unionists realised that they had the potential to immobilise the infrastructure of the country.

The imposition of direct rule had a unifying effect on the unionist community. As Paul Dixon argues, unionists were angered by what they perceived to be a soft approach adopted by the Conservative government with the introduction of direct rule, which had been a key IRA demand. Later on, the talks between the government and the PIRA in July 1972 also infuriated unionists, especially as the Conservatives had said that they would not negotiate with terrorists.[89] Unionists saw the government's attempts to achieve some sort of settlement with the PIRA as treachery.

After direct rule

When direct rule was imposed, the British declared their intention to end internment but also maintained, 'We must still be free to intern if there is a clear case for internment on security grounds.'[90] A programme of phased ending of internment was undertaken, and, inside five months, the number of persons detained or interned was reduced to 239. The pace of releases was dictated by the risk of released internees reoffending and a possible Protestant backlash if too many internees were released too soon.[91] In April, the *Irish News* reported, 'The unconditional release of seventy-three internees and detainees, and the decision to stop using the *Maidstone* as a prison ship, was welcomed in non-Unionist circles yesterday.' The men were released from Long Kesh, Magilligan and the *Maidstone*; bonfires were lit in celebration in parts of Counties Armagh, Derry and Tyrone.[92] The releases were applauded by the SDLP, and the party began to change its position on internment. It no longer insisted upon the ending of internment before entering into discussions on the political situation.

The destruction of the Stormont parliament had been a declared PIRA war aim from the outset, but they could no longer claim to be fighting a war against a bigoted unionist regime in Stormont. They had achieved one of their main aims, and, as such, to continue on with the military campaign meant they risked losing the backing of less militant Catholics who up until now had given them their tacit support.

On 15 May 1972, republican prisoners in Crumlin Road began a phased hunger strike, with five new men joining the protest every week. The prisoners were demanding political status equal to those who had been interned. The tactic of a phased hunger strike was also to be adopted in 1981 in Long Kesh. The prisoners stated that they were prepared to continue their protest 'until the end, realising full well that it can end only in victory or death'.[93] By June, the protest had expanded to include prisoners in three prisons: Long Kesh, Crumlin Road and Armagh. In the same month, the PIRA announced a ceasefire and entered into talks with the British in July. Two of the key preconditions for entering the talks were the granting of demands of the hunger-strikers and the release of Gerry Adams from internment to take part in the talks. The prisoners were granted de-facto political status or 'special category status'. Whitelaw maintained, 'I have made it perfectly clear that the status of political prisoner is not being granted. What has been granted is similar to the facilities provided in the Parkhurst and Leicester wings in this country.'[94]

Some commentators contend that the 1972 hunger strike laid the foundations for the 1981 hunger strike. There can be little doubt that both strikes were connected. As McKeown outlines:

> Following a hunger strike by sentenced republican prisoners in Crumlin Road Prison, similar conditions as those enjoyed by internees were granted to all convicted in the courts who claimed to have been politically motivated. This 'special category status', or 'political status' as the prisoners called it, was introduced at a time when the British government was holding talks with the IRA in the hope of convening a truce. The truce came and went but 'status' remained until a new ruling by the Labour government in 1975 ended it for all prisoners convicted of offences after 1 March 1976. From that date onwards anyone found guilty by the courts was to be treated as an ordinary prisoner ... the policy became known as 'criminalisation' and it laid the ground for five years of intensive protest by sentenced republican prisoners who demanded the return of political status.[95]

The prison dispute of the late 1970s and early 1980s was to have far-reaching effects on the Troubles and began when

> the first republican prisoner to be sentenced under the new legislation, Kieran Nugent, was taken to the H-Blocks and ordered to wear the prison uniform and do prison work he simply refused and for several days was held naked in solitary confinement before being given a blanket to wrap himself in.

Furthermore, in '1981 after a long protest, which bore no fruit, it was felt that a hunger strike was the only option left. This tactic had been considered throughout the protest particularly because of its success originally in winning political status from the government in 1972.'[96] The internment experience established a new conflict within the prison system, as '[u]p until the Gardiner Report in 1975, the management of paramilitary prisoners in Northern Ireland was underpinned by the de-facto recognition of the political character of the inmates.'[97] When this was removed, republicans were determined to get recognition for their status as political prisoners. So it can be seen how the introduction of internment resulted in political status being granted to internees and then subsequently to anyone convicted of political offences, a decision that ultimately led to the prison dispute of the 1980s.

The animosity between the army and republicans was as fierce as ever, with each side becoming increasingly hostile. Loyalists were also intensifying their campaign using men like Albert Baker who deserted from the Army and rejoined the UDA; within a year he was in prison for the brutal murder of four Catholics. Baker was later to allege that the UDA had close links with British intelligence and support from the RUC.[98] The killings associated with Baker and his gang were to be a forerunner for the gruesome murders carried out by the Shankill Butchers.

Decline of the PIRA

Talks between the British government and the PIRA took place on 7 July 1972. The PIRA team consisted of Seán Mac Stíofáin, Seamus Twomey, Ivor Bell, Dáithí Ó Conaill, Martin McGuiness and Gerry Adams. The British side included William Whitelaw, Paul Channon, Philip Woodfield and Frank Steele. The PIRA demanded that the British government recognise that it was for the people of Ireland to decide the country's future, the British should also make a declaration of intention to withdraw from Ireland by 1 January 1975, and that internment must end, with an amnesty for all political prisoners and wanted persons.[99] The PIRA had obviously believed that they were operating from a position of strength, but they had made impossible demands. So it was that the 'British governments talks with the IRA in the summer of 1972 confirmed the latter's commitment to the "armed struggle" and this ensured that the government's focus switched to the constitutional parties.'[100] In addition, around this time, the British government felt that 'the moral high ground and military advantage was slipping away', and 'it was probably at this point that the British administration finally realised that it could no longer continue to conduct a colonial policing policy.'[101] They firmly believed that they needed to isolate the PIRA. Around the time of the talks, the British were also assessing 'military operations in the event of a renewed IRA campaign'. The assessment judged that the OIRA and the PIRA had approximately 2,000 men. It also outlined that they had used the ceasefire 'to recruit, reorganise, retrain and re-equip'. Furthermore, the British believed that the IRA would 'hope to carry-out a major car bomb offensive as a curtain raiser to their new campaign'.[102] Unfortunately, this assertion was to materialise on Bloody Friday. Around the same time, the British had come to the conclusion that

[w]hile few Catholics outside the IRA really believe in a united Ireland achieved by force, even fewer I suspect would be prepared to agree now to a prolongation of total unionist domination and to a system which does not give them either a guarantee of non-discrimination or a proper share in the government of their country.[103]

In July 1972, the British were also considering 'a possible future arrest and detention policy'. They believed that

[o]ne of the lessons from Operation Demetrius was that little purpose is served by arresting so many people at one time that the interrogation machine is completely swamped. To attempt such an operation ... based on little or no up to date intelligence, will result in a large and indiscriminate number of arrests, many of which will subsequently prove to be valueless.

The future policy was envisaged to consist of two phases. In the first forty-eight hours, the Army would swamp republican areas and pick up known IRA men, especially anyone on the arrest lists, which consisted of 300 individuals. The arrest operation was to include members of all groups including the IRA and the UDA. The second phase was to entail the opening of holding centres for interrogation and detention. It was estimated that the arrest operation would have a 50 per cent success rate; 'minnows' were not to be detained. The British realised that the outcome of a new internment operation was uncertain. Nevertheless, the final recommendations included the establishment of suitable screening centres with accommodation for possibly 600 detainees. Additional accommodation would be needed for up to 1,400 prison/detention population, and a reinforcement of the prison service and the appointment of a senior official to act as a commissioner for internment would also be needed.[104]

The ceasefire broke down on 13 July, with Lord Balniel stating, 'The current IRA propaganda is to lay the blame for the ending of the ceasefire on the shoulders of the Army. This is done with the intention of alienating the Army from the Catholic community.'[105]

Up to 21 July 1972, the PIRA, although it had carried out disastrous operations, retained most of the support it had gained when internment was introduced. There had also been developments on the military front that gave the IRA reason to believe that it could stretch the British further; such as the armalite, car bomb and landmine. Moreover, the increase in membership that it had received since the previous August gave the PIRA the manpower and infrastructure it needed to carry out an operation like it did on Bloody Friday, when it detonated twenty car bombs in Belfast, killing nine people. The revulsion at the bombings was widespread, and, as a consequence, the PIRA went into decline afterwards. They could no longer rely on the general support of the nationalist community.

The bombing also saw a further hardening of attitudes in the loyalist community. David Ervine, a future prominent figure in the Troubles, recalls that 'I was increasingly getting fed up with attacks on my community … That culminated on the day of my nineteenth birthday, witnessing "Bloody Friday". The following Sunday I joined the UVF.'[106] On Bloody Friday also Francis Arthurs, a Catholic, was viciously murdered by some of those who it is believed became involved with the Shankill Butchers at a later date.[107] There seems no doubt that 'Bloody Friday was the unionist equivalent of Bloody Sunday, and it was an unmitigated disaster for the IRA … it had a speedy political impact. Moderate nationalists put even more distance between themselves and the IRA and intensified efforts to seek negotiations with the British and Faulkner's unionists.'[108] However, it should not be concluded that the PIRA had lost all support or that they were doomed to defeat.

Ten days after Bloody Friday, the security forces launched Operation Motorman. The revulsion at the murders created the right atmosphere for them to enter the 'no-go' areas that had existed in some nationalist areas since the introduction of internment. Twelve thousand soldiers entered these areas in an attempt to restore control. Previously these areas had been controlled by the paramilitaries, which made it hard for the security forces to gather intelligence and build up a relationship with those communities. However, as Smith and Neumann outline,

> When the organisation rashly escalated its campaign, culminating in the Bloody Friday outrage, the government initiated Operation Motorman to contain the conflict within acceptable boundaries … In particular, we can see how the IRA's campaign was contained at a lower level of violence, which we may deduce impacted on its future judgements about the efficacy of its armed struggle.[109]

It seems clear that a year after Operation Motorman the British believed they had significantly reduced the level of violence. According to their figures, security-force murders had been reduced from twenty-one for the month of July 1972 to just three for August 1973. Sectarian murders had been reduced from thirty-six to thirteen for the months in question; shootings and bombings had also been drastically reduced.[110] Leaders of the republican movement were coming under more and more pressure. As Gerry Adams admits, 'In 1969–70 there had been a popular uprising … By late 1972 the popular uprising had receded to some degree … As a consequence of a mixture of sheer, hard repression and coercion by the Brits, and mistakes made by republicans, the struggle had entered a defensive mode.' In a telling comment he also admits, 'Quite sizeable demonstrations against internment were taken place, but the big weakness of our situation, was that we created no political alternative to the SDLP. Neither did we seek any accommodation with them.'[111] In hindsight, Adams was admitting that the weakness of the Provisional movement was that it could not provide a clear political alternative to the military campaign. As a consequence, when operations went wrong, the organisation was bound to lose support within the nationalist community.

The SOS, despite his declared intention of phasing out internment, 'after the collapse of the PIRA ceasefire, the Belfast bombing and Motorman … resumed detention in September by signing orders against 26 republicans'.[112] Although it was clear to the authorities that there was widespread opposition to internment in the nationalist community, it was also apparent that PIRA atrocities made it easier to use stricter security measures.

More mistakes were to follow from the PIRA. On the very same day as Operation Motorman, it detonated a bomb in the village of Claudy, Co. Derry, killing eight people – although senior republicans have denied any responsibility for the bombing. Political initiatives were also ongoing. In an attempt to bring together moderates and to isolate the extremists, the British held a conference in Darlington in September 1972, attended by the UUP, the Northern Ireland Labour Party (NILP) and the Alliance Party, which was boycotted by the SDLP because of internment. Internment still remained somewhat of an obstacle as far as most constitutional nationalists were concerned. Although the intelligence of the security forces had improved, and there were few, if any, innocent men being detained or already interned, in many ways the damage had already been done. The flawed nature of Operation Demetrius, which made it easy to portray as an indiscriminate act against the nationalist community, had turned nationalists against any detention procedure perceived as an attack on civil liberties. This in turn had made many nationalists wary of political initiatives proposed by the authorities.

The government was pursuing avenues to find an alternative to internment, which they still intended to phase out. In July 1972, the British suggested a way of improving the internment system: 'The most promising possibility is to create a system of special courts whose function would not be to convict accused persons of criminal offences, but to judge whether they were guilty of certain specified conduct and commit them to "preventive detention" if they were.'[113] One of the major problems that the authorities faced was the intimidation of witnesses by the PIRA. A prime example of witness intimidation was the PIRA murder of Sydney Agnew, a forty-year-old Protestant, who was due to give evidence in a hijacking case; his eighty-two-year-old mother-in-law was also wounded in the attack.[114] The government appointed Lord Diplock to investigate alternative legal procedures, and his report was released in December 1972.[115] The report found that '[t]he main obstacle to dealing effectively with terrorist crime in the regular courts is intimidation by terrorist organisations of these persons who would be able to give evidence for the prosecution if they dared.' Its proposals included that '[t]errorist offences were now designated Scheduled Offences and trials for Scheduled Offences were to be heard by a High Court or a County Court Judge sitting alone with no jury and the usual rights of appeal'. Furthermore, the onus of proof was changed and '[a] confession made by the accused should be admissible as evidence in cases involving the Scheduled Offences unless it was obtained by torture or inhumane or degrading treatment.'

Since it was established, the Diplock system has come in for much criticism from republicans. Of course, the fact that no jury trials were to take place leaves any legal system open to criticism. However, if the PIRA intended to intimidate and indeed murder witnesses, they were hardly in a position to 'cry blue murder' about such measures which had been introduced to make sure that this did not occur and to replace internment.

At the same time, throughout 1972, internment was still in use. By February, 383 cases had been heard by the Advisory Committee, with 291 internees refusing to appear before the committee. Of the 383 cases heard, 345 had been recommended for internment, with thirty-five being released and three adjourned.[116] There seems little doubt that in 1972 virtually all the detainees were members of the IRA and that the MOD had more faith in the RUCSB intelligence, which was now scrutinised by a senior army-intelligence officer. Nevertheless, not all internees were considered to be 'hard-core paramilitaries. Indeed 25 per cent of the detainees were considered to be in the category of least dangerous.' These detainees 'could be progressively released if political considerations made this desirable and provided that the political initiative was not followed by a major setback'.[117]

1973–75

Throughout 1973–75, internment continued to be an issue despite the declared intention of the government to phase out the measure. The manner in which Operation Demetrius had been carried out, allowing it to be portrayed as an indiscriminate attack on the nationalist community, allied to the fact that internment was an attack on civil liberties, ensured that opposition to the measure would continue. However, increasingly, its importance began to dissipate, especially as intelligence improved, with the result that virtually all internees by this stage were paramilitaries. One government minister attributed this to improved intelligence:

> [t]here must be no doubt in the first instance that co-operation on the part of the whole population with the security forces is a vital feature in the security of any state. Co-operation from the population of Northern Ireland ... has been increasing all the time, is still increasing, and is a major factor in the improving success of the security forces.[118]

The use of internment was still proving useful for the authorities, and it was used as a bargaining tool by the government in negotiations for the Sunningdale Agreement in December 1973. For example, the SOS repeated his 'declared aim of releasing all persons detained without trial in November 1973 when he also announced the creation of the new power-sharing Northern Ireland Executive'. This increase in releases in December 1973 was part of the strategy to get the SDLP to make concessions and join the power-sharing executive. Equally, the increased use of ICOs in April 1974 can be seen as a sop to Unionists prepared to participate in the executive, although Merlyn Rees maintains this increase was due to an upsurge in PIRA violence. It also seems possible that detention operated differently for many republicans who were suspected of marginal involvement in the PIRA. Their detention was sought by security forces so that they would be tainted with suspicion among those who remained at large, and, once released, they would not be readily accepted by the PIRA. They would not be easily accepted because of the very fact that they had been released and were therefore suspected of possibly collaborating with the security forces. It seems as though Whitelaw developed one regime for those peripherally involved and another for 'hard-core' activists. As he outlined himself, 'I had no case against a lot of people who were very well known to be high up in the IRA and they were very active terrorists. And yet we had no case against them. So internment to that extent, something to get them off the streets, was necessary.'[119]

Internment also provided an arena for direct conflict between the authorities and republicans, as happened on 15 October 1974 when a riot broke out in Long Kesh and the security forces were accused by republicans of using CR gas to contain the riot. Some internees to this day believe that they have health problems which they associate with the use of the gas during the riot.[120] It is known that the gas had been moved to prisons in Northern Ireland in July 1974.[121]

The beginning of 1973 saw internment take on a new dimension when the first woman was detained. It is apparent that women played a more important role in the republican movement after the introduction of internment. As a consequence, the security forces began to take more of an interest in their involvement in paramilitary activities. The first woman interned on 1 January 1973 was Liz McKee. The strong reaction in the local papers suggests that the interning of 'girls' was shocking to the Catholic population whatever their political affiliation. Political and community organisations made public statements denouncing what they considered 'callous disregard for human rights' and a step 'before children end up in Long Kesh as well'.[122]

It was February 1973 when the authorities interned the first loyalist paramilitaries. The first two loyalist internees included Edward 'Ned' McCreery (UDA) and John McKeague (UVF). However, the detention of loyalists never reached more than seventy, and this was at the height of the Ulster Workers' Council (UWC) strike in May 1974; otherwise, it stabilised at around fifty at any one time.[123] When the government began detaining Protestants in February 1973, the opposition to detention became more widespread.[124] The Loyalist Association of Workers (LAW) and the UDA components of the Ulster Loyalist Council staged a one-day strike on 7 February 1973 in protest against the first application of internment of loyalists.[125] The earlier Vanguard strike and the LAW strike were to be the forerunners of the UWC strike, which was to bring down the power-sharing executive in 1974.

The British government regarded the ending of internment as a positive step forward, which they hoped would bring the two communities together and help reach a political settlement.[126] However, for many internees, the internment experience had hardened their resolve to oppose British rule. Indeed, '[t]hese men emerged from the internment centres … with more training in weaponry and explosives than they possessed before they were interned, and with a strong sense of camaraderie, of being part of a large organisation stretched across Ireland.'[127] Men such as Gerard 'Bloot' McDonnell, who was interned from 1972 to 1975, maintains that his experience only served to make him more determined to oppose British rule.[128] This certainly seems to be the case as McDonnell was subsequently imprisoned a number of times. Brendan Hughes remembers him being in jail in the late 1970s, recalling,

> Some just refused to come out of their cell, people like Big 'Bloot' McDonnell. I had heard his voice, oh, for months and never saw his face,

didn't know what he looked like. He was one of those who refused to take any sort of visit or even come out of his cell to go to mass.[129]

His refusal was a hard-line stance against any conformity with the prison authorities. He was jailed again in 1986, along with the Brighton bomber Patrick Magee, for conspiring to cause explosions on the mainland. It was also during internment that Magee remembered

> Gerry Adams lecturing in Long Kesh in 1973. Does anybody here think this war will be over in two years? … Does anybody think this war's going to be over in twenty years … He was very much aware that this was a long haul.[130]

So it may have been that the PIRA strategy of a long war was born in the internment camp.

The experience of prison for the internees has been further analysed:

> The prison experience itself can catalyse leadership potential. The experience intensifies the individual's grievance, and also provides, for many, an opportunity to study and examine in depth tactical and ideological issues attendant upon revolution. Leadership ability also crystallizes within the institution, as certain individuals become respected among their fellows and their advice and behaviour become models for others.[131]

Of course, the psychological effects of internment also should not be underestimated. According to Rona Fields, a psychologist who visited Long Kesh internment camp between 1972 and 1973 and conducted a series of tests on the internees, 'The only conclusions to be extracted from these findings are that the majority of those interrogated and interned were probably damaged permanently.'[132] Internment had other social effects; indeed, 'The strain that internment exerted on family members of interned men and those "on the run" has passed into folk memory; stories of loneliness, depression, and prescription sleeping tablets characterize many discussions about women's experience of the period.'[133] There is no denying that internment brought hardship on those who endured the experience.

On 9 February 1975, the PIRA announced an indefinite ceasefire. Merlyn Rees, SOS for Northern Ireland, admits that he successfully accomplished one of his objectives during the truce, which was to 'end internment without trial in Northern Ireland, which would probably have been politically impossible in the middle of a major PIRA bombing campaign.'[134] Internment was brought to an end on 5 December 1975.[135] In total 2,060 suspected republicans and 109 suspected loyalists were interned between 1971 and 1975.[136] Curiously, and perhaps significantly, as Gerry Fitt noted,

On 9 August 1972, 73, 74 and 75 the PIRA lit bonfires on the streets of Belfast to celebrate the introduction of internment – the greatest weapon in its armoury – and that there were no bonfires on the streets of Belfast when internees and detainees were released last week.[137]

The period of internment was to produce other consequences, which have not been adequately highlighted. One result of the measure was that younger, more radical members were becoming more involved in acts of violence. Important figures, including most of the 1981 hunger-strikers, joined republican paramilitaries during this period, many of them in their formative teenage years. But these were not the only young people to be affected by the introduction of internment. Indeed, during 1972, twenty-eight youths between the age of fourteen and sixteen were charged with scheduled offences, and seventeen were found guilty.[138] By the end of October 1973, forty-five under-eighteens had been returned for trial, with four on murder charges, while forty-four were on remand, four of whom were on murder charges.[139] It can also be observed that the list of ex-internees reads like a 'who's who' of the republican movement and includes Gerry Adams, Danny Morrison, Freddie Scappaticci, Denis Donaldson, Patrick Magee, Martin Meehan, Leo Martin and Dominic McGlinchey, to mention just a few.

Another significant legacy which followed the introduction of internment has not been given sufficient consideration. Internment resulted in a huge growth in support for the IRA, and after direct rule this support did shrink considerably; however, enough republican activists remained in the movement to ensure that the Troubles would not be over quickly. It was the internment period that left militant republicans with enough support to carry on a prolonged campaign. The key aspects needed for militant republicanism to survive had been established by the time internment was ended. The use of formal and informal repression combined with an institutionalised denial of any wrongdoing only served to increase support for and membership of republican paramilitaries.

The sense of injustice and the actions of the authorities clearly contributed to this situation being established. As one army officer recognised,

We were turning those on the periphery of the IRA into the IRA or at least into their active supporters. In those early days, we failed to appreciate the difference between Belfast and Borneo ... By this time we'd done sufficient damage to keep the IRA going for the next ten years.[140]

In the battle for 'hearts and minds', the authorities, through some of their actions, had lost the war in the eyes of some.

In the final analysis, it is arguable that internment 'should be available but should be used most sparingly because it entails the grossest infringement of procedural rights and liberty'.[141] Some forty years later, the legacy of internment has still not faded away, as recently some of the ex-internees have set about taking a case against the British government. The case will be based on 'the physical and mental treatment of the internees and the fact that the policy was used overwhelmingly against nationalists'.[142] The case has been inspired by the recent application for compensation from Mau Mau ex-internees from Kenya.

Overview

Chapter 2 demonstrated that Operation Demetrius could have been carried out in a more balanced and targeted manner. This chapter has developed this contention further by suggesting that the timing of the introduction of internment could also have influenced the reaction to the measure within the nationalist community. It has also advanced the argument that internment has not previously received proper academic attention by examining both the short-term and long-term consequences of the period for the conflict. The proposition that internment gave rise to an increase in support for the IRA has not been fully analysed; it is clear that other factors also contributed to the increase in support for the IRA and consequently to an escalation of the conflict. In this study, White and White's analysis of internment as a form of formal state repression has been employed; in addition, examples of state repression such as the brutality of the initial arrest operation, the Ballymurphy killings and Bloody Sunday have been provided. Furthermore, an additional problem associated with state repression, which is the institutional denial of any wrongdoing by the authorities as exemplified by the Compton and Widgery Reports, has been identified. There can be no doubt that nationalists were right to consider the Widgery Report as a 'whitewash', especially as it demonstrated that there was a lack of accountability in relation to the actions of state forces. Additionally, by comparing the findings of Widgery and Saville, the inadequacies of the former have been highlighted, which emphasises the point that Widgery convinced many nationalists that there was no hope of fair treatment from the authorities, and it may have even persuaded some of the necessity of armed resistance. All of these aspects of state policy contributed to the increase in support received by the IRA.

It seems obvious that the increase in republican activity derived from the introduction of internment also led to a hardening of unionist

attitudes and increased paramilitary activities by loyalists. How internment influenced the position of constitutional nationalists, including the
attitude of the SDLP on negotiations with the authorities, has been considered. The British, after direct rule, gradually phased out internment
until it was finally ended in 1975. This was part of their steady change
of policy which gave a political settlement priority over a security solution to the conflict, exemplified by their willingness to enter negotiations
with the PIRA. However, during this period, they did find the measure
useful to use as a bargaining chip with both nationalists and unionists.
They also found that internment could be used to imprison paramilitaries who they could not prove a case against and to isolate those on the
peripheries of militant activities.

The colonial aspects of British policy such as the use of SD during
interrogations have been identified. It is also evident that a greater interest on the international arena in the conflict in Northern Ireland developed following the introduction of internment. While many of these
aspects have been recounted elsewhere, this book has examined these
areas together so as to provide a more comprehensive, coherent analysis
of the use of internment than has been previously provided.

How had internment changed the IRA? What was the main long-term
legacy of internment for the conflict in Northern Ireland? As previously
stated, undoubtedly internment resulted in an increase in support for
the IRA which gave the organisation an increased capacity to carry out
operations. This increase in support included more active participation
by young people and women in the republican movement. It was helped
in no small manner by the ability of republican paramilitaries to portray
internment as an indiscriminate attack on the nationalist community.
Immediately following the introduction of internment, they proclaimed
'The North Raped' and describing the measure as a 'grisly bordering
on barbaric political weapon peculiar to Northern Ireland'.[143] Over the
years, republicans maintained their narrative regarding the impact of the
measure, which, in their view, 'came as a crucial indication that the road
to reform was blocked off and had a major effect in making people conscious participants in the struggle' and that after its introduction 'large
parts of Northern Ireland were becoming virtually ungovernable'.[144] In
their narrative, this indiscriminate policy mobilised a whole community
in support of their armed campaign, which lasted for the duration of
the Troubles. However, this was not the case. There is no doubt that
internment was introduced in a flawed manner and this increased support for the IRA, but the increased levels of support could not be maintained by the IRA. The resulting growth in capacity led to atrocities like
Bloody Friday. Although the nationalist community had since August

1971 perceived itself under attack, and indeed in many ways it was, it was clear that there was little support for such atrocities. From Bloody Friday onwards, the PIRA was on the back foot and would not receive as much popular support again until the hunger strike of 1981. Perhaps one of the most lasting legacies of internment was that it helped to leave militant republicanism with enough support to bridge this decade. As Joseph Ruane outlines:

> The 'republican analysis of the situation' consisted of the following propositions which for republicans had the status of axioms: the British government was an imperial presence in Ireland; partition was a denial of the Irish right to self-determination; as long as the British remained there would be people who would resist by force of arms; Northern Catholics could never get equality while partition remained; the British government and establishment could not be negotiated with or trusted; only violence would persuade it to withdraw; the campaign of the IRA was a war, and as in all wars innocent people would die; this time the war had to continue until the British left; the war would succeed. Not all nationalists, still less all Catholics, could be persuaded to accept each and every one of these propositions. But enough were persuaded to constitute a core republican community.[145]

Admittedly, the creation of this core militant republican community was the result of a number of factors. Support for or involvement in republican paramilitaries depended on friendships, family connections, location, tradition, the desire for a united Ireland and the rejection of decades of unionist domination, but it was also connected to the actions of the authorities in the early 1970s. The use of state repression, mistakes made by the state, and the institutionalised denial of any wrongdoing also contributed to the establishment of such a community and, in turn, to a continuation of the conflict.

The events described by no means provide a full analysis of the political situation between 1971 and 1975. However, this chapter has attempted to provide a more comprehensive account of the repercussions that followed the flawed introduction of internment. It is certainly true to say that the introduction of internment resulted in an increase in support for the IRA; additionally, many other consequences which came after the decision to introduce the measure have been detailed. So far, this analysis of internment has concentrated mainly on events in Belfast and, to a lesser extent, Derry. Very little serious academic research has been undertaken that examines the evolution of the Troubles outside of these two cities before and after the introduction of internment. This is an area which will now be explored.

Notes

1 Secret Perimeter (n.d.), TNA: PRO CJ/4/57.
2 Taylor, *Brits,* p. 60.
3 *Irish News,* 11–13 March 1971.
4 S. J. D. Collins, 'British security policy in Northern Ireland since 1969', PPE FHS thesis, Exeter College Oxford, 1991; LLPC, P5008.
5 R. J. Spjut, 'Executive detention in Northern Ireland: The Gardiner Report and Northern Ireland (Emergency Provisions) (Amendment) Act 1975', *The Irish Jurist,* 10 (1975): 272–99.
6 Robert W. White and T. F. White, 'Repression and the liberal state: The case of Northern Ireland', *Journal of Conflict Resolution,* 39 (2) (1995): 330–52.
7 Padraig O'Malley, *The Uncivil Wars: Ireland Today* (Belfast, 1983), p. 208.
8 John Whyte, *Interpreting Northern Ireland* (Oxford, 1990), p. 121.
9 Taylor, *Brits,* pp. 127–28.
10 Carver, *Out of Step,* p. 412.
11 *Irish News,* 10 August 1971.
12 'The campaign' (n.d.) *Ballymurphy Massacre,* available online at www.ballymurphymassacre.com/campaign2.htm (accessed 4 May 2011).
13 Wharton, *Bloody Belfast,* p. 174.
14 *Irish News,* 12 August 1971.
15 *Northern Ireland House of Commons Debates,* 13 October 1971, vol. 82, col. 1311–12.
16 Anderson, *Joe Cahill,* pp. 231–38.
17 *Hansard,* 3 July 1972, vol. 859, col. 232.
18 Patterson and Kaufmann, *Unionism and Orangeism,* p. 137.
19 Gerald McElroy, *The Catholic Church and the Northern Ireland Crisis* (Dublin, 1983), p. 114.
20 Bardon, *History of Ulster,* p. 685.
21 McElroy, *The Catholic Church,* p. 83.
22 Also commonly known as the 'five techniques'.
23 'Torture Files': RTÉ Investigations Unit, *RTÉ 1,* 4 June 2014.
24 Eunan O'Halpin, 'A poor thing but our own: The Joint Intelligence Committee and Ireland 1965–72', *Intelligence and National Security,* 23 (5) (2008): 658–80.
25 Memo from GSO1 to BGS, Interrogation requirement NI, 30 March 1971, TNA: PRO DEFE/24/1214.
26 Loose minute on NI interrogation, 6 July 1971, TNA: PRO DEFE/24/1214.
27 Memo from CLF to CGS ON British military assessment of internment in 1971, LLPC P15935.
28 J. M. Parkin, Head of C2 (AD) to T. H. Sergeant, Civil Adviser to GOC, 8 March 1972, TNA: PRO DEFE/24/1215.
29 Note on Operation Calaba from A. P. Hock to CGS, 18 October 1971, TNA: PRO DEFE/24/1215.
30 *Hansard,* 9 December 1971, vol. 827, col. 1680.

31 C.A. Whitmore, Secretary HQ Organisation Committee, to Private Secretary of Permanent Under-Secretary, 17 November 1971, TNA: PRO DEFE/24/1215.

32 McGuffin, *The Guineapigs*, pp. 36–40.

33 John McGuffin, *The Guineapigs* (2nd edn, San Francisco, 1981), pp. 62–63.

34 [Compton Report] *Report of the enquiry into allegations against the security forces of physical brutality in Northern Ireland arising out of events of 9th August* 1971. Cmnd, 4823 (London, HMSO, 1971).

35 *Hansard*, 16 November 1971, vol. 826, col. 216.

36 Interview GSOI D116/ MAJ GEN J McGhie DA Psych, Psychiatric aspects of interrogation, 7 December 1971, TNA: PRO DEFE/24/1215.

37 Kevin J. Kelley, *The Longest War: Northern Ireland and the IRA,* 2nd edn (London, 1988), p. 156.

38 [Parker Report] *Great Britain committee of privy councillors to consider authorised procedures for the interrogation of persons suspected of terrorism.* Cmnd 4901 (London, 1972), p. 22.

39 O'Halpin, 'A poor thing but our own'.

40 *Hansard*, 9 December 1971, vol. 827, col. 1681.

41 Copy of draft parliamentary statement on the publication of Lord Parker's Report 29 February 1972, TNA: PRO CAB/129/161/25.

42 De Baroid, *Ballymurphy and the Irish War*, p. 74.

43 Brian J. Brady, Denis Faul and Raymond Murray, *Internment, 1971–75* (Dungannon, 1975), p. 4.

44 McGuffin, *The Guineapigs*, p. 159.

45 McGuffin, *The Guineapigs* (2nd ed.), pp. 63–65.

46 McGuffin, *The Guineapigs*, p. 68.

47 Taylor, *Brits*, p. 69.

48 Craig, *Crisis of Confidence*, p. 105.

49 Brigadier J. M. H. Lewis to VCGS, Future interrogation policy, 25 February 1972, TNA: PRO DEFE/24/1215.

50 *Belfast Telegraph*, 22 June 2012.

51 McGuffin, *The Guineapigs*, pp. 135–36.

52 Northern Ireland contingency planning: Interrogation, 28 March 1973, TNA: PRO DEFE/25/283.

53 *Irish News*, 14 September 2010.

54 Note of Home Secretary's meeting with Faulkner at Home Office, 6 December 1971, TNA: PRO PREM/15/484.

55 'Research' (n.d.) *McGurk's Bar*, available online at www.mcgurksbar.com/research (accessed 9 July 2012).

56 Public statement by the Police Ombudsman under Section 62 of the Police (Northern Ireland) Act 1998: Relating to the complaint by relatives and victims of McGurk's Bar, Belfast on 4 December 1971(n.d.), *Police Ombudsman*, available online at www.policeombudsman.org/Publicationsuploads/McGurk's–finalreport.pdf (accessed 7 April 2011).

57 Paul Dixon, *Northern Ireland: The Politics of War and Peace* (New York, 2001), p. 119.

58 *Irish Press*, 17 August 1971.

59 Shanahan, *The PIRA and the Morality of Terrorism*, p. 207.
60 P. J. McLoughlin, '"… it's a United Ireland or Nothing"? John Hume and the idea of Irish unity, 1964–72', *Irish Political Studies*, 21 (2) (2006): 157–80.
61 People's Democracy, *Internment '71–H-Block '81: The Same Struggle* (Belfast, 1981), p. 7.
62 Michael Farrell, *Northern Ireland and the Orange State* (London, 1976), p. 285.
63 John Conroy, *Belfast Diary: War as a Way of Life* (Boston, Mass., 1987), p. 37.
64 Kelley, *The Longest War*, p. 169.
65 O'Halpin, 'A poor thing but our own'.
66 Gerry Bradley and Brian Feeney, *Insider: Gerry Bradley's Life in the IRA* (Dublin, 2009), p. 128.
67 *Newsletter*, 18 January 1972.
68 *Newsletter*, 24 January 1972.
69 *Northern Ireland House of Commons Debates*, 25 January 1972, vol. 83, col. 1903–4.
70 Hennessey, *Evolution of the Troubles*, p. 299.
71 *Irish News*, 20 April 1972.
72 [Widgery Report], *Report of the tribunal appointed to inquire into the events on Sunday 30th January 1972, which led to loss of life in connection with the procession in Londonderry on that day.* 1971/72 HC. 220/1971/72; HL 101. (London, 1972), p. 38.
73 'Bloody Sunday: PM David Cameron's full statement' (2010) *BBC News*, available online at www.bbc.co.uk/news/10322295 (accessed 23 October 2014).
74 [The Saville Inquiry]. *Report of the Bloody Sunday Inquiry / The Bloody Sunday Inquiry; Lord Saville of Newdigate (chairman), William Hoyt, John Toohey.* HC 2010–11; 29 Vol. 1.
75 *Hansard*, 19 April 1972, vol. 835, col. 523.
76 Michael Mansfield, *Memoirs of a Radical Lawyer* (London, 2010), p. 170.
77 English, *Armed Struggle*, p. 156.
78 Brian Hanley and Scott Millar, *The Lost Revolution: The Story of the Official IRA and the Worker's Party* (Dublin, 2009), pp. 176–81.
79 Robert W. White, *Ruairi O'Bradaigh: The Life and Politics of an Irish Revolutionary* (Bloomington, 2006), p. 181.
80 *Northern Ireland House of Commons Debates*, 7 March 1972, vol. 84, col. 931–32.
81 *Newsletter*, 6 March 1972.
82 *Republican News*, 12 March 1972.
83 *Newsletter*, 16 March 1972.
84 Eamon McCann, *War and an Irish Town* (London, 1980), p. 245.
85 McGrattan, *The Politics of Entrenchment*, p. 46.
86 Heath, *The Course of My Life*, p. 436.
87 *Hansard*, 24 March 1972, vol. 833, col. 1859–60.

88 *Hansard*, 24 March 1972, vol. 833, col. 1873.
89 Paul Dixon, 'Contemporary unionism and the tactics of resistance', in Maurice J. Bric and John Coakley (eds) *From Political Violence to Negotiated Settlement: The Winding Path to Peace in Twentieth-Century Ireland* (Dublin, 2004), p. 141.
90 *Hansard,* 28 March 1972, vol. 832, col. 242.
91 Spjut, 'Internment and detention'.
92 *Irish News*, 8 April 1972.
93 *Irish News*, 27 May 1972.
94 *Hansard*, 6 July 1972, vol. 840, col. 741.
95 McKeown, *Out of Time*, p. 14.
96 McKeown, *Out of Time*, pp. 17–18.
97 McEvoy, *Paramilitary Imprisonment*, p. 225.
98 Ken Livingstone, *Livingstone's Labour: A Programme for the Nineties* (London, 1989), pp. 126–33.
99 English, *Armed Struggle*, p. 158.
100 Cunningham, *British Government Policy*, p. 12.
101 Snedden, 'Defence research paper'.
102 Tuzo to Whitelaw, 'Military operations in the event of a renewed IRA campaign', 9 July 1972, TNA: PRO FCO/87/81.
103 Memo from Home Secretary, 2 March 1972, TNA: PRO CAB/129/162(26).
104 Secret draft on Internment/Detention, 20 July 1972, TNA: PRO DEFE/24/1215.
105 *Hansard*, 20 July 1972, vol. 841, col. 883.
106 Moloney, *Voices from the Grave*, p. 306.
107 Paul Bew and Gordon Gillespie, *Northern Ireland: a Chronology of the Troubles, 1968–1999* (Dublin, 1999), p. 54.
108 Moloney, *A Secret History*, p. 117.
109 M. L. R. Smith and Peter R. Neumann, 'Motorman's long journey: Changing the strategic setting in Northern Ireland', *Contemporary British History*, 19 (4) (2005): 413–35.
110 Major General P. J. H Long to Howard-Drake, Army's method of operations, 10 September 1973, TNA: PRO CJ/4/668.
111 Adams, *Before the Dawn*, pp. 214–15.
112 Spjut, 'Internment and detention'.
113 Letter from 10 Downing Street to Cabinet Office with attached Paper on Preventive Detention, 31 July 1972, TNA: PRO WO/296/71.
114 *Newsletter*, 19 January 1972.
115 [Diplock Report] *Report of the commission to consider legal procedures to deal with terrorist activities in Northern Ireland*. Cmnd 5186 (Belfast, 1972).
116 Note on Advisory Committee from R. Wilson, 17 February 1972, TNA: PRO CJ/4/844.
117 R. A. Curtis (MOD) to P. L. Gregson, Esq., Northern Ireland: Internment, 6 March 1972, TNA: PRO DEFE/24/1215.

118 *Hansard*, 10 May 1973, vol. 856, col. 726–27.
119 Spjut, 'Internment and detention'.
120 Interview with Gerard McDonnell, 24 March 2010.
121 *Guardian,* 23 January 2005.
122 Begona Aretxaga, *Shattered Silence: Women, Nationalism, and Political Subjectivity in Northern Ireland* (Princeton, NJ, 1997), pp. 75–76.
123 McEvoy, *Paramilitary Imprisonment*, p. 212.
124 Paddy Hillyard, *'Law and Order' in Northern Ireland: Background to the Conflict* (Belfast, 1983), p. 38.
125 Patterson and Kaufmann, *Unionism and Orangeism*, p. 157.
126 *Hansard*, 8 December 1975, vol. 902, col. 36.
127 Bradley and Feeney, *Insider*, p. 76.
128 Interview with Gerard McDonnell, 24 March 2010.
129 Moloney, *Voices from the Grave*, pp. 219–20.
130 English, *Armed Struggle*, pp. 162–63.
131 Rona M. Fields, *A Society on the Run* (Harmondsworth, 1973), p. 167.
132 Fields, *A Society on the Run*, p. 78.
133 Tara Keenan-Thompson, *Irish Women and Street Politics, 1956–73* (Dublin, 2010), p. 226.
134 Christopher Andrew, *The Defence of the Realm: The Authorised History of MI5* (London, 2009), p. 626.
135 *Hansard*, 8 December 1975, vol. 902, col. 74.
136 McEvoy, *Paramilitary Imprisonment*, p. 212.
137 *Hansard*, 8 December 1975, vol. 902, col. 33.
138 *Hansard*, 16 May 1973, vol. 856, col. 330.
139 *Hansard*, 9 November 1973, vol. 863, col. 274.
140 Taylor, *Brits*, p. 141.
141 Gerard Hogan and Clive Walker, *Political Violence and the Law in Ireland* (Manchester, 1989), p. 95.
142 *Irish News*, 13 September 2010.
143 *Republican News*, August 1971.
144 Adams, *Before the Dawn*, p. 178; Tommy McKearney, *The Provisional IRA: From Insurrection to Parliament* (London, 2011), p. 86.
145 Joseph Ruane, 'Contemporary republicanism and the strategy of armed struggle', in Maurice J. Bric and John Coakley (eds), *From Political Violence to Negotiated Settlement: The Winding Path to Peace in Twentieth-Century Ireland* (Dublin, 2004), pp. 121–22.

4

Regional dynamics before internment

Many commentators regard the Falls Road Curfew as a watershed in the relationship between the security forces and the nationalist community.[1] As McLoughlin outlines,

> From the burning of Bombay Street in August 1969, through to the draconian Falls Road Curfew of July 1970, militant republicans had established a significant foothold within the minority community, a position from which they were able to promote their interpretation of the emerging political conflict, and so attempt to set the agenda for nationalist politics.[2]

Perhaps unsurprisingly, this analysis is also favoured by many Belfast republicans.[3] Admittedly, this version of the curfew has been contested. Geoffrey Warner believes that 'the Falls Road Curfew, while undoubtedly traumatic for those directly involved, was not as crucial a turning-point in the Troubles as many have claimed'.[4] It may or may not be true that the Falls Road Curfew was the 'last straw' for many nationalists in Belfast. However, this view is centred on the situation in the city and does not adequately reflect the position outside of Belfast. In fact, militant republicans did not establish 'a significant foothold' within the nationalist community across the whole of Northern Ireland until after the introduction of internment. Indeed, as late as September 1971, Faulkner could not believe that Roman Catholics in Northern Ireland were as totally opposed to the government as was being suggested by nationalist politicians. However, he did concede that 'it was probably true in certain limited areas of Belfast and Londonderry that the IRA were able to muster a considerable degree of support'.[5]

It is important to note that Operation Demetrius was the first repressive measure to be applied, simultaneously by both Stormont and Westminster, towards the nationalist community across Northern Ireland since the onset of the civil-rights crisis. This was the first time that nationalists outside of Belfast and Derry had experienced state repression on such a scale. Included in the initial arrest operation were men from every part of the country: '86 from Belfast, 60 County Derry [sic], 20 Newry, 20 County Armagh and 40 each from counties Fermanagh and Tyrone'.[6] Moloney contends that

> The effect of this was to antagonise a broad swathe of rural Catholics and to energise the IRA outside Belfast, in Counties Tyrone, Armagh and Fermanagh in particular, where new units, battalions, and brigades of Provisionals formed or expanded ... Internment enlarged the IRA into a 6-county wide army and transformed it into a force that could now seriously challenge British rule in Northern Ireland.[7]

However, Moloney provides no detailed analysis of the growth of militant republicanism or the dynamics of the conflict, across Northern Ireland, after the introduction of internment. This area will now be addressed.

In their recent study of how the conflict developed, Prince and Warner contend that the Troubles started in earnest in Derry and Belfast with the Battle of the Bogside and over the weekend of 27–28 June 1970 respectively.[8] However, Ó Dochartaigh provides a more nuanced account of how the dynamics of the conflict developed differently in Derry as opposed to Belfast. He states:

> Given the high levels of disorder, it is surprising that, as July 1971 began, neither the IRA nor the British Army had yet killed anyone in Derry. Although there was continued severe rioting in the city in the first half of 1971, the situation had not escalated to a shooting war as it had in Belfast.

He concedes that Derry was experiencing violence before July 1971 but argues that following the army killings of Seamus Cusack and Desmond Beattie and the subsequent introduction of internment, the conflict in the city moved on to a new level. As he outlines, 'It was perceived that the army was wilfully and blatantly "covering up" the shootings and that the British government was weighing in behind them.' For Ó Dochartaigh, these killings changed how the conflict developed in the city: 'The killings by the army had brought the Provisionals in Derry a long way.' Furthermore, he maintains that, after the introduction of internment, 'the conflict moved on to a new plane'.[9] He also outlines how for many nationalists in Derry the issue of law and order had dominated the situation in the city since 1969.[10]

It was not until after the introduction of internment that the dynamics of the conflict extended across the whole of Northern Ireland. It was at this stage that many nationalists across the country believed they were under attack from both the unionist regime and the forces of the British state. Prince and Warner accept that, in their analysis, 'we have simply presented the most convincing interpretation of what happened in Belfast and Derry at the start of the troubles ... We will not pretend that we have produced a general history (a history of its capital and second cities is not a history of Northern Ireland).'[11]

It is the area outside of these two cities that will now be examined. Consequently, the evolution of the conflict across the rest of Northern Ireland before and after the introduction of internment will be outlined. This study will take a closer look at the towns of Lurgan (Co. Armagh), Dungannon (Co. Tyrone), Newry (Co. Down) and Enniskillen (Co. Fermanagh) and their surrounding areas, for the period January 1970 to December 1972. Indeed, a total of thirty-three towns and villages will be included in this research. These four towns have been chosen because they are major towns in their respective counties, and they all contain both nationalist and unionist populations. The following local newspapers from each town will be examined: the *Lurgan and Portadown Examiner*, the *Lurgan Mail*, the *Fermanagh News*, the *Fermanagh Herald*, the *Dungannon Observer*, the *Tyrone Courier* and the *Newry Reporter*.[12] The papers represent both nationalist and unionist viewpoints, which will alleviate some of the problems of bias. In addition, the use of newspapers will provide a real-time account of events, which will help to overcome problems of memory. Another benefit of using the local press is that it is unlikely that any significant event will be overlooked. As Michael Wheatley advocates in his localised study of nationalism and the Irish Party in the early twentieth century, it is possible to construct, taking into account problems of bias, 'a reliable narrative of local events' using local newspapers as a source.[13] Statistical data from these local newspapers will be compiled to complement this analysis. I have established eight types of Troubles-related incidents: murders, deaths, bombs, shootings, riots, rallies, arms finds and bomb scares. Rallies have been included in this analysis to demonstrate the level of street protest that occurred before and after the introduction of internment.[14] Local political issues, before and after the introduction of internment, in the four provincial towns will also be examined in detail. In essence, a minute reconstruction of the situation across these four towns will be undertaken, which will give us with a better understanding of the intimacy of local events and also how the momentum of the violence evolved. This approach will demonstrate the stark contrast between the localised situation before and after the introduction of internment.

In March 1971, the British government saw internment as a live issue. Accordingly, MI5 was considering the various options open to them regarding its introduction. It is interesting to note that they suggested that it could be applied to a limited area, 'say within the boundaries of greater Belfast'. A number of advantages of introducing the measure in this manner were outlined. MI5 considered that 'the fact that the Province as a whole was not included would emphasize the government's determination to use the internment weapon as sparingly as possible'. It would also 'deter undesirable visitors from entering Belfast where most of the really bad trouble occurs'.[15] It is likely that the proposal that internment should be confined to the greater Belfast area indicates that the security forces believed that the IRA posed no major threat in areas outside of Belfast at this time. This research on the evolution of the conflict outside of Belfast and Derry will be divided into two chapters. This chapter will examine local politics and regional security before the introduction of internment, while Chapter 5 will explore these areas in the period immediately after the introduction of the measure.

Local politics before internment, 1970[16]

The issue of internment did not figure significantly in the local politics of the four towns under consideration during 1970. Nevertheless, in April, Mr T. Caldwell, a moderate unionist MP from Fermanagh, suggested that the 'Special Powers Act should be invoked to intern "extremists" in our midst.' However, the nationalist *Fermanagh News* countered his argument:

> Fair enough, but who is going to define what constitute an extremist? In the not too distant past, men were interned whose only crime was that they would not give a formal undertaking 'to be good little boys' in the future ... For insisting on what they considered to be their civil rights, these men were incarcerated in Crumlin Road jail for lengthy periods. Are we to go back to that state of affairs? Let's hope not ... No, internments will not solve the mighty problems that confront the north. That sort of coercion has been tried before and failed miserably. Indeed, many of the men who were interned in the 40s and 50s played a leading role in the civil rights campaign of the 60s.

Obviously, the paper did not agree with the general consensus that internment had worked before. This debate over the use of internment was clearly in response to events elsewhere in Northern Ireland, as up until August 1970 there were no paramilitary attacks in the Fermanagh area. Indeed, across the four towns, other issues dominated local politics. An interesting dispute was brewing in Newry Rural Council over the rights of female council staff to get married. 'The Cupid Controversy' centred on whether 'female staff should be permitted to marry and hold on to their posts or marry and get out'. The existing rule did not allow women to retain their posts once they got married. One member of the council, Councillor Trainor, who was obviously against allowing female staff to marry and keep their employment, stated, 'If you decide to go to a joint session and change this rule, then you can start right away drawing up plans for a new children's nursery up here for the use of our staff.' He added 'Maybe they'll be taking the pill', pointing out that if the rule were changed and the staff were permitted to marry and keep their posts the council would have the added problem of finding replacements every time an employee 'went on the sick to have a baby'. Eventually the marrying ban was lifted, on a motion passed by twenty-six votes to two. The Newry area had also been waiting for the delayed report into the development of the town, and, on 17 February, Faulkner outlined to the Chamber of Commerce that the Newry Development Plan would be presented to the council 'in a few weeks'. Indeed, the economic situation in the town was the major concern of most local politicians.

Of course, the underlying tensions between nationalists and unionists still existed. Captain L. P. S. Orr, Unionist Westminster MP for South Down, was warning that 'The safety of Ulster is in our hands and in our hands alone.' The internal divisions within unionism were also highlighted at this time, with the election of Ian Paisley and William Beattie, Protestant Unionists, to Stormont on 16 April 1970.[17]

At the Easter commemoration on Easter Sunday in Newry, calls were made for a uniting of all anti-unionist movements. Events in Belfast were also not going unnoticed. On 9 April 1970, the Newry Civil Rights Association (NCRA) issued a statement condemning 'the indiscriminate use of CS gas in Ballymurphy last week'. PD held a meeting to complain about the high unemployment rate in Newry, with Bernadette Devlin as one of the guest speakers. In other moves, three candidates announced that they would be standing in the forthcoming June Westminster election. They were Captain L. P. S. Orr (Unionist), the sitting MP since 1950, Hugh Golding (Unity) and John Quinn (Liberal).

Elsewhere, in Dungannon, in January 1970, the nationalist *Dungannon Observer* was celebrating the successes of the civil-rights campaign: 'Welcome to the inquisitive '70s – No longer can anyone, irrespective of rank or position, make a statement in public and expect it to be accepted without question.' According to the paper, proof of the new playing field was apparent:

> on the very last day of the old decade when six defendants on civil rights summonses appeared at Dungannon court … and manfully queried the magistrate as to why they were being prosecuted … Gone are the days when a man was scared, afraid or reluctant to stand up in public and speak in his own defence. Gone too, are the days when the word of a policeman

or for that matter any other controversial figure in the establishment, was accepted without question as the gospel truth.

Meanwhile, Clogher Rural Council was among the first councils to allocate houses on a points system. This was seen as an important move in the Dungannon area, as, in the early 1960s, 'not one Catholic family had been offered a permanent house' for decades.[18] The Public Order Bill was also a key issue, and Seamus Mallon, nationalist politician, stated that 'the government had been forced to proceed with the Public Order Bill in order to satisfy the fanatics in their own party'. The Public Order Act had been introduced in 1951 but was amended in 1970 in response to the Troubles. The amendment made it an offence to take part in an illegal procession, to hinder a legal procession and to sit, kneel or lie in a public place to hinder any lawful activity.[19] The differences within unionism were also apparent in local politics. Tom Caldwell, an independent unionist, stated,

> The hardliners of the grass roots of the Unionist Party can do what they like by flooding their constituencies in order to ensure that only hardliners are nominated at the next election. What these people do not realise is that the vast centre of opinion in Northern Ireland is becoming more intelligent and more moderate as each year comes and goes.

The Omagh Civil Rights Association announced that it was opposed to the new UDR, and approximately 1,000 people attended a rally in Dungannon in opposition to the regiment. The regiment was due to go into service on 1 April 1970, and the B-Specials were due to be disbanded on 30 April. John Hume and Austin Currie, who were supposed to put the case for joining the UDR, could not attend the rally. At the rally, Michael Farrell (PD) expressed the hope 'that the day would not be far off when they in Ireland would see the establishment of a thirty-two county workers' and farmers' republic'. Around this time, moves were also being made to 'normalise' policing, and on the 26 March the Police Act (NI) came into effect. Under the Act, Stormont accepted the principle of an unarmed police force.

Not all local nationalists were initially opposed to the UDR. A local civil-rights supporter, P. J. McKernan, stated that he would be pleased to see his eight sons joining the UDR and 'taking their part in helping to make our province a place where each of us could live in peace and prosperity'. Indeed, many nationalist politicians initially encouraged Catholics to join the UDR and RUC reserve. However, they became less supportive of both new forces when they learned that application forms had been sent out to every member of the B-Specials. By the time the regiment was due to go into service, its strength was '2,440 men, including 1,423 ex-Specials. Catholics numbered 946.' It would be hard to convince nationalists of the impartiality of the new force with so many former members of the B-Specials in its ranks.

The fallout from disagreements among members of the NICRA was being lamented by the local nationalist press: 'Unity among the Indians, disunity among the chiefs ... It was a week above all when the civil rights supporters throughout mid-Ulster were saddened to read newspaper reports of discord, disunity and disarray in the leadership of this once solidly united, broad-based movement.'

In the June 1970 General Election, Neville Thornton, a right-wing unionist, was selected to stand for the UUP in mid-Ulster but was defeated by Bernadette Devlin. She was elected, along with Frank McManus in Fermanagh–South Tyrone, and Gerry Fitt in West Belfast. Commenting on Devlin's re-election, the *Observer* remarked that 'Mid-Ulster voted for the singer not the song.' According to the paper, both sides had something in common: there was no particular affection for Thornton among unionists, and there was no particular understanding of Devlin's views among nationalists. As elsewhere, unemployment, which stood at 11.2 per cent, was an important local issue.

Across in the west, in Enniskillen, at the start of 1970, the nationalist *Fermanagh News* reported that 'All is quiet on the political front in Fermanagh, or so the stranger would think, but we who live here know to the contrary. Unionists, republicans, nationalists, labourites and liberals are all concerned about something.' Unionists were concerned about the fight between right and left wings while nationalists were considering who would be the candidate for the next election. In Enniskillen, the government took out an advert proclaiming that it had 'built 12,000 new homes, modernised local government, established votes for all, provided a fair deal for the citizen, improved community relations and created the Londonderry Commission'. PD was warning that the imprisonment of Bernadette Devlin could be an indication that Stormont was about to start a campaign to intimidate fervent opponents of the government. The civil-rights campaign was clearly continuing. The Fermanagh Civil Rights Association (FCRA) held a meeting attended by a 1,000 people, which passed a motion for a boycott of the UDR. Increasingly, the regiment was being besmirched by allegations of favouritism towards Protestants, especially former B-Specials. As one former Catholic member said, 'It was made clear we weren't wanted.' Additionally, the loyalty of Catholic UDR men was being called into question by unionists, despite the fact that they had taken an Oath of Allegiance to the Queen.[20]

The Macrory Report on Local Government was published in 1970 but was not implemented until 1973 after direct rule, when the new twenty-six councils found their powers drastically reduced.[21] In the intervening period, nationalists were to make many protests regarding the retention of the old structures. For example, in January 1970, the anti-unionist members of Fermanagh County Council (FCC) signed a petition calling for a special meeting of the council. The meeting would consider a motion for the abolition of the county council on the grounds that it was not representative of the people and that its affairs had been conducted along bigoted and sectarian lines. However, the council voted twenty-eight to ten against dissolving itself. The issue was a central demand of the local civil-rights association's campaign. In April, following a protest outside FCC offices in Enniskillen, there were scuffles between the police and about 150 civil-rights protesters. Meanwhile, at Stormont, local hard-line MP Harry West was expelled from the UUP for his criticism to government policies.[22] In June, the Chairman of FCRA, Frank McManus, won the constituency of Fermanagh–South Tyrone in the Westminster general election by just over 1,400 votes. He shared some of Provisional Sinn Féin's policies, including abstentionism, and was eventually to become the Chairman of the NRM.[23] Following his election, a Union Jack was torn down from Enniskillen Town Hall, and stones were thrown at police during his victory parade. McManus, who came from a strong republican family and was well known in Gaelic Athletic Association (GAA) circles, was to become a central figure in local politics in Enniskillen in the next few years.

Meanwhile, in Lurgan, in August 1970, unionists were making calls for tougher security measures. R. J. Mitchell, MP for North Armagh, threatened to resign if the government did nothing to quell the ongoing violence, and the local UUP branch issued a strongly worded statement criticising the Prime Minister and his government. Nationalists were also mobilising: PD and the republican clubs had both held protests in the town.

In June there was good news in Newry on the economic front with the announcement that a £12 million hydro-electric plant was to be built in Camlough, just outside the town. The textile manufacturer Courtaulds were also to set up a factory which would provide 400 jobs. A local nationalist politician, Michael Keogh, who was to become a key figure during the anti-internment campaign in Newry, commented, 'At last the government have been generous to this area … and hundreds of men who have never known the luxury of a steady job will now lift their heads a little higher.'

It certainly seems that in the later part of 1970 political opposition to the authorities in Newry was beginning to become more organised. A series of protest meetings took place in the town just as Bernadette Devlin was about to begin her prison sentence. A protest took place against the imposition of the Falls Road Curfew; on the platform were representatives of the old IRA, NILP and Irish Labour. Despite this protest, it should not be assumed that the alienation of the Catholic community from the security forces across the whole of Northern Ireland was uniform because of the curfew. As Hennessey states, 'Catholic opinion was more complex than a simple blanket, Province-wide alienation as was demonstrated by the re-entry of the RUC into the Bogside, later in July.'[24]

Nevertheless, other protests against the security forces were ongoing. In July, a rally at Newry UDR base was attended by around 200 people. The protest was organised to highlight objections to the use of repressive measures by the security forces. In August 1970, the Newry and District Civil Rights Association held a meeting to commemorate the first civil-rights march held in the town. This meeting proposed five motions. It called for all public representatives to resign if Bernadette Devlin was sent to prison; it resolved to pursue full and fair employment; it called on all government ministers and policemen to resign from the Orange Order; it declared its opposition to the Special Powers Act and the Public Order Amendment Act; and, finally, those at the meeting deplored the establishment of the UDR, which was described as the 'B-Specials under a new title'. At a protest rally organised by the NICRA, it was stated that Newry people would not accept internment. A republican rally was held in the town, which called for the release of Irish political prisoners held in jails in Britain, the release of Bernadette Devlin, the release of those held under the Criminal Justice Act, and the repeal of the Special Powers Act. The 12 July commemorations in 1970, in Newry, was reported as being the quietest ever in the district. All the local Orange Order brethren were away at parades in Moira, Kilkeel and Newtownhamilton. All the clubs, pubs and hotels had been closed down by order, and, as a result, 'the town had a deserted appearance, save for the heavy flow of passing holiday traffic'.

Likewise, the Twelfth in Enniskillen was reported as being 'the best-guarded, most publicised, best attended and most subdued twelfth in the history of the Orange Order. Yet, the first twelfth of the 70s was to all intents a non-event.' In July also, the nationalist members of the FCC decided to continue indefinitely their boycott of the council. In the same month, the government had banned all parades, with the exception of those on Remembrance Sunday, until the end of January. In September

1970, a conference was held at London University, hosted by Professor Burton, to discuss the causes of the conflict in Northern Ireland. The conference was attended by trade unionists, community leaders and representatives of the different churches. At the end of the conference, the desire was expressed that:

> Fermanagh could become the crucible for a dynamic and high-powered get-together of Protestant and Catholic community and youth leaders, sportsmen, trades unionists, politicians and clergymen, who would put all the problems and hostilities, which are wrecking the north, under a microscope, and forge a new style of living and relationship for the future.

The civil-rights campaign was still ongoing, and twenty FCRA members were imprisoned for non-payment of fines arising out of a protest earlier in the year when they had occupied the FCC chamber. Local unionist MP Harry West, leader of the West Ulster Unionist Council (WUUC), warned that if the forthcoming civil-rights parade planned for Enniskillen in late November 1970 took place that it would bring 'serious confrontation' to the town. He stated, 'If the government is unable or unwilling or afraid to stop these people breaking the law and disrupting the peace of the community then a serious confrontation will take place.' The WUUC had been established in April 1970 and had 'united local right-wing unionist associations in the west of Northern Ireland in a right-wing faction within the Unionist Party'.[25] However, the parade passed off without incident.

Local politics before internment, January–July 1971[26]

At the start of 1971, the nationalist *Lurgan and Portadown Examiner* ran an editorial expressing the desire that nearby Armagh City be calm and peaceful: 'No civil strife or street violence, housing needs met, more employment, no drugs, less road accidents, more amenities for young people, prominence in sport, more church interest, financial support for the voluntary and charitable sector and 1971 to be a peaceful, happy and memorable year for all.'

Armagh was less than fifteen miles from Lurgan and had been the site of many disputes since the start of the civil-rights era. At the same time, the local unionist branch passed a motion of no confidence in the Prime Minister and the government. Shortly afterwards, 170 delegates of the Ulster Unionist Council called for Chichester-Clark's resignation.[27] The unionist Mayor of Lurgan, William Gordon, issued a hopeful New Year message in 1971:

In the year that has just past, people have had their shares of happiness and misery and Lurgan didn't altogether escape the turmoil of the street confrontation. It is up to all our citizens to pull together for an overall betterment of the community and for my part I will do what I can to assist. The past is gone the Province has an opportunity to start anew and the future could be bright if it does.

Unfortunately, the Mayor's hopes for the upcoming year were to prove unfulfilled. In his New Year message he admitted that Lurgan has been touched by some violence but clearly he hoped that this phase had passed. However, the security situation was to deteriorate drastically, especially after the introduction of internment. In January 1971, the local unionist weekly newspaper, the *Lurgan Mail,* reported that Ian Paisley had visited Lurgan and had spoken to the local unionist branch. He informed them that he had obtained information that the RUC had received a 'secret document' which claimed that the IRA was to increase its campaign in the next three months. Ironically, he also claimed that RUC intelligence indicated that leading IRA members in 'the South' were contemplating moving to safe areas in the North to avoid the threat of internment. At the same time, R. J. Mitchell, local Unionist MP, was warning that 'disorder in Ulster will bring poverty' and that 'people are not prepared to go on supporting any form of government that tolerated the continuation of recent disorder'. Mitchell also believed that the sooner internment was introduced the better.[28] Local unionists were also making calls for 'The Specials' to be brought back. Despite the deteriorating situation elsewhere, Lurgan was looking forward to decimal day on 15 February, and it was also announced that three interdenominational youth centres were to open in the town.

After the PIRA murder of Gunner Robert Curtis on 6 February, the first British soldier to be murdered in the Troubles, the nationalist *Examiner* declared that '[t]he terrible happenings in Belfast are a form of madness which one finds difficult to associate with a so-called Christian and civilised community. There are few people in this area who would disagree with this view and fewer still who appear to know what the solution is.' The paper interviewed a cross-section of the community to try and find out what people thought could be done. The responses of the interviewees proved to be quite revealing.

One person replied, 'Sure as far as we are concerned the trouble in Belfast is as far away as the Apollo 14 astronauts are now from the moon.' Other responses varied from 'Intern the leaders. But then who are the leaders? Then there's another problem finding them. I just don't know' to 'It's the mothers and fathers I blame, not the children.' A number of other comments were made:

'I wouldn't be surprised if it wasn't part of a worldwide Communist conspiracy.'

'I couldn't care less if they murder each other in Belfast.'

'I'll tell you one thing I'm awfully glad I don't live in Belfast.'

'Stormont should pack it in and hand over the running of Northern Ireland to Westminster. There won't be peace here until that happens.'

'To my mind Belfast is a place apart. It is a problem that cannot be solved.'

'The British troops should withdraw and the United Nations should be asked to send in a peace-keeping force.'

'It was a wise man who said, "Ireland unfree shall never be at peace" … The key to the whole situation is the border. It must go it will go sooner or later.'

'Internment is the answer, once the leaders are behind bars the trouble will die down.'

All of the interviewees had been guaranteed anonymity. In the responses we see a wide variation in people's perceptions of the unfolding situation. The fear that a Communist plot was behind the violence was expressed, as was the belief that social problems were contributing to the situation. Constitutional nationalist aspirations of bringing in the UN or perhaps direct rule were also conveyed. Republican and unionist solutions of reunification and internment respectively are also expressed. Interestingly, a significant number of the interviewees regarded the events in Belfast as being isolated from Lurgan. Clearly there was a belief that the town had not yet reached the same level of violence that existed in the capital city. There were further indications that events in Belfast did not have the approval of the local community. Members of both communities gathered at the war memorial to lay wreaths in respect of the three Scottish soldiers murdered in Belfast. A number of local factories also held a two-minute silence as a mark of respect. In another development, Kilwilkie Tenants' Association had become affiliated to the Northern Ireland Tenants' Association. This was perhaps a surprising move, given the estate's reputation for being a republican stronghold.

As part of the annual republican commemorations in Lurgan, it was announced that the Easter 1971 parade would consist of two parades on two consecutive Sundays. The first parade, which consisted of both republicans and nationalists, was described as an 'anti-internment parade'. Even before the introduction of internment, nationalist opposition to the measure was being mobilised. The proposed parade was regarded by unionists as an attempt to heighten tensions in the town. A local unionist umbrella group made representations to the police and Faulkner over the proposed parades, asking that they be prevented from entering the Church Place area of the town, which was the site of the local Church of Ireland. The 'anti-internment parade' went ahead without incident, although it was faced by a loyalist counter-demonstration, under the watchful eye of a large contingent of police. The counter-demonstration had been attended by over 600 people, including Ian Paisley; a wreath was laid at the war memorial in memory of the British soldiers killed in Dublin in 1916. Nevertheless, afterwards the police praised the nationalist organisers of the parade, which they said had passed off peacefully and had been attended by 2,000 people. The local press commented that '[a] feature of this years [sic] Easter commemoration ceremonies was the number of young people who attended. They were well to the fore among the marching thousands.'

In July 1971, Faulkner met local Orange Order leaders to discuss forthcoming Twelfth of July parades, in an effort to make sure they passed off peacefully. A notice was placed in the *Examiner*, with Faulkner asking, 'Do I look like I want to be herded around?' In response, the paper outlined its belief that the Unionist Party had two leaders: Faulkner and Craig. This was an obvious reference to the threat that Craig posed as a hard-liner to Faulkner's leadership. Since the onset of the civil-rights era, there had been an ongoing dispute between moderate and right-wing unionists over the pace of reform. Both of Faulkner's predecessors had been forced to resign, essentially over their inability to appease the 'hawks' within the UUP. These strands have been further defined as assimilatory (those who believed it was possible to achieve Catholic support for the union) and segregatory (those who believe Catholic unionism would be undesirable).[29]

As it happened, there was some trouble in the run-up to the July parades in Lurgan. Police had to use a water cannon to disperse nationalist rioters in Edward Street, and there was also rioting in the Kilwilkie and Shankill estates. The authorities estimated that both traditions held approximately 1,500 traditional marching ceremonies across Northern Ireland from April to August in 1971. The parades were considered to be less likely to cause trouble in country districts. It was noted that, '[h]owever, several hundred are due to take place in Belfast, Londonderry and certain towns and villages among divided communities with a history of mutual antagonism.' It was considered that this was liable to produce violence or provide the paramilitaries with opportunities to exploit the situation.[30]

In Newry, the New Year began with good news with the opening of Newry's new £100,000 swimming pool. However, the NCRA was not content, and it was demanding that local council elections take place in 1971. It also dismissed *Festival '71* as a 'party political stunt'. Planning for the festival had begun in 1968 under the premiership of Terence O'Neill and was envisaged as the highpoint of his civic week project. It was designed to celebrate and promote Northern Ireland on the fiftieth anniversary of the foundation of the state.[31] However, it was obvious that nationalists would be opposed to any such celebration.

As early as March 1971, it seems that nationalists in Newry were in no doubt that internment was imminent. A civil-rights parade was held in Camlough protesting against the activities of the Army and against any possible introduction of internment. Furthermore, several hundred people attended a NCRA protest in Newry; the guest speaker was Bernadette Devlin. She stated, 'Let them try internment and then they will see what trouble really is. They can frighten us, gaol us and shoot us, but they can't stop us.' Kevin McCorry of NICRA added that 'Chichester-Clark was going to go down in the marass [sic] of right wing pressure.' Around the same time, Protestant shipyard workers from Belfast took part in a march demanding the introduction of internment for members of the IRA. At the Newry protest, Michael Farrell of PD commented on the murder of the three Scottish soldiers in Belfast: 'He was sure that everyone regretted the death of the three soldiers and other deaths which had happened in Northern Ireland and that the authorities knew the soldiers were not shot by the IRA but by extreme unionists.' In what seems to be a recurring theme, some nationalists were trying to lay republican atrocities at the foot of loyalists, who they suggested were trying to intensify the conflict. There is no doubt that the murders caused widespread revulsion in Newry. Indeed, a fund had been set up for the dependants of the murdered soldiers. The fund had been subscribed to by both Protestant and Catholic members of the community in the Newry district.

Republicans were active in the town, and they gave a hostile reception to Jim Callaghan, Shadow Home Secretary, when he visited Newry in March. They were refused admission to the meeting that Callaghan was attending and stood outside singing 'Go Home You Bum' for twenty minutes. Callaghan had been on a tour of Northern Ireland and had held meetings with political representatives in Belfast, Lisburn, Portadown, Lurgan, Armagh and Dungannon as well as Newry. He recalls of his visit that 'we had very useful and helpful meetings and there was a striking contrast between the extremists who jostled and jeered on both sides, and the sensible, sober, well-meaning but troubled people who met me inside the halls.'[32]

There were two republican Easter parades in Newry in 1971. Over 2,000 people attended the PIRA Easter Parade. At the OIRA parade, a call was made for unity between the PIRA and OIRA, unity between anti-unionist groups and between Catholic and Protestant working-class people. Meanwhile, 10,000 loyalists had gathered in nearby Kilkeel for the annual Easter Parade of the Apprentice Boys of Derry. Edward Irvine, Chairman of the Mourne branch of the Apprentice Boys said,

> Now that we have a new administration which has shown within limits by its tougher policy in the law and order field, that it means business, it is our duty to co-operate and to refrain from any action which might hinder the determined efforts of one who has shown that he understands the situation and that he has the interest of Ulster at heart.

These were sentiments that Ian Paisley obviously did not agree with. On a visit to Bessbrook, he stated, 'We will shake this weak-kneed government, remove the Lundy's and get a Protestant unionist government.' The local Alliance Party agreed with Paisley on the need for a new government, but for totally different reasons. The Alliance Party had been formed on 27 March 1971.[33] They stated, 'We in Alliance realize that the only way to change the situation in Northern Ireland is to introduce a new government and that is why the Party accepts as its principle aim and object the provision of an alternative government.' However, David Bleakley, Minister of Community Relations, clearly did not agree. He was advocating the retention of the administration and suggested that the worst of the violence might well be over: 'The gloom of the last two years is at last beginning to lift and it may well be that we are beginning to see the end of the worst of our community confrontations.' Meanwhile, the plight of Newry's unemployed was still prominent in the minds of those who attended a march to highlight the problem in July 1971.

In January 1971, the issue of local government was very much to the fore in Dungannon. Members of both communities in the town joined forces to launch a campaign to have urban and rural councils abolished and replaced by a commission. As a first step, a seven-man community council was set up to consider appropriate steps to achieve this objective. In June, Jack Hassard, a Labour member of the Dungannon Urban Council, resigned because 'he can no longer accept collective responsibility for the acts of maladministration, which he alleges, were being perpetrated by the council.' Civil rights and other social issues such as housing were also very prominent. The Housing Executive body for Northern Ireland was established in February.[34] In a progressive step, Stormont had appointed a former nationalist councillor from Dungannon, James Donnelly, to the executive. Indeed, even some prominent republicans admit that at this time there was still some hope in the Dungannon area that sufficient reforms would be introduced.[35] However, local residents in Coalisland were still making complaints regarding housing issues and proposed rent increases. A large civil-rights march from Coalisland to Dungannon took place; one of the banners carried at the parade demanded 'British Army Out'. In early morning raids, the security forces searched the home of Paddy Joe McClean, Secretary of the Tyrone branch of the National Graves Association; he was later to be interned and subjected to SD during Operation Demetrius. At a civil-rights executive meeting in Omagh in July, it was claimed that by 9 o'clock the next morning internment would have been introduced in Northern Ireland. Concerns were also expressed over high levels of unemployment, which had reached 18.9 per cent in Dungannon and was still on the increase in Tyrone as a whole.

The Revd William McCrea was arrested by the Army and handed over to the police at a pro-Paisley rally in Dungannon in June 1971. The Revd Michael Patrick, also at the rally, pronounced that 'we intend to oppose every lundy, every traitor, every compromiser. I want to tell John Taylor from this meeting that come what may he will be opposed.' He also criticised Stormont for allowing republican parades while banning loyalist parades. In other moves, a branch of the Alliance Party was formed in Dungannon. However, hecklers had foiled an attempt by Austin Currie to form a branch of the SDLP in the town.

At the start of 1971, the nationalist *Fermanagh News* reflected on 1970 in Enniskillen. According to the paper,

> it was a year in which the RUC made most intensive efforts to win the confidence of the people only to see their efforts come to naught with the revelation of a conspiracy of silence on the part of certain members of the RUC over the death of Samuel Devenney. Alliance fought hard to gain a foothold. SDLP made its debut with a 'brave flutter of wings which failed to gain momentum as the months passed'.

In March, Harry West was appointed back to his old position as Minister of Agriculture in Faulkner's new cabinet. Before his appointment he had criticised the government on its failure to introduce internment: 'The government are clearly afraid to take this step.' However, once back in the fold, West resigned from the WUUC, stating, 'I felt I could not continue with a body which had passed a vote of no confidence in a government to which I belong.' Once again, the Twelfth passed off peacefully in Enniskillen.

Civil-rights organisations remained very active, and the FCRA called for a massive campaign of passive resistance to any move to reintroduce internment or to rebuild the B-Specials. It was this period which saw the Local Government Act become law and the launching of the Ulster '71 exhibition.[36] Social issues also remained central in Enniskillen, especially unemployment. John Corran, Nationalist MP for South Fermanagh, stated, 'It does not matter two hoots whether the factory is in Derrygonnelly or is in Derrylin so long as these people are employed. It is only by keeping people in employment that the government can expect full co-operation in those areas.' Proposed rent increases were also being strongly condemned. Frank McManus was due to be released from prison; he had been jailed in connection with a civil-rights march in December. His brother, Revd Sean McManus, was also in trouble, as he refused to fill in his census form in protest at 'the general injustice perpetuated by the Unionist government in the north of Ireland.' Father McManus eventually moved to the USA in 1972 and founded the Irish National Caucus, an Irish-American lobby group that campaigned for the introduction of the MacBride Principles in Northern Ireland from 1984 onwards.[37]

Regional security before internment, 1970[38]

The first part of 1970 saw virtually no Troubles-related incidents in Newry; the only exception being two bomb scares in April. Similarly, there were no violent actions in Lurgan in the early part of the year. The fact that the Troubles had not yet come to Newry is reinforced by the many appearances of local security-force members in the local press. For example, it was announced that a local man, Lieutenant Colonel John Furniss, was to be appointed as Senior Education Officer in the Army. It was also reported that Douglas Hogg, a Newry RUC Constable, was awarded the British Empire Medal for chasing a gang who had raided two Newry banks. He had also been given permission to keep his beard, which he grew while on a month's leave. He was pictured in the local press, who reported that he had become the first RUC man on the beat in Northern Ireland to sport a beard. In another newspaper report, it was revealed that two local policemen, District Inspector Michael McAtamney and District Inspector William Edgar had both been promoted. The fact that these members of the security forces were openly named and photographed in the local press surely demonstrates it was not felt that their lives were in any danger. In stark contrast, twenty-nine people lost their lives in 1970, with the vast majority of these deaths occurring in Belfast.[39] These articles also reflect the efforts being made to normalise the RUC, a key element of the Hunt Report, which was to be implemented from October 1969 onwards. It appears that, in July 1970, some nationalists in the Newry area were trying to work with the police. At a meeting of nationalists in the nearby village of Rostrevor, a call was made for a constable to be based in the village. There was criticism at the meeting of the new arrangements which had come into place that resulted in the closing down of most of the rural police stations. As a consequence, there had been an absence of police in the area, which was also criticised. Nationalists in this area clearly still felt the need for a police presence and felt little animosity towards the RUC. The situation could hardly have been more different than the one that existed in Belfast at this time.

In the capital, the weekend of 27–28 June 1970 was when the 'PIRA was able openly to demonstrate its growing strength.'[40] During this weekend, Belfast saw the first sustained military action by the PIRA when fierce rioting broke out in north and east Belfast. During the clashes, the PIRA fired from St Matthew's Catholic Church for five hours. At the end of the confrontation, five Protestants and one Catholic were shot dead.

In Dungannon, 1970 started peacefully; so much so that police news reports in the local press were dominated with concerns over sheep worrying, and dog-owners were advised to keep their pets under control at night. Locals were also being encouraged in the press to join the new UDR. However, Harry West (Enniskillen MP) had stated that 'nationalists who joined the UDR would be working with two faces.' It also seems that the republican clubs retained a presence in the area, but, when asked about this, Sir Arthur Young, RUC Chief Constable, replied, 'I don't know anything about these.' The Thomas Clarke Republican Club in Dungannon was reorganised and pledged its support for the PIRA, saying, 'We deny the right of any Irishman to take seats in Westminster, Stormont or Leinster House.' The situation in Dungannon was, however, entirely different from Belfast, which had seen the first major clashes between the Army and nationalists in early April. Around the same time, the Army had adopted a new get 'tough policy', warning that petrol-bombers 'were liable to be shot dead'.[41]

There were only two paramilitary attacks in the Dungannon area in early 1970, and both these attacks were carried out by loyalists. On both occasions they had targeted the home of local nationalist politician Austin Currie. In June, a bomb was planted by loyalists at his house. However, local unionists made light of the attack, and William Scott, unionist member of Dungannon Rural Council, stated that, 'There wasn't enough gelignite to blow up a balloon.' Shots were also fired at Currie's house in the same month.

There was controversy surrounding the annual Easter parades. For the first time in many decades the Tricolour was carried at the republican commemoration through Dungannon. The nationalist *Dungannon Observer* remarked:

> Those who have died since the proclamation of the 32-county Irish Republic in 1916, must have looked down from heaven in utter amazement at the sight of British soldiers and members of the RUC assisting members of the republican movement directly or indirectly, in enforcing measures which, whether their aim or object ensured the flag for which the patriots had paid the supreme penalty would not be defiled, insulted or interfered with in any way.

The RUC, commenting on the parade, issued a statement that they had received assurances beforehand that the flag would not be carried.

There were some signs of the impending deterioration in the security situation. In early May 1970, the security forces launched Operation Mulberry. This was a full-scale joint Army and UDR search operation involving more than 2,000 men, which took place in border areas in Fermanagh, Tyrone and Armagh. It was the UDR'S first operation and involved 400 of its members. The operation entailed an all-night search for terrorist weapons through the setting up of checkpoints on border roads.[42] The exercise was the first real test of the regiment's operational capabilities.

It is clear that the Troubles had not yet come to Fermanagh in the first half of 1970 as there were no Troubles-related incidents of any description. The nationalist *Fermanagh News* led with an article on 'Fermanagh's golden opportunity to become the playground of the north. By the end of the 70s we should see the development of Lough Erne as the north's major tourist attraction with Enniskillen as the power house of a vast area.' Paradoxically, another editorial posed the question,

> Where is it all going to end? The events of the past week have made the majority of people stop and think long and hard about the situation … On the other hand, the civil rights campaign for equal rights and justice for all, has become overshadowed by the ominous threat of civil war and the British soldier, at first welcomed, or, at least tolerated has now come under a certain degree of suspicion.

Clearly there were fears that Fermanagh would soon be drawn into the ongoing violence. However, the situation was quite unlike Belfast in June 1970, when 'the first small Provisional IRA bombs went off'.[43] Local unionists were also warning about the dangers of militant republicanism. In what at first may seem a surprising comment, Joe Burns, Unionist MP (North Londonderry), described the IRA in the following terms: 'In the main they are honest, genuine and sincere men … they are tremendously good guerrilla fighters.' However, his reasoning becomes much clearer when he added:

> Many people are under the impression that the IRA is an organisation of hooligans ... They are fighting for a cause which is very dear to their hearts and they regard it as an honourable business. It is because of this because they are not hooligans, because they are genuine and sincerely believe that this is so that they are so dangerous. If they were only a lot of hooligans running about the place they would not be dangerous at all. But these people are well disciplined, well armed and well drilled. Let us make no mistake about it.[44]

There can be no doubt that the major Troubles-related incident in the greater Newry area prior to internment was the murder of two RUC men in nearby Crossmaglen in August 1970. Indeed, the car used in the murders had been stolen from the Ardmore Hotel in Newry. The non-aligned *Newry Reporter* reported widespread condemnation of the incident. Michael Keogh called 'on every public leader to express their abhorrence and condemnation of this sickening crime'. He also accused Faulkner of being too quick to accuse republicans and suggested that it may have been the responsibility of loyalists. Again, the dubious accusation that loyalists might be prepared to murder members of the security forces in order to exacerbate the situation is apparent. Gerry Fitt said, 'I appeal to all sections of the community to do everything possible to ensure that those who have been guilty of this crime are brought to justice as quickly as possible.' The CCDC said 'that those responsible for the killings are neither Protestant nor Catholic and not worthy of any cause'.[45] At the funeral of one of the RUC men, Samuel Donaldson, there were ten wreaths from the Crossmaglen area, including wreaths from the Border Lakes Festival Committee and the St Oliver Plunkett Youth Club Crossmaglen.[46] Indeed, it has been suggested that '[a]t the time, Crossmaglen, although staunchly nationalist, was not the IRA stronghold, it was later to become. Local people sent wreaths to the policemen's homes, something that would not happen in the years ahead.'[47] The murders were also condemned by Cardinal Conway, John Hume and many representatives from the nationalist community.[48] However, the murders of the two RUC men should not be seen as the start of a concerted military campaign by the PIRA in the greater Newry area. Indeed, after this attack, the PIRA did not murder anyone in the area until September 1971, instead concentrating on bombing commercial targets until after the introduction of internment; in this period there were eighteen such attacks. As Kelley outlines,

Danny O'Hagan became the first Catholic to be murdered by the British army … The killing of O'Hagan and the 'Rape of the Falls' prompted retaliatory attacks by the Provisional IRA. Two RUC men were blown up by a booby-trap car bomb on 11 August in Crossmaglen.[49]

It is probably more precise to see the murder of the two RUC as an isolated incident, in response to the ongoing violence in Belfast, which the South Armagh PIRA carried out to get recognition. As Patrick Regan outlines, this is a tactic which has been employed by many rebel groups who 'must overcome the problems of recruitment. They must get the attention of … potential rebel recruits. The insurgency would start slowly, by blowing up a bridge or a police station, some action that would put them on record as a group to contend with in the area.'[50] This is not to suggest that there was no violence in the Newry area at this time. Indeed, three bombs were planted: one at the British Legion, one at the Ulsterbus depot, and a third at the electricity offices (which failed to explode). There were three more bombs in greater Newry, two in South Armagh and one in South Down before the end of the year.

Nevertheless, the security situation had not deteriorated to the point where the practice of naming and publishing photographs of local security-force personnel ceased. In September, it was reported that Constable Winifred Stevenson, Killeavy Road, Newry, had recently passed out of the RUC Training Centre in Enniskillen. She was pictured with her brother, Constable John Stevenson, who was stationed in Belfast.

The murders in Crossmaglen also brought condemnation in Lurgan. The Thomas Harte Republican Club issued a statement: 'We condemn unreservedly the unwarranted attack on unarmed Constables Donaldson and Miller by a booby-trap bomb at Crossmaglen late on Tuesday night. We extend to their families our deepest sympathy.' The statement went on to allege that Craig, Faulkner and Chichester-Clark

> see it as an excuse to the Westminster Government to once again allow internment without trial under the sleeping clauses, of the despicable Special Powers Act bolstered up by the wave of genuine sympathy of all sections of the community at the death of these young Irishmen. Let us state clearly that this condemnation as the sympathy we extend to the bereaved families is given sincerely to our fellow Irishmen. As republicans we are determined to remove the basic cause of these tragic deaths by breaking the link with Britain.[51]

At the same time, the first Troubles-related incidents occurred in the town. In that month, the local electricity-board offices were blown up, as well as an electricity transformer beside the Goodyear factory. Rioting had also occurred in the Shankill and Kilwilkie estates. The Kilwilkie estate was to become the centre for republicanism in the town during the Troubles; it is still to this day a base for so-called dissident republican factions. In September 1970, trouble also flared after a meeting addressed by Ian Paisley, and troops used teargas for the first time in the town to disperse demonstrators. In the same month, during a 'planned search' in the Derrymacash area, the army found guns, bomb-making materials and training manuals. In another security development, the newly formed UDR manned its first checkpoint in the town.

Nonetheless, levels of violence remained relatively low in the Lurgan area, and there were signs that the republican paramilitaries had no substantial support. In August 1970, neighbourhood policing was being introduced in nearby Craigavon. The idea behind the creation of the 'New City' of Craigavon had been to link the existing towns of Lurgan and Portadown, which were only three miles apart, with a new urban area. However, the plans never came to fruition, and the new urban area that was built, while retaining the name of Craigavon, was never developed sufficiently to join the two towns together.[52]

It does seem that some semblance of normality also existed in Lurgan. Indeed, it was announced, in response to the calls from local residents, that the police were to go on the beat in the Kilwilkie estate. Furthermore Lurgan was to get its first RUC reserve constables: Thomas Patton, Norman Sands, Ivan Calender and Dennis Uprichard. Again, the very fact that these local men could be named was evidence that the town was not yet on a war footing. When the Troubles did come to the town, naming local policemen in the press could have compromised their security. It has to be admitted too that the town was beginning to see some violent acts.

In Dungannon, unlike in Belfast, which experienced extensive rioting, the first Twelfth of the 1970s passed off peacefully. However, a series of violent incidents did occur in the greater Dungannon area following the arrest of Bernadette Devlin. There was serious rioting in Coalisland between the Army and protesters, and, once again, Austin Currie's home was attacked. Devlin had been arrested on 26 June 1970 to serve a six-month sentence for involvement in rioting during the battle of the Bogside in Derry. According to Ó Dochartaigh, her imprisonment 'was seen as an assertion by the Unionist government that the thousands of people in Derry who had rioted in August 1969 were all criminals and the defence of the Bogside had not been justified.'[53] Tommy McKearney, years later, believes that

> [n]ot only did her arrest reinforce an impression that the government was
> not impartial but that it also had a plan to settle Northern Ireland by siding

with the Stormont regime and its supporters on order to crush the campaign for social justice and democracy.[54]

In August 1970, the republican clubs condemned the burning of an Orange hall, which they said had the sole purpose of escalating an already inflamed situation in the Dungannon area. There were also calls being made for an independent and impartial inquiry into the death of seventy-six-year-old John Haughey, who had been hit on the head, allegedly by a police baton, on 1 July 1970 in Coalisland. Haughey died two months after the incident; he was a veteran IRA man and an ex-internee. However, his inquest heard that the blow might have been caused by a stone thrown from a loyalist crowd. A doctor examined him on 18 August, and he told the inquest, 'At the time he had had a stroke and I inspected the wound on his head. There was no fracture of the skull and the wound had healed up very well, but the stroke and the wound he received on 1 July were in no way connected.' Despite the results of the inquiry, demands were being made for another impartial investigation.

Even though there was a low level of violent incidents, as happened in other towns, the security forces still appeared regularly in the local press. It was reported that Samuel Douglas and Ronald Morrow were the first RUC reserve constables to go on service in Dungannon. Their pictures, as well as a full page of pictures of Dungannon RUC Christmas dance, were published. It was also reported that three new RUC officers were to commence duties in the local area: Kenneth Curran (Cookstown), Hilary Holmes (Dungannon) and Hammond Nesbitt (Dungannon).

In July 1970, in Enniskillen, there was disbelief at violence elsewhere in Northern Ireland. The *Fermanagh News* opined that 'this is the thought uppermost in the minds of many people throughout mid-Ulster today as the north, for a second time within a year, is engulfed by a form of madness which has already claimed six lives and done ir-repairable[sic] harm to community relations.' There was also condemnation of the Crossmaglen attack. However, the first Troubles-related incidents occurred in Fermanagh, in August, when the PIRA bombed three border customs posts. Local unionist Captain Jack Brooke, MP (Lisnaskea), seemed to apportion some of the blame for the violence across the country on the media: 'I am among those who believe that the hooligans who are causing so much damage today get a perverted pleasure in seeing themselves and the destruction they cause on television.' In the local area there were four bomb attacks on British Customs posts between August and October. Troops in armoured cars had also been used to protect a meeting of FCC.

Regional security before internment, January–July 1971[55]

In the lead-up to August, preparations for internment were being undertaken in Newry. A holding centre was established at the UDR base
in the town. It was also intended to arrest forty-three men from the
town.[56] In April 1971, in response to violence in the town, a local judge
made an appeal at Newry County Court for the public to assist police
in capturing evil-doers. He made the appeal while hearing numerous
claims for damages arising out of bombs and other malicious acts.
Judge Brown said 'it was in the interests of the citizens to restrain if
possible the perpetrators and to give information to the police to have
evil-doers apprehended and brought to trial.' However, Michael Keogh
was adamant that the Army should stay out of Newry if they genuinely
wanted to prevent trouble. His sentiments were echoed by Provisional
Sinn Féin, which condemned the Army. They also stated that they
deplored the recent wanton damage of business premises in the town
and wished to state that none of its members were involved in the van-
dalism. 'We call on the people of Newry not to be misled into this sort
of action.' Attacks on the security forces continued in the build-up to
August and included the shooting of an off-duty paratrooper, who was
slightly injured. Army patrols also came under attack from gunmen in
the Killeen border area.

Meanwhile, in August, full-scale searches were carried out by the
security forces, and a quantity of arms and ammunition was discovered.
A torchlight protest was held in the town against army raids; afterwards,
minor disturbances took place, and nine policemen were hurt. Indeed,
around '2,000 people accompanied by bands took part in the procession
through the town to the RUC station … where after speeches … 600
demonstrators marched to the Army and UDR centre where protests
were made against raids and searches of houses in Newry.' The arrests
made were part of Operation Linklater, which had been conducted as
part of General Tuzo's plan to arrest 'a number of known IRA leaders,
taking them away for questioning for forty-eight hours and searching
their homes. Intelligence had suggested that repeated swoops of this kind
would have a substantial effect.'[57]

In the period leading up to August 1971, the authorities were also
making preparations for the introduction of internment in Lurgan, where
they intended to arrest thirty-three men. An establishment and recognition centre was also set up by the Army at Kitchen Hill Barracks in the
town. After processing, detainees were to be brought to Ballykinler interrogation centre, which was code-named Leg Slip and then on to Crumlin
Road (Top Hat) or the *Maidstone* (Full Back).[58]

In the run-up to August, levels of Troubles-related incidents in Lurgan remained relatively low. A nine-day weapons amnesty, which was introduced across the whole of Northern Ireland, produced forty weapons in the town. It also seems that the police were receiving intelligence from the community. Acting on information received, they discovered an arms cache, which included guns, ammunition and bomb-making material. A quantity of explosives was also discovered in April. Around the same time, there was 'more violence in Belfast which was to continue sporadically throughout the summer'.[59] The PIRA was continuing a bombing campaign in the Lurgan area, with bombs at the offices of the Craigavon Development Commission and the local police station. In response to this attack, the Army reinforced the protection of the station as part of a number of security precautions being implemented across Northern Ireland.

In the aftermath of Operation Linklater, rioting in the town became more sustained, with trouble lasting for several nights. The nationalist *Lurgan Examiner* reported 'Now Lurgan knows what it is like in Belfast … Tension and terror gripped the people of Lurgan when riots broke out on Friday night and continued sporadically for long periods over the weekend.' The riots erupted after protests by republicans over the swoop-and-search tactics being employed by the security forces across Northern Ireland. The Thomas Harte Republican Clubs claimed that the authorities wanted confrontation to justify further raids. In their statement, the political wing of the OIRA condemned

> unreservedly acts of vandalism and actions aimed at stirring up sectarian strife and calls for all its supporters to avoid any provocation from any source. It appeals to their misguided fellow workers of a different political viewpoint to restrain from actions suggested by those who wish to keep the Irish working class disunited on a sectarian basis in order to maintain the ascendancy class in its privileged position of power.

By far the worst Troubles-related incident in the Dungannon area came when five men were murdered in a landmine explosion near Trillick, Co. Tyrone, in February 1971. Their jeep had undoubtedly been mistaken for an army vehicle. Three of the men came from Kilkeel, where one local resident said, 'the three young men were highly respected by all the community, where the relationship between the Roman Catholics and Protestants was amicable, and the deepest sympathy of the entire community would be expressed to the family of these three young men.' Thousands attended their funerals, and the unionist *Tyrone Courier* echoed the feelings of revulsion in the community: 'The savage murder of five working men by the IRA booby-trap on a lonely country road brought reactions of horror and revulsion throughout Britain last night.' These murders can, like the murders of two RUC men in Crossmaglen, be seen as an isolated incident in the Dungannon area. They were clearly an attempt to murder members of the security forces, probably as a reaction to events in Belfast. However, the murders did not mark the beginning of a concerted campaign. Indeed, it was nine months before the IRA murdered again in the Dungannon area. In the intervening period, their operations mainly consisted of bombing commercial targets. Additionally, it is likely that the attack was an attempt to promote the profile of the PIRA within the area, in order to increase support and recruitment as the membership of the PIRA in Tyrone was very small at this stage. As has been admitted by some senior republicans, by mid-1971 the PIRA had established only 'a basic skeleton organisation in the county'.[60] Furthermore, Tommy McKearney maintains that, before internment, the PIRA retained a significant presence only in Belfast.[61] Nevertheless, Dungannon was not to escape the internment swoop. The authorities intended to arrest thirty-five men in the area, and, as in other towns, an identification centre was set up for detainees who were to be sent to Ballykinler holding centre for processing, 'or in the case of selected individuals for interrogation as directed by the RUCSB'.[62] Revulsion at the murder of the three Scottish soldiers in Belfast was also being expressed by the nationalist *Dungannon Observer* in March 1971:

> It was well nigh unbelievable that such a thing could happen in this day and age in so-called Christian Ireland. Most people just could not bring themselves to believe that anyone could be so callous, so heartless and so cowardly as to murder three young unarmed men in cold blood. Under no circumstances, whatsoever, could their action be justified. No never! This is our reaction, and indeed, the reaction of practically everyone in this country to the horrible events in Belfast.

There was one shooting incident, in the Dungannon area, in the first half of 1971. It occurred when two UDR men had their car attacked by a crowd of thirty youths in Dungannon. In response, they shot and injured two of their attackers. The bombings that took place included four bombs in Dungannon and Coalisland. Loyalists were also active and had planted a bomb at the Garden of Remembrance in Carrickmore, which was due to be opened formally on Easter Monday by Mrs Nora Connolly O'Brien. The opening ceremony went ahead, and calls were made for both factions of the republican movement to come together and settle their differences. Other bombings took place at Eglish GAA Club, at Pomeroy police station and at the home of a detective sergeant in Dungannon. During the mini-Twelfth (a day of parades held shortly before 12 July) in Coalisland, despite a heavy military presence, a bomb containing five pounds of gelignite was planted. Despite the ongoing violence, it was announced that a local neighbourhood constable, George Lambe, would go on patrol on his own beat in Cookstown.

Meanwhile, in the west, in April 1971, loyalists bombed the Fermanagh GAA grounds in Irvinestown. In Garrison, ten armed republicans hijacked a police land-rover; however, the policemen involved escaped unharmed. Faulkner believed that they had been unharmed because of the RUC's policy of remaining unarmed. The nationalist *Fermanagh News* commented on the violence across the country: 'Shock, sadness and anger. These are just some of the reactions to yet another weekend of killings, bombings and robberies. The existing situation is intolerable. It cannot be allowed to continue. And yet, people ask, who can stop it? What is the solution?' There were also rumours at the time that PIRA leaders had gone over the border to avoid internment and that arms had been hidden both in country areas in Northern Ireland and across the border in Co. Donegal.[63]

Overview

So it was that internment gradually became an issue in the four provincial towns where the political and security situation was remarkably similar. However, in 1970, the measure was not of major importance. Conventional issues such as housing, unemployment and economic development were the areas of main concern. Traditional tensions between unionists and nationalists did still exist, as did the divisions within unionism over reform. The annual Twelfth of July parades in 1970 were to be non-events with virtually no trouble. Civil-rights issues did still figure in the political landscape, with opposition to the formation of the UDR proving to be a particularly divisive issue. Another important issue was the reform of local government with nationalists agitating for speedier change. These political debates were about reform within Northern Ireland, and the issue of reunification of the island did not feature to any great extent. All of these conflicts continued into 1971, but, as the year progressed, the prospect of the introduction of internment began to dominate local politics. As violence increased in Belfast, its introduction became even more likely, and local nationalist politicians across the country began to mobilise in opposition to it. Equally, local unionist politicians were making ever increasing calls for action.

The security situation across the four provincial towns remained relatively peaceful throughout 1970. Indeed, the only attacks of any note were carried out by loyalists in the Dungannon area. As the year progressed, Troubles-related incidents did gradually increase, with the worst attack undoubtedly being the murder of the two RUC men in Crossmaglen. However, this attack did not mark the start of a concerted IRA campaign. It is clear that the levels of violence in the four towns were much lower than in Belfast. As McKearney contends, 'Due to the origins of the Provisional IRA and the conflict that gave rise to it, the initial focus was in Belfast.' The first half of 1971 did see an increase in Troubles-related incidents, with the Tyrone murders being particularly deplorable. However, the IRA's activities did not demonstrate that an all-out campaign had been launched. In reality, the incidents of violence remained fairly isolated across the four towns.

It is clear that

> [a]t the beginning of the Provisional IRA campaign, many rural units developed almost as a collection of self-contained semi-autonomous groups, rather than anything resembling conventional military structures. Small ASUs were usually located in a particular district or area and the membership was often made up of a handful of friends or workmates.

The main thrust of their campaign remained the bombing of commercial targets. Of course republicans did see the benefits of this type of campaign as they believed that

> the destruction of commercial property ... served several purposes. In the first instance, it undermined the local commercial and administrative infrastructure. More significantly perhaps, it demonstrated to the people of Ireland and the world beyond that the northern part of the island was a troubled area where an insurrectionary movement was engaged in conflict with the state.[64]

It is true to say that traditional political tensions and limited security problems existed in the four towns, but these difficulties were simmering well below boiling point. The situation in the four provincial towns was quite unlike Belfast, where 'the Provisional IRA had begun to systematically shoot at troops in early 1971'.[65] Or, for that matter, in Derry, where Ó Dochartaigh maintains that, '[b]y early 1971, the Provisional Republicans were very definitely on the offensive'. However, he does add that 'the Provisionals were making "slow progress" in Derry up until July 1971'.[66] The spark that brought the conflict onto a new level in Derry was the killings of Cusack and Beattie in July 1971. However, these killings had no effect on the situation in Lurgan, Newry, Dungannon or Enniskillen. It should also be noted that loyalist paramilitary activity, although not insignificant, could not be considered as a substantial threat to security. So, the development of the dynamics of the conflict was certainly more gradual and appeared less inevitable than was the case in Belfast and, to a lesser extent, Derry. Despite the relatively low levels of violence in the four towns, it is patently clear that preparations for the introduction of internment across the whole of Northern Ireland were well advanced.[67]

Notes

1 See Keenan-Thompson, *Irish Women and Street Politics*, p. 224; Bew, *Ireland*, p. 499; Paul Dixon and Eamonn O'Kane, *Northern Ireland since 1969* (Harrow, 2011), p. 29; Hennessey, *Evolution of the Troubles*, pp. 38–47; Hanley and Millar, *The Lost Revolution*, pp. 158–59.
2 McLoughlin, '…it's a United Ireland or Nothing?', pp. 157–80.
3 Adams, *Before the Dawn*, pp. 140–42: Anderson, *Joe Cahill*, p. 208.
4 Geoffrey Warner, 'The Falls Road Curfew revisited', *Irish Studies Review*, 24 (3) (2006): 325–42.
5 Note of a meeting at Chequers, Heath, Faulkner, Political Developments, 26 September 1971, PRONI, CAB/9/R/38/8.
6 People's Democracy, *Internment*.
7 Moloney, *A Secret History*, p. 103.
8 See Simon Prince and Geoffrey Warner, *Belfast and Derry in Revolt* (Dublin, 2011), Chapters 8 and 10.
9 Ó Dochartaigh, *From Civil Rights to Armalites*, pp. 265–69.
10 Ó Dochartaigh, *From Civil Rights to Armalites*, pp. 311–12.
11 Prince and Warner, *Belfast and Derry in Revolt*, p. 260.
12 This analysis will also consider the environs of the four provincial towns. The *Newry Reporter* was the only local paper published in Newry at this time. It is also the only local newspaper which can be considered as non-aligned to either nationalist or unionist community. References from the local news-papers have been grouped, including direct quotes, into chronological time periods and endnotes added at the start of each section.
13 Michael Wheatley, *Nationalism and the Irish Party: Provincial Ireland, 1910–16* (Oxford, 2005), p. 21.
14 All figures will be taken from the local press of each of the four provincial towns. The deaths category includes any person who was not murdered but whose death was directly or indirectly related to the security situation. I only count rallies where more than 100 people were in attendance and which were not part of traditional parades such as the Twelfth of July or Easter Commemorations.
15 PO Box 500 (MI5) to Robert North (HO), Note on internment, 16 March 1971, TNA: PRO CJ/4/56.
16 For local references in this section, see the *Dungannon Observer,* the *Fermanagh News,* the *Fermanagh Herald,* the *Lurgan Mail,* the *Lurgan and Portadown Examiner,* the *Newry Reporter* and the *Tyrone Courier*, 1 January 1970–31 December 1970.

17 'A chronology of the conflict 1970' (n.d.) *Cain,* available online at www
   .cain.ulster.ac.uk/othelem/conflict/chron,htm (accessed 8 November 2010).
18 Bew, *Politics of Enmity,* p. 488.
19 Public Order Act (NI) Amendment 1970.
20 Chris Ryder, *The Ulster Defence Regiment* (London, 1991), pp. 32–46.
21 Bardon, *A History of Ulster* (2nd edn), p. 715.
22 'A chronology of the conflict 1970'.
23 Kelley, *The Longest War,* p. 162.
24 Hennessey, *Evolution of the Troubles,* p. 47.
25 Ó Dochartaigh, *From Civil Rights to Armalites,* p. 252.
26 For local references in this section, see the *Dungannon Observer,* the
   Fermanagh Herald, the *Fermanagh News,* the *Lurgan Mail,* the *Lurgan
   and Portadown Examiner,* the *Newry Reporter* and the *Tyrone Courier,* 1
   January 1971–31 July 1971.
27 'A chronology of the conflict 1971'.
28 *Northern Ireland House of Commons Debates,* 2 June 1971, vol. 81, col.
   39–40.
29 Marc Mulholland, *Northern Ireland at the Crossroads: Ulster Unionism in
   the O'Neill Years, 1960–9* (Basingstoke, 2000), p. 7.
30 Notes on Security information/Assessment of operations in Northern
   Ireland, 1 May 1971–1 November 1971, PRONI, HA/32/2/51.
31 Jeremy Shields, 'Northern Ireland's civic festival that was overshadowed
   by turmoil' (n.d.) *BBC News,* available online at www.bbc.co.uk/news/
   uk-northern-ireland-13839746 (accessed 5 April 2012).
32 Callaghan, *A House Divided,* pp. 158–59.
33 'A chronology of the conflict 1971'.
34 'A chronology of the conflict 1971'.
35 Skype interview with Tommy McKearney, former prominent member of the
   PIRA, 10 February 2012.
36 Bew and Gillespie, *A Chronology of the Troubles,* pp. 34–35.
37 Religion and Politics (2010), *Irish Press Releases,* available online at www
   .irishpressreleases.ie/2011/04/04/fr.sean-mcmanus.
38 For local references in this section, see the *Dungannon Courier,* the
   Fermanagh Herald, the *Fermanagh News,* the *Lurgan Mail,* the *Lurgan
   and Portadown Examiner,* the *Newry Reporter* and the *Tyrone Courier,* 1
   January 1970–31 December 1970.
39 McKittrick et al., *Lost Lives,* p. 47.
40 Prince and Warner, *Belfast and Derry in Revolt,* p. 233.
41 Bew and Gillespie, *A Chronology of the Troubles,* p. 26.
42 'Forums' (n.d.) *Military Images,* available online at www.militaryimages
   .net/forums/archive/index.php/t-1640.html (accessed 5 April 2012).
43 Ó Dochartaigh, *From Civil Rights to Armalites,* p. 204.
44 *Northern Ireland House of Commons Debates,* 7 May 1970, vol. 76, col.
   204.
45 *Belfast Telegraph,* 12 August 1970.

46 *Belfast Telegraph*, 14 August 1970.
47 Taylor, *Brits*, p. 57.
48 *Irish News*, 13 August 1970.
49 Kelley, *The Longest War*, p. 148.
50 Patrick M. Regan, *Sixteen Million One* (London, 2009), p. 103.
51 *Irish News*, 13 August 1970.
52 Martin J. McCleery, 'The creation of the "New City" of Craigavon: A case study of politics, planning and modernisation in Northern Ireland in the early 1960s', *Irish Political Studies*, 27 (1) (2012a): 89–109.
53 Ó Dochartaigh, *From Civil Rights to Armalites*, p. 210.
54 McKearney, *The Provisional IRA*, pp. 70–71.
55 For local references in this section, see the *Dungannon Courier,* the *Fermanagh Herald,* the *Fermanagh News,* the *Lurgan Mail,* the *Lurgan and Portadown Examiner,* the *Newry Reporter* and the *Tyrone Courier*, 1 January 1971–31 July 1971.
56 Confidential operational instructions from HQ 19, 8 August 1971, TNA PRO, WO/296/71.
57 Hennessey, *Evolution of the Troubles*, p. 113.
58 Operation instructions, 8 August 1971, TNA PRO, WO/296/71.
59 'A chronology of the conflict 1971'.
60 McKearney, *From Resurrection to Parliament,* p. 85.
61 Interview with McKearney.
62 Operation instructions, 8 August 1971, TNA PRO, WO/296/71.
63 Conclusions of meeting held at Stormont Castle, 1 August 1972, PRONI, CAB/9/G/27/6/4.
64 McKearney, *From Insurrection to Parliament*, pp. 112–16.
65 Ó Dochartaigh, *From Civil Rights to Armalites*, p. 234.
66 Ó Dochartaigh, *From Civil Rights to Armalites*, p. 237.
67 Troubles-related incidents for period: Lurgan, twenty-six; Newry, forty-four; Dungannon, twenty-six; Enniskillen, twelve. Total, 108.

5

Regional dynamics after internment

Local politics after internment, August–December 1971[1]

Following the introduction of internment, in August 1971, a civil-rights campaign was initiated across Northern Ireland when 'the Northern opposition parties met on 9 August at Dungannon, Co. Tyrone. The combined meeting of SDLP, Nationalist and Republican Labour parties expressed great concern at the direction events were taking and called for the withholding of all rents and rates.'[2] Those assembled agreed on a number of demands. All those in public positions should oppose internment by withdrawing from office; the public should withhold all rent and rates; everyone should support all the organisations who called meetings to oppose internment; the military should protect people against sectarian attacks pending a political solution; and, finally, Westminster should suspend Stormont. Tyrone was also to be the setting for the formation of the NRM, at a conference organised by the Tyrone Central Civil Resistance Committee, in Omagh on 17 October 1971.[3] The committee appears to have been a body set up to coordinate the different groups involved in the civil-resistance campaign in Tyrone.

After the introduction of internment, Coalisland, near Dungannon, was described as being a virtual 'ghost town', with shops, factories and even banks being closed as a consequence of the one-day strike in connection with the civil-disobedience campaign. By September 1971, 95 per cent of tenants in the town were withholding rents.[4] In early September, John Hume and Austin Currie visited Dungannon, pledging that they were determined not to take part in any negotiations until every internee had been released. NICRA also held a conference in the town, vowing that the civil-disobedience campaign would be intensified. As part of this campaign, fourteen people, including four priests, were fined £5 and £8.55 each for failing to fill in census forms at Dungannon court. The opposition to internment was coming from every section of the local nationalist community. According to some republicans, the introduction of the measure 'was the straw that broke the camel's back', and the nationalist community perceived that any further reform was impossible.[5]

In unionist circles, John Taylor, local MP, praised internment and called on the government in the South to introduce the measure also. Unionists were also claiming that 'threats and intimidation had failed to persuade a quarter of Catholics in the Dungannon Urban Council area to join the rent and rates strike'. However, not all unionists were in favour of internment. At Stormont, moderate unionist David Bleakley resigned as Minister of Community Relations in protest at its introduction.[6] Nonetheless, local Dungannon unionists expressed their support for Taylor's views on the lack of security; he had made calls for the UDR to be used in border patrols. They also urged him not to support the proposed reintroduction of PR in local elections. Later in the year, Taylor, referring to the Compton Report, criticised certain papers for believing the IRA's 'far-fetched allegations which have now been exposed'. The Compton Report had been commissioned to examine the SD techniques used by the security forces during the interrogation of detainees. A rally in Dungannon was attended by 5,000 unionists who pledged their loyalty to the union and condemned the destruction and violence. Shortly afterwards, Ian Paisley and Desmond Boal launched the DUP, 'which would be on the right of constitutional issues and the left of social issues'; at the same time a branch of the party was formed in Dungannon.[7] At a local DUP rally, the Revd William Beattie referred to internment. He emphasised that instead of being soft his party would be tougher than the government 'because we want these men dealt with effectively by the law. We want them charged and put behind bars not allowed to be released on to the streets.'

Immediately following the introduction of internment, the Lurgan Civil Rights Committee initiated a rent and rates strike. By October 1971, the civil-disobedience campaign was in full swing, with 4,000 tenants in the town refusing to pay rent at an estimated cost of £10,000 per week.[8] In total, across Northern Ireland, over 25,000 tenants were withholding their rent out of some 135,000 public-authority tenants. The weekly loss was estimated at £50,000, with thirty-two out of sixty councils affected.[9] At the same time as the civil-disobedience campaign was launched, an anti-internment committee was set up in the town. The committee was a broad-based leftish group of people. It included members from PD, the Communist Party and both the Provisional and Official movements and men like Paddy McNally of the trade-union movement and Brian Tipping, a member of the Official republican movement. The committee's functions included organising anti-internment protests, helping people move because of sectarian intimidation and publishing a newsletter, *The Lurgan Campaigner*.[10]

Amid the violence in the town, approximately 1,000 people attended an anti-internment rally at a local GAA ground. Speakers at the rally included Bernadette Devlin and Joseph French, Chairman of the County Armagh GAA Board. A large number of factory employees stayed away from work so they could attend the rally. Meanwhile, a branch of the SDLP was also formed in the town.

It is also clear that unionists in the town were equally committed in their support of internment. R. J. Mitchell, local unionist MP, stated at Stormont:

> Internment is justifiable. We must ensure bandits of the worst type cannot carry on their activities ... Many more people should be interned. Indeed the members of the house [sic] who have been stumping around the country and inciting people from one end of it to the other to break the laws of the land and defy the authority of the Government and of local authorities should be brought within the confines of Long Kesh or some other internment camp.[11]

Mitchell also made appeals for more men to join the UDR and suggested that a 10 p.m. curfew should be introduced. He also believed that the use of 'the birch was badly needed'. He proposed that the death penalty be introduced for anyone found guilty of causing explosions and suggested that the right to vote could be withdrawn from anyone found guilty of other offences including the withholding of rents. He stated that 'the CRA had called for one man one vote and they should be made to value that right'.

Concerns were also expressed by unionists of reports that members of the RUC were taking part in the civil-disobedience campaign. On a visit to Lurgan, Ian Paisley urged every man over eighteen to join the Citizens' Defence Corps, which, he stated, was 'not a military or paramilitary organisation'. He added that 'no one can prevent us from taking steps to protect ourselves, our families and our property. Make no mistake the present situation is all too serious. The die has been cast and the time has come for loyalists to stand together.' He went on to condemn the decision to disband the B-Specials. There is very little information available on the Citizens' Defence Corps, although it does not appear to be a group of any significance. Some local unionists were more moderate in their demands. Samuel Magowan, MP, made calls for a referendum on the border to take place every ten years 'to take the border out of politics'.

Following the introduction of internment, an audience of 2,000 people attended a meeting in Newry Town Hall to launch a civil-rights campaign.[12] The meeting expressed anti-unionist sentiments and called for the non-payment of rent and rates. The Chairman of the Urban Council, Patrick McMahon, indicated that he was 100 per cent behind the campaign, as were councillors, S. Ruddy, J. McKevitt, M. Murphy, M. McKeown, H. Golding and T. Markey. By October, it was estimated that approximately 16,000 households were withholding rent and rates from council houses across the North.[13] In Newry, as early as September it was estimated that 95 per cent of tenants were refusing to pay rent and that Newry Urban Council (NUC) had lost £150,000 in ten weeks.[14] All the nationalist councillors in the town resigned from NUC, leaving it with only six unionist members. Patrick McMahon, a local nationalist councillor, commented on the boycott:

> On that black Monday morning when thirty of our local men were taken roughly from their beds I thought the time had come to quit and take no more part in the affairs of Newry Urban Council. I will not return to the council until the last internee is released.

A branch of the Catholic Ex-Servicemen Association (CESA) was formed in the town for the defence of the area. However, its chairman, John Henry, was soon sacked from his civil-service post for being a member of the association, and the local branch was also banned by Faulkner from honouring its former comrades on Remembrance Day. The CESA was formed by 'Philip Curran, a Belfast accountant, who had resigned from the Ulster Defence Regiment following internment'.[15] It was established as an organisation purely for the defence of the nationalist community.

Intimidation was also taking place in the strongly nationalist Derrybeg estate. For example, the four Protestant families who still lived there moved out after receiving threats. This was a common occurrence in the wake of internment. It has been estimated that as many as 7,000 people, many of them Catholics, were forced to flee their homes.[16] John Hume visited the town and called on people to reject violence:

> It is time we used our brains instead of our brawn. It is difficult for an Irishman to keep his temper. It is not part of our character to turn the other cheek but this is no time for throwing stones, bombs or bullets because the only people that will suffer are ourselves.

These sentiments were echoed by G. B. Newe when he addressed Newry Chamber of Commerce: 'The Irishman who engages in physical violence does no service to Ireland. On the contrary he does this proud nation, north and south, a graver and more harmful injury than ever an invader could do.' Newe had been appointed to Faulkner's cabinet in October and was the first Catholic to hold a ministerial position at Stormont. The President of Newry Chamber of Commerce was worried that 'it will take a long time to wipe these scars away but they must also show the outside world that the vast majority of people wanted to live in harmony and peace.' To preserve harmony, members of Newry Rural Council decided not to vote on 'the issue of protesting against internment ... To consider only important matters'. The government was trying to combat the civil-disobedience campaign, proclaiming that '[b]y helping to end the present campaign, you will help yourself, your family and your fellow citizens. Do not be misled, civil wrongs secure no rights, civil disobedience will not build houses, or bring jobs. The rent and rates strike is a self-inflicted wound.' There were some small signs of hope as an interdenominational prayer meeting for peace was held in November 1971, attended by over 2,000 people.

In the west, Frank McManus got married a few days before the introduction of internment, and, as a result of its introduction, 'the couple had cancelled their honeymoon on account of the crisis in the north.' In Co. Fermanagh, twelve men were arrested on 9 August. They were Paul Corrigan and Francis Doherty (Macken), Paddy McCaffrey and Eamon Anderson (Kinawley), Brendan Burns (Garrison), Maurice McGrath and Danny Barr (Ederney), Eamon Goodwin, Columba Fitzpatrick and Malachy McEroe (Enniskillen), Patsy McBrien (Derrygonnelly) and Tom Flatley (Coa) who was Director of Fermanagh Citizens' Bureau. It is not clear if all of these men were eventually interned.

A protest meeting was held in Enniskillen, at which Frank McManus said, 'if these men are terrorists then he was a terrorist also'. He said they were not 'prepared to knuckle down under Faulkner' and warned him to be aware of 'a risen people'. He added that 'Edward Heath had stirred up a hornets [sic] nest that would be too hot for him.'

The Alliance Party had also condemned internment, amid reports of the Irish Army setting up camps for refugees. Stormont's move was met with organised protests against internment, and local nationalists also launched a civil-disobedience campaign. The Catholic Church in Fermanagh believed that 'Abhorrence of internment without trial, and particularly its one-sided application was deep and widespread, among the great majority of Catholic people.' However, not long after this, Cardinal Conway was to be equally critical of the IRA, describing them as a 'small group of people' with unrealistic aims.[17]

In early September, a one-day strike in Fermanagh in protest against internment brought businesses in Enniskillen almost to a standstill. Over 1,000 people had marched in protest at a rally at which the FCRA said it would name the employers in the county 'who have sacked and victimised their workers who had participated in the strike'. It seems that the civil-disobedience campaign was receiving substantial support in Kinawley, Ederney and Newtownbutler, while it had also been established in other places such as Lisnaskea, Irvinestown and Belleek. A number of people were also in court for refusing to fill in census forms. Indeed, across the country, it was not long before nationalists were refusing 'to pay gas and electric bills, car tax, ground rent, TV licences and fines to courts'.[18] Father Sean McManus was fined £20 for obstructing a policeman. He refused to recognise the court, stating, 'I do not, I never have, and never will recognise the colonial state of British-occupied Ireland.' Meanwhile, his brother Frank condemned the Compton Report, stating, 'I regard the Compton Commission as a whitewashing operation from start to finish.' In September 1971, the proposed new shape of district council was announced. There were to be a total of twenty councillors, in single-seat wards. The ward electorate would average 1,750, with a total electorate in the county of 35,226 on the new franchise of eighteen and upwards. It was expected that the new district council would meet for the first time in May 1973. Coincidently, the DUP won its first seat on the county council in a by-election.

Local politics after internment, 1972[19]

At the start of 1972, unionists in Lurgan were calling for the resignation of local unionist MP, Jack Maginnis. The dispute was over his appearance in a BBC programme about Northern Ireland, *A Question of Ulster*. Maudling also attacked the BBC over the programme, and Alistair Black, Chairman of County Armagh Unionist Association stated that 'the BBC has so prostituted itself before the aims of republicanism that no unionist should have taken part in a programme that was obviously so utterly prejudiced.'

Maudling's attack was not the first time the government had attacked the BBC. In August 1971, Lord Carrington had accused the corporation of political bias.[20] On one of his visits to Lurgan, Ian Paisley said, 'I believe that the leaders of the Tory party now see just exactly what we are up against.' He also criticised the disbandment of the B-Specials and the disarming of the RUC. On a later visit, he claimed that many Protestants in the town were being intimidated out of their homes in areas close to nationalists. He asked Whitelaw to visit the town to see for himself the intimidation, and he also advised all unionists to write to the BBC and ITV calling for a programme to be made regarding the intimidation of Protestants. He was accompanied on his visit by Desmond Boal, and both men made calls for the full integration of Northern Ireland into Great

Britain. Indeed, amid the intimidation of both Catholics and Protestants, Whitelaw did visit the town. He was welcomed by a hostile crowd of about 200 loyalists, who pushed and spat at him. William Corden, the unionist mayor, condemned the attack but stated, 'At the same time their feeling was understandable considering the damage caused to our town.'

In February 1972, the unionist *Lurgan Mail* ran an editorial, 'A Time for Peace', in which it posed the question 'Could not a fresh start be made? Each side believes itself to be an innocent victim of the other and the hate and mistrust goes on.' In March, the imposition of direct rule was welcomed by the local Alliance Party, while local unionist R. J. Mitchell departed Stormont declaring 'no surrender'. The Alliance Party's optimism was displayed by Oliver Napier when on a visit to the town he declared that 'the situation is not worsening but may be even improving slightly'. However, the Lurgan Anti-Internment League was not so optimistic and was highly critical of both Whitelaw and Faulkner. It mocked Faulkner's indecisiveness, who, according to them, had said, 'I won't speak or co-operate with Mr. Whitelaw.' However, one week later, he stated, 'I will co-operate with Mr. Whitelaw.' The *Lurgan Campaigner* also commented:

> Mr. Whitelaw has only been here a few weeks ... and he is trying to portray himself as a fair and liberal man ... he has suspended Stormont for one year ... This does not completely incense the unionists as they hope and will strive to be in power again within the year. It gives the anti-unionist population some hope they have got rid of the unionist system for good and gives Whitelaw more time to work ... He releases a few internees and hints at a fair and just society ... Lifts ban on parades (which has already proved ineffective anyway).[21]

By March, the Craigavon branch of the CESA membership had grown to 150. Its stated aims were threefold:

> to offer aid and support to the whole community, to protect minority areas in the North if the long-awaited Protestant backlash became a reality and to give leadership to the minority ... We have just purchased a Ford Cortina car for the sole purpose of conveying the dependants of internees to Long Kesh, Crumlin Road, the *Maidstone* prison ship or any other place internees are likely to be held.

An anti-internment rally took place in January with over 3,000 attending the march in defiance of the government's ban on parades. This was one of a series of large anti-internment rallies held across the country before Bloody Sunday. There had been a rally in Belfast on 2 January and one in Magilligan on 22 January.[22] The protest was held a few days before Bloody Sunday, and the guest speakers included Austin Currie and Paddy Devlin. Currie stated that Faulkner was relying on the British and was hoping that after Easter he could say to Orangemen, 'I have beaten the rebels on the ground. I have stopped their marches. Their leaders are in jail. The government is in control.' The march was stopped from entering the centre of the town with well over 1,000 security personnel on duty; a counter-demonstration of 300 loyalists also took place. In February, a day of disruption was organised by the Civil Rights Campaign. As part of the protest, a group of local women organised a protest outside the police station proclaiming their support for the 'men behind the wire'. In May, two internees from Lurgan, Gerry and Barry McKerr, were released on compassionate parole for thirty hours to visit their parents who had been injured in a hit-and-run accident.

Whitelaw's general amnesty 'for all those convicted of breaking the former Unionist government's parade ban' was largely welcomed. Meanwhile, it was estimated that there was £50,000 owed in rent arrears in the greater Lurgan area. It was also reported that the 'peace wall' in the Shankill estate was unlikely to come down. At the end of May, the members of Craigavon Area Hospital Committee who had resigned in protest over the introduction of internment returned to their positions. Economically, unemployment was on the rise, and 1,164 people in Lurgan were on the dole.

At the start of 1972, the Catholic Bishop of Dromore, Eugene O'Doherty, expressed his desire that

> Every one of us must make a determined effort to get back to the straight and narrow road that we have left. We might begin by taking a critical look at our town and what has happened here and what is happening here. The main streets, the principal shopping centre, is a sorry caricature of what it once was. Now there are blackened walls, sightless windows and an enormous loss of employment.

The Bishop's desire for a return to normality was to prove forlorn following the events in Derry. In the aftermath of Bloody Sunday, Newry was described as 'a deserted town a high percentage of shops, offices and businesses were closed on Monday, Tuesday and Wednesday'. Sean Hollywood, a local schoolteacher, who had been at the march in Derry, said 'I was one of the people to survive. I feel privileged to have been in Derry over the weekend because in the Bogside and the Creggan I saw the spirit of a people who will never be beaten.' In response to the murders, a massive protest was held in the town with estimates of between 20,000 and 50,000 people attending. The rally passed off peacefully. The security forces on both sides of the border were fearful of major trouble at the Newry demonstration. As Craig's examination of the Irish Military Archive reveals, 'On 4 February the Irish Army recorded that Provisional IRA men are filtering into Newry. "It is known that about 30 Army uniforms stolen over period. Known to have explosives. Some men missing from home addresses here."' Additionally, an intercepted British Army communication shows that danger was not far away: '1620: Barriers being put up in Monaghan Street. RUC est. [sic] is 10,000 participants. Sniper reported on roof in Monaghan Street and men in black berets at St. Colman's Church.'[23]

The deepening involvement of the GAA in the opposition to internment was also reflected by the Newry Mitchels football club, which organised a Long Kesh tournament in April. In the same month, the Easter Parade went ahead despite the government's ban, and nine internees received £3,900 damages, including Newry man Kevin Lonergran.

Newry Urban and District Council was dismissed, as, following the boycott by nationalist councillors, the council had not met since December. In a government statement it was explained that, 'The Minister of Development has, as a temporary measure, appointed the Secretary of his department to exercise for the time being the functions of Newry Urban District Council and to ensure that essential services in the town continue.'

In February, a Vanguard rally was held near Newry, which was attended by several thousand people, the main speaker was William Craig. They pledged themselves 'to assert our right to take whatever action we consider best to preserve majority rule in Ulster, such action to include, if there is no alternative, the establishment of an independent British Ulster'. The Vanguard movement advocated a semi-independent Northern Ireland and had been formed just prior to the imposition of direct rule. However, it seems that the Vanguard strike protesting at the introduction of direct rule was ineffective in Newry, as 'Most shops stayed open, most factories closed because they had no electric, hospitals were unaffected and there were no street demonstrations.' Constitutional nationalists in Newry welcomed direct rule, as Michael Keogh stated: 'I hope the Westminster decision will lay the foundation for a lasting peace.' However, Rory McShane of the NCRA, was wary of any nationalist triumphalism: 'We must look to the Protestant population and must say to them, not that we have had a victory over you, because we have not, but that we have had a victory over the establishment and over the Orange-Unionist link which has misled Protestants for too long.'

The involvement of the GAA in the anti-internment campaign was also quite obvious in the Dungannon area. In January 1972, Paddy Joe McClean, one of initial internees to undergo SD during interrogation, was made an honorary member of Tyrone GAA, and a challenge game to aid the internees' dependants fund was held in Coalisland. Two local internees were released in April: Brendan Girvan and Pat McCaffrey. It was reported that they received an 'enthusiastic welcome home in Coalisland for the first of the "men behind the wire". Please god, the remainder will be released very, very soon.' Not long after, four more internees were released, including McClean, whose release was welcomed by the Alliance Party. A large crowd attended a rally in Coalisland to show solidarity with the hunger-strikers in Crumlin Road Prison. These men were demanding to be held under similar conditions as those under which the internees were detained, a de-facto political status.

In unionist circles, Clifford Smith, formerly a young unionist, defected to the DUP in February. Following direct rule, work in all factories in the Dungannon area was brought to a standstill, in response to the Vanguard strike. The local weekly unionist newspaper, the *Dungannon News and Tyrone Courier* described the strike as being 'more effective than any strike hitherto experienced'. A protest meeting was also held, which was addressed by John Taylor on his first public appearance since being shot. The OIRA had attempted to murder him in February 1972 in retaliation for Bloody Sunday. He was 'shot six times in the head and body as he sat in his car in Armagh'.[24] He commented on the government's ban on parades: 'The unseemly events of this weekend, when many republican parades were allowed to proceed in defiance of the law, without apparent action being taken by the security forces has brought the ban into complete disrepute ... The general ban should now be lifted.' At a later Vanguard rally in the town, Craig stated, 'Civil war is inevitable unless there was a speedy restoration of power to the democratic government in Ulster.'

At the same meeting, Austin Ardill, former unionist MP, proclaimed himself 'proud that the tartan gangs were playing such an important part, and they will be a well disciplined and organised body to help us'. The tartan gangs were made up of young loyalists and aligned with the UDA. Some of the gangs numbered as many as 150, and they 'identified themselves by tartan scarves or patches on their denim jeans'. This may have been in tribute to the three Scottish soldiers murdered by the PIRA in Belfast in February 1971, or the Scottish pop band the Bay City Rollers.[25] The tartans were much feared by the Catholic community as they carried out sporadic attacks on nationalists and nationalist areas.

In the west, in January 1972, the opening of the new internment camp in Magilligan faced much criticism from nationalists – as did Bloody Sunday, which was described in the local nationalist press as 'Ireland's Sharpeville'. Schools were closed, and work stopped across much of the county. The murders were described as a 'ghastly and bloody attack on innocent civilians'. Following this, a large anti-internment march, organised by the NRM, took place in Enniskillen. In April, at the welcome-home reception for internee Brendan Burns, Frank McManus stated,

> All the internees must be released immediately ... Now is the time to continue the resistance struggle so that Ted Heath will be forced to give not concessions, but to give the Irish people their just demands and rights and freedoms that should have been theirs many, many long years ago.

Burns had been one of the 200 internees released by Whitelaw in his first six weeks in office.[26] McManus, along with Bernadette Devlin, was soon to be jailed for six months for their part in anti-internment march in Enniskillen the previous February. The local anti-internment committee's news-sheet *Concerned* was calling for people to support the hunger-strikers, stating that 'Whitelaw will let them die if he thinks they are alone.' A protest meeting in support of their demands was held outside Enniskillen RUC station on 13 June.[27]

In June, the SDLP was considering asking local councillors and public representatives to return to their positions; this was a move that drew criticism from McManus. Additionally, the FCC turned down an offer by nine opposition members to return to active membership. The nationalist councillors stated that their absence has been 'in protest against the undemocratic system of election to the council as a result of gerrymandering and the unfair discrimination practised by the council majority down the years'.

Following the imposition of direct rule, factories in Fermanagh closed down because of the lack of electricity. Vanguard had called for a two-day protest, which resulted in electricity cuts and the stoppage of public transport. Many firms also closed across Northern Ireland.[28] However, the *Irish Times* commented, 'the fact that the unionists have all the key jobs in most areas of employment made the Vanguard aim of bringing industry practically to a standstill very easy indeed'.[29] The nationalist *Fermanagh Herald* hoped

> [t]hat peace should be given a chance to prevail to see whether the British initiative can be used to ensure justice for all sections of the community seems, from investigation, to be the prevailing mood of Fermanagh on both sides of the political divide, leaving out the extremists on both sides of the political spectrum.

There were some glimmers of hope as a number of cross-community meetings between young people were taking place. On another front, for the first time in many years, there was no Easter Commemoration

in Sean McDermott's native town of Kiltyclogher, on the Fermanagh–
Leitrim border due to the republican split.

In Lurgan, the anniversary of the introduction of internment in August
1972 was marked with a parade of over 1,000 people. By the end of the
year, there were six Lurgan men still interned. They were Sean Hughes,
Gerard McKerr, Owen Callaghan, Patrick McKeever, Francis John Green
and former Lurgan man Art McAlinden. Despite the civil-disobedience
campaign continuing, there were some small signs that the campaign was
beginning to dissipate. For example, in the Wakehurst housing estate, the
rent and rates strike was called off. Ian Paisley, on one of his many visits
to his home town, stated that '[i]nstead of releasing the remaining internees they should be brought before the courts, properly tryed [sic] and if
found guilty sentenced to fifteen years or more.' He also called for the
introduction of capital punishment for terrorists and rejected the idea of
an amnesty for those engaged in the civil-disobedience campaign.

On Remembrance Day, 1972, a ceremony was organised by Craigavon
CESA, which was attended by over 800 people, with wreaths being
laid at the grave of Lance Corporal J. E. Shanks, who died during the
Second World War. Also in November, the government green paper, 'The
Future of Northern Ireland' was published, and Whitelaw suspended the
local-government elections until after the border plebiscite. These elections eventually took place on 30 May 1973.[30] Jack Maginnis believed
that the Border Poll 'would not stop the war but would give people the
right to say where they stood as regard to their future within the UK'.

The rattling of dustbins marked the first anniversary of internment in
Newry. One of the hooded men, Sean McKenna, who had been recently
released, stated, at a Sinn Féin anti-internment rally,

> There are those who have been willing to talk to Whitelaw to get a seat at
> the peace conference table. If the members of the IRA are not sitting at the
> conference table the conference will not be worth two pence. It will mean
> nothing to us and the fight will go on while the Union Jack flies in any part
> of the country.

The rally was attended by over 1,000 people, and speakers at it were also
critical of the SDLP for talking to Whitelaw before the ending of internment. Shortly afterwards, approximately 10,000 Royal Black Institute
members attended their annual demonstration in Newry. The divisions
that had developed in the civil-rights movement manifested themselves
in Newry when both the Secretary and the Public Relations Officer of
the NCRA resigned. They stated:

> We believe in non-violent mass protest. We believe that the CRA must
> condemn and work positively against attempts from whatever source, to

impose a solution to our troubles by violent means. In light of last week's events, and the absence of such an approach, we can no longer be identified with the leadership of the CRA movement.

John Hume and Paddy O'Hanlon also visited the town and arranged a meeting to establish an SDLP branch.

In Dungannon, in July 1972, the PIRA ceasefire was welcomed by the local civil-rights movement, and the East Tyrone Brigade of the PIRA pledged complete loyalty and obedience to the Army Council's directive. However, John Taylor warned that 'Loyalists must once and for all appreciate that British policy was neither to defeat the IRA nor strengthen the union.' In Coalisland, hundreds attended an anti-internment rally. It was also reported that, despite the introduction of PR, the new Dungannon electoral district was still likely to be in unionist control. In other moves, only one person from Tyrone attended the Darlington Conference; he was Tom Gormley, MP for Mid-Ulster. He attended the conference as an adviser to the Alliance Party. The conference was attended by the UUP, NILP, the Alliance Party and Whitelaw but was boycotted by the SDLP.

In Fermanagh, Frank McManus withdrew from Westminster, stating that he would not return 'until Britain changed her policy of military repression in Northern Ireland', although he did continue to draw his salary. In September 1972, two local internees, Danny Barr and Maurice McGrath, were released, and a welcome-home party was organised for them in Enniskillen.[31] Approximately 2,000 people attended the rally, which was held at the local GAA pitch. Frank McManus addressed the crowd and criticised the new system of detention, saying that, 'under all the fog talk it amounts to internment in a new way'. Tom Flatley, an ex-internee, commented, 'We are all overjoyed at the release of these two Ederney men, but we are not going to thank Whitelaw. We all know that these men, like all the others, were unjustly held, and are still being held as bargaining fodder.'

In August 1972, the proposals for the future of local government of Fermanagh were also announced. There would be five electoral units, of four wards each; election would be by PR. The authorities were keen for the elections to be held using PR, as Whitelaw explained:

If simple majority vote was retained, very few councillors would be returned who were not supporters of one of the two extreme parties, Ulster Vanguard or Sinn Fein. The reintroduction of PR might not wholly prevent such a polarisation; but if PR was still withheld, the blame for the polarisation would be placed upon the government by those moderate elements in Northern Ireland whom it was most desirable to encourage …

Mr. Faulkner had indicated that there would be strong objection to PR within the Unionist Party.[32]

Shortly afterwards, Whitelaw visited Enniskillen and defended the actions of the security forces: 'I think that it has been shown that the security forces have been absolutely impartial against all those people who have been breaking the law.' Austin Currie and John Hume also attended a meeting in Enniskillen at which they faced much criticism. Hume was questioned over his failure to march on Bloody Sunday, to which he replied, 'he had been at Magilligan and had realised the potential for violence and he did not want to lead his own people into violence.'

Meanwhile, the local anti-internment committee, somewhat sarcastically, gave its analysis of the political landscape:

Stormont Park Political Stakes (2 y.o. and upwards)

1. Ted Heath – White gelding by Sailor boy out of Organ grinder – inexperienced and knows little about the game.
2. Faulkner – A black colt of doubtful pedigree was run out of it in his last race.
3. Internee – By Game Spirit out of Freedom – will do better over fences.
4. Military – By Slayer out of Brit-Bum – falls quite often, not a safe bet.
5. Alliance – By Unionist out of Unionist – fades rapidly under pressure.
6. Whitelaw – By Invader out of Order – not expected to stay.
7. Lynch – By Stand out of Idly By – a greatly over-rated animal.
8. Paisley – By Churchman out of Own Making – needs strong handling, will try to get to the front early.
9. Harry Curry – By Cop out of Piglet – has not been out for some time.[33]

Regional security after internment, August–December 1971[34]

After the introduction of internment, widespread violence erupted in Lurgan with the nationalist *Lurgan and Portadown Examiner* commenting, 'The tragic events of this week in August 1971 in which internment was introduced in the North will be remembered in Ireland for a long time to come.' There were many riots and demonstrations, with local women at the forefront of the protests. As a result of the violence, a local travel agent reported being inundated with inquiries about emigration to Canada and Australia. Violence in Lurgan, which had been at a low level prior to internment, continued to escalate with the attempted murder of two unarmed off-duty soldiers in October. Loyalists were also clearly active in the town, with the local nationalist press reporting that 'Tartan Terrorists Roam Lurgan's Streets'.

The first murder of a member of the security forces in Lurgan took place in November 1971. Two soldiers were shot near Lurgan hospital. One of the soldiers, Paul Genge (eighteen) from Cheshire, died instantly; the other soldier was seriously injured. Both men had been unarmed when attacked. They saw their attackers approaching and attempted to escape, as their commanding officer outlined: 'They started to run for it but there was no cover and they were shot down in cold blood.' This incident was followed up by bomb attacks in Craigavon and Lurgan. Despite the Remembrance Day ceremony being cancelled that year, it went ahead, with over 4,000 attending as a mark of respect to the war dead and the murdered soldier. In the aftermath of the shooting, the Army was accused of running amok in Kilwilkie. Up to thirty British soldiers, in full battle gear, with their faces blackened, went on the rampage in the estate. They 'smashed and terrorised their way through the estate'. Liam Carville, fifteen years old, said, 'A crowd of twenty soldiers surrounded me. They grabbed me by the hair and kicked me over a garden wall. Then they pinned me to the ground. One deliberately dropped his rifle on my face smashing my nose. Another pushed his rifle into my throat.' After the attack on the estate, 500 women protested at Kitchen Hill Barracks.

Towards the end of 1971, the violence in Lurgan continued unabated and resulted in another two deaths. Warrant Officer Colin Davies (thirty-nine) from Wales was killed trying to diffuse a bomb in William Street. The bomb itself did not kill him, but he was fatally injured by the collapsing building. The PIRA suffered its first fatality in Lurgan when Michael Crossey, a local shop assistant, was killed by his own bomb. He was described by the PIRA as being a 1st Lieutenant of the Lurgan Company Óglaigh na hÉireann. More than a fortnight after the explosion, the weapon used to kill Signalman Genge was found in the debris of the explosion, fully loaded in a tattered coat pocket. At the end of the year, the British Army conducted search-and-arrest operations in Catholic areas, detaining seventeen men, including a sixty-six-year-old army pensioner. It seems as though the security forces were still acting on inconsistent intelligence as the Army also called at a house in Kilwilkie to arrest a young man who had died in a car crash seven months previously.

Internment's introduction was described as 'Newry's Nightmare' when arson and rioting broke out in the town and continued for three nights. There were numerous fires, bombs, lootings and shootings, and hundreds of soldiers were brought into the area to take control of security. It was initially believed that around 100 men had been arrested. The PIRA claimed that it had been active in the violence that affected the town. It was reported,

> There was a siege like atmosphere in the nationalist Derrybeg estate with shots being exchanged between snipers and the army during the night. Two soldiers were injured in Hill Street, one of them seriously. A new security tactic was tried out and proved to be successful ... All street lighting was switched off and a helicopter flew overhead and the crew searched the darkened town by using a powerful searchlight.

Local MP Michael Keogh stated that '[a]n atmosphere of despair pervades the streets of the town, allied to terror in the housing estates-every night bringing fear of invasion by an undisciplined British Army. They are hated today, as were the Black and Tans.' The local fire service was stretched to its limits, as one fireman remembers 'feeding when and where they could, the firemen snatched an hour's sleep, sometimes sitting or lying down in their wet uniforms and boots, on station or even out on the street'.[35]

Just outside the town, in South Armagh, a gun battle took place between the Army and fifteen to twenty gunmen in the Flagstaff area near the border. It was also claimed that there had been a great increase in the number of applications to join the UDR. However, after a week of rioting, it seems that Newry was slowly returning to normal. The security forces had had some successes, and there were a number of arms finds in the town which included four revolvers, 3,000 rounds of ammunition, three Luger magazines and some bomb equipment. The OIRA and the PIRA in Newry issued a joint statement condemning a petrol-bomb attack on the home of a Catholic UDR man in nearby Newtownhamilton. They stated, 'We wish to inform the general public that our intelligence staff ... are carrying out an immediate investigation into this cowardly crime.' It seems that attacking Catholic members of the security forces was not yet considered acceptable although this was soon to change.

The first murders of members of the security forces in the Newry area since August 1970 came in September. A soldier, Ian Armstrong (thirty-two), was shot dead in a border ambush near Crossmaglen. Following this, Trooper John Warnock (eighteen) was killed in a landmine blast in the Derrybeg estate. Two other soldiers were seriously injured in the attack, which was carried out by the OIRA. Following this, two suspected IRA men, Eamon Henry and Brian Hamill, burned to death in a drapery-store fire in Hill Street that caused £300,000 worth of damage.

Then, in October, three Catholic men were shot dead in the town in controversial circumstances. They were John Ruddy, Thomas McLoughlin and Robert Anderson. Eamon Collins recalled, in his account of his life in the PIRA, that following the incident, he had become involved in rioting along with another PIRA member, Raymond McCreesh, future 1981 hunger-striker, because everyone in the area felt that the Army was lying about the incident.[36] A report from the Historical Enquiries Team in 2011 ruled that the killings 'were a tragedy that should not have happened'. The men had been drinking and, on the spur of the moment, had decided to rob two men lodging cash in a night safe. The Army had intelligence that an IRA team was going to bomb the bank. On hearing the commotion, the Army observation unit had shot the men as they ran away, despite the fact that an arrest team had been in place at the scene.[37] Meanwhile, across the whole of Northern Ireland, in the three months up to November, twenty-three soldiers, seven RUC/UDR men and fifty-six civilians were killed, and there had also been 383 explosions. In the run-up to Christmas, two customs' officers were shot dead during an IRA attack on the Army at Killeen; they were Ian Hankin and James O'Neill. The year ended with the government asserting, 'Tonight the men of the UDR will be on guard. You should be with them.' However, not long afterwards, Sean Russell became the first Catholic member of the UDR to be murdered when he was shot dead in his home in Belfast.[38]

Violence also broke out immediately after the introduction of internment in the Dungannon area. A group of 100 people attacked Pomeroy police station following a republican meeting, with teargas being used to disperse the crowd. The nationalist *Dungannon Observer* commented that the

> [m]edicine was worst [sic] than the disease. The deep-rooted antagonism aroused in Tyrone on Monday by the news of the introduction of internment spilled over into the streets of two towns that night and was followed up on ensuing nights by further protest demonstrations and, in some cases, confrontation with the British army.

Indeed, in the second half of 1971, there were sixteen bombings, six shootings and seven major riots. In another move, local publicans were warned by republican paramilitaries that they must not serve the British Army. There is no doubt that the introduction of internment had a huge impact on many individuals in Tyrone. As Tommy McKearney, who was born in 1952 in the small town of Moy, recalled:

> My reaction to internment was one of outrage … It demonstrated clearly that the state, Stormont and its sponsor, the British, were acting arbitrarily,

beyond the law. They were not, amenable to any peaceful, political, demo-cratic or electoral initiative. So internment had a tremendous impact in terms of intellectual analysis and the morality of the situation. It also demonstrated to me, because of the overwhelming response from the Nationalist community, that in practical terms, a substantial section of the population was willing to act against an anti-democratic state.[39]

Indeed, the Troubles in Tyrone entered into a new phase almost imme-diately. In September 1971, Private John Rudman (twenty-one) became the first soldier shot dead in Dungannon; two other soldiers were also injured in the incident. A year later, his brother, also a serving soldier, was murdered by the IRA. Loyalists were also active in the area, and, once again, shots were fired at the home of Austin Currie.

It is surprising perhaps, given the escalating violence, that Constable Cairns Culbert, from Dungannon, was abducted by the IRA but released a short time later. He had been kidnapped by four armed gun-men and taken across the border. He said that he had been 'treated well and had even been given a cup of tea'. He added that he would rather not say anything about what had been discussed between himself and the kidnappers. On first sight, it does seem unusual that he was not executed by his captors, although, on closer examination, the fact that he was about to retire probably saved his life. It seems that execut-ing pensioners was, at this stage at least, unacceptable to republican paramilitaries. However, this is not to say that members of the security forces were safe in Tyrone. The situation was similar to Derry, where, '[i]n May 1971, off-duty soldiers had still been able to walk into the Bogside to visit friends; by August 1971, the only way they could enter was in groups several hundred strong, at the dead of night'.[40] This fact was reinforced by the attempted murder in October of Constable James Craig in Dungannon.

Amid the violence, John Taylor called for the UDR to patrol the bor-der. He was also adamant that 'the security forces were making serious inroads into the strength of terrorist organisations as a result of infor-mation from the internees and also because people now felt free to tell the security forces because internment had removed the intimidators.' The security forces did have some success when five men were arrested in town with three Claymore mines in the boot of their car. It was also announced that a new battalion of the UDR had been established, the 8th Tyrone Battalion.

The situation across Northern Ireland was deteriorating depressingly. Between 4 July 1971 and 13 December 1971 there had been 380 shoot-ings; 1,932 rounds fired by the Army; 364 rounds fired in reply; 1,741 pounds of explosives used; 211 explosions; and 180 nail bombs.[41] The year was to end with more murders in the Dungannon area. UDR man Denis Wilson (thirty-one) was shot dead as he lay in his bed by three armed men in nearby Caledon.

In December, a sixteen-year-old boy, Martin McShane, was shot dead by the Royal Marines in Coalisland. The Army said that he had been acting suspiciously: 'he had taken the aim position, whereupon he was shot'. Austin Currie refuted their claims saying, 'There had been no trouble in the area and the children had been playing for a considerable time before the shooting took place.' There was serious rioting in the area after the shooting. In 1975, a High Court judge found that McShane had only a toy gun, but 'a commando captain who had fired 30 shots from a sub-machine gun had acted reasonably and had honestly believed he was faced with a gunman with a real weapon'.

There is no doubt that after the introduction of internment the security situation in Fermanagh deteriorated. Enniskillen exploded into violence during an anti-internment rally. The rioting was so serious that tear gas had to be fired to disperse the crowd. Across the whole of Northern Ireland, a similar pattern had developed. On 9 August 1971, when he was returning from the Fastnet race, Heath heard 'that violence had broken out on the streets of Belfast and Londonderry, subsequently spreading to smaller towns which were normally relatively peaceful'.[42] This was certainly true in Fermanagh, as there were reports of widespread violence across the county in protest against internment.

In September, the first member of the security forces to be murdered was UDR man Frank Veitch (twenty-three) from Kinawley. There was widespread condemnation from all community leaders in Fermanagh of the murder. Frank McManus condemned the murder: 'My heart goes out to his family at this time.' Just over a month later, Corporal David Powell (twenty-two) of the 16/5 Lancers became the second member of the security forces to be murdered, in Fermanagh, when his Ferret armoured car was blown up.

Following the introduction of internment, there was another issue which was to prove just as contentious in Co. Fermanagh. Feelings of deep resentment were expressed by nationalists in the border areas when the British Army blew huge craters in three unapproved roads at the border, 'the aim being to prevent IRA infiltration along hundreds of country lanes that zig-zag back and forth across an arbitrary boundary line'.[43] Lord Carrington concluded at a meeting, with Heath and Faulkner, immediately after the introduction of internment:

> Provided reasonable peace was restored on the streets following the immediate aftermath of internment, the army intended to concentrate on border

security. Because of the flight south of a number of IRA men who had escaped the net it was expected that border incidents would increase and there was already evidence of this. The question of closing unauthorised roads was raised and Faulkner said … large scale cratering might prove more effective. Heath felt that the time had come to make further strong representations to Lynch about better co-operation from his security forces, which Faulkner described as being of little practical value at present.[44]

It seems clear that it was Faulkner who suggested that the policy would prove beneficial. As Moloney outlines, unionists blamed the border for the deteriorating security situation, and, as a result, the Army continued to crater border roads, which angered local farming communities and led to confrontations with the security forces.[45] The nationalist *Fermanagh Herald* proclaimed, 'The stupid and unnecessary escalation of trouble by the blowing up of border roads has led, as predicted, to an extension of the six-county armed conflict to Fermanagh, hitherto comparatively peaceful'. As a result of the policy, there were numerous confrontations between the Army and local nationalists. At one such confrontation, Frank McManus was arrested, along with twenty-five other people 'near the Tyrone-Monaghan border … after people from both sides of the border had filled in a crater on an unapproved road'. In December there were two shooting incidents at border crossings which had been spiked by the Army. The blowing up of border roads was a 'most stupid and most detestable action' according to John Carron MP. He added:

> Apart from the outrage of internment, nothing was liable to antagonise or alienate the people more than this vandalism to their roads and their means of communication. All it did was seriously interfere with the ordinary lives of decent, peaceful people. No one could concur in their wildest dreams that the cratering of roads would stop easy access across the border by anyone who wished to engage in illegality.

In response, farmers launched a campaign of filling in the craters in the border roads. In December 1971, there was a confrontation between the Army and farmers at Derryvullan; a riot ensued, and the Army used teargas and rubber bullets. The local press was in no doubt: 'It is evident from the mood of the people that they have, by reason of these incidents, come literally to hate the troops and all they mean in Ireland.' During the trouble, shouts could be heard coming from the crowd of 'Here are the IRA', which sent the soldiers running for cover. Even infamous loyalist paramilitary John McKeague did not agree with the policy of cratering, instead proposing that 'All border roads should be closed … They should be sealed off entirely with effective customs barriers at each road, and an obligation on everyone entering the Northern state to carry a passport.'[46]

Cratering was only one part of the security forces' tactics to be used after internment in rural areas. Other measures employed included patrolling, vehicle and pedestrian checks and searches. However, the use of surveillance in these areas was less prevalent than in Belfast and Derry.[47]

Meanwhile, Stormont was asking that people '[w]ork with the men who are working for peace: Join the UDR'. The momentum of the violence continued, and the IRA and the Army fought a twenty-minute gun battle at Belleek police station. In another development, it was announced that claims totalling £17,135.97 were granted for damage to property between December 1970 and September 1971 in Fermanagh. It also seems that the ordinary RUC sergeant was unwittingly benefiting from the violence. The average sergeant received £345 overtime in August to bring his gross pay to £525, while the monthly pay for a superintendent was £264. It is doubtful that the extra money was worth the risk that the ordinary rank-and-file RUC personnel now had to take.

Regional security after internment, 1972[48]

At the start of 1972, the OIRA in Lurgan shot and injured a local loyalist youth. They believed he was a member of the tartan gang in the town. After the attack, they issued a statement threatening to kill members of the gang 'if it persists in its campaign of terror'. Amid the violence, a Vanguard parade of over 500 men wearing dark glasses and masks took place in nearby Craigavon. Loyalist paramilitaries were also active in Lurgan, as hoax bomb alerts occurred at the Gaelic League, Irish National Foresters and a local GAA club premises. In addition, the Special Powers Act was used, during a search operation, for the first time in the New City. However, the security forces still had to be careful regarding their procedures during such operations, as evidenced by the award of £300 at Lurgan County Court against the Chief Constable and the MOD for wrongful arrest and assault.[49] Five men from the town were interned at this time. They were Gerry McKerr, Hugh Neil, Gregory Creaney, Barry McKerr and Francis Green.

Many senior army figures, such as General Tuzo and Field Marshal Carver, maintained that internment was having a debilitating effect on both wings of the IRA by January 1972 in Belfast. Hennessey states that 'in January 1971, IRA activity had been reduced with internment grinding down many IRA units in terms of personnel and material ... But these successes were soon to be nullified by the events of January

1972.' His argument that internment was having an adverse effect on the IRA prior to Bloody Sunday is also clearly based on their activities in the Belfast area. Moreover, Major General Ford and Field Marshal Carver both acknowledged that there had been a switch of IRA activities away from Belfast to rural areas in this period.[50] What is clear is that this alleged reduction in IRA operations post-internment certainly did not take place in the four provincial towns; indeed, the momentum of the violence was sustained in these towns and increased further following events in Derry on 30 January 1972.

Bloody Sunday was described, in the nationalist *Lurgan Examiner*, as a 'Horrible massacre of 13 innocent civilians by British military'. Workers in the town went on strike for two days, with shops and schools also being closed. For the first time, a local unionist politician was targeted by republicans. Former Mayor of Lurgan Alex Greer was shot and his house petrol bombed. In the immediate aftermath of the tragedy in Derry, incidents in Lurgan included the attempted murder of two policemen, shootings, rioting, hijacking and bombings. Deadly attacks continued also, and a soldier, Michael Prince (eighteen), was shot dead just outside the town in the village of Moira, Co. Down. His patrol had come under bomb and bullet attack from an overhead bridge as it travelled along the M1.

In March, the PIRA shot dead UDR sergeant Harry Dickson (forty-six). He was the first member of the regiment to be shot dead in Lurgan. A former B-Special, he was murdered as he answered his front door. His eleven-year-old daughter witnessed his murder. He had been recently threatened and told to leave the force, but he had refused to do so. The getaway car used in the murder was found burnt out in the nearby sprawling nationalist Taghnevan housing estate. The murder certainly influenced an editorial in the unionist *Lurgan Mail*, which proclaimed:

> Daily throughout Northern Ireland the bombings continue daily the shootings go on and some politicians in high places clutch at every straw in trying to assure a sickened and increasingly impatient population that 'things are on the turn'. Judging by recent events its [sic] a turn for the worst and no amount of verbal bilge will make ordinary people think different. They can see for themselves and unless peace is quickly restored they will clamour for the right to act defensively and collectively to protect themselves and their families and their homes.

The implication of the editorial was that Protestants had no other choice but to resort to violence, in self-defence, as politicians were clearly failing their community. Additionally, it is clear that loyalists were carrying out military actions in Lurgan. Just before the imposition of direct rule, a loyalist bomb, containing ten pounds of gelignite, exploded in the underground toilets in Market Street, Lurgan. It appears that the bomb had been intended for use on a Catholic pub but had been discarded because of the police presence in the town. The bomb killed Helen Carmel Knox (twenty-two) instantly. She had been on her way to a St Patrick's Day dance nearby.

After the imposition of direct rule, the Vanguard strike proved effective in Lurgan. During the protest, gangs of loyalists had 'smashed and looted shops' in the town. There were two large protest meetings, attended by approximately 1,000 people. Local unionists denounced the Heath government and pledged total resistance to the new Whitelaw administration in the North. A crowd of several hundred loyalists attacked the RUC station and burned a Union Jack. The mob also bombarded the British Army with stones, screaming, 'Go home you British bastards.' They had also attempted to invade Catholic areas on several occasions. Intimidation was also rife during the strike, and fifty-one Catholic families fled their homes in the mainly Protestant Mourneview estate. The strike was so effective that there was no bread from Saturday to Wednesday in the town. The intimidation continued, and in June the UDA forced another sixty Catholic families out of Mourneview. They also erected barricades, cars were hijacked and burned, and there were clashes with the Army. Around the same time, it was announced that a peace line was to be established between the mainly Catholic Shankill estate and the largely Protestant Wakehurst estate.[51]

Vigilantism was also prominent in republican areas. The nationalist estates' committee issued a warning to squatters in the area that they risked being evicted, pronouncing, 'you have been warned'.[52] An attempt was made in March 1972 to establish people's courts to replace the vigilantes. It was declared, 'The sentences of this court will not be physical. Sentences will take the form of restitution or work tasks to benefit the community.'[53] At the same time, the anti-internment league was highly critical of Jack Lynch: 'It must be evident now to the people struggling in the north for their national identity that they expect no help whatsoever from Jack Lynch or any of his associates.'[54]

Militant republican actions continued, and the centre of Lurgan was demolished, with two huge bombs that caused an estimated £250,000 of damage. Following this, the town centre was made a pedestrian-only area. More violence was to follow when three soldiers, Sergeant Major Arthur McMillan, Sergeant Ian Mutch and Lance Corporal Colin Leslie were killed in a booby-trap bomb on the outskirts of the town. The bomb had been placed at the home of a former internee who had not returned to the cottage after his imprisonment. An anonymous caller had reported 'suspicious activity around the house of Sean Moore', which the three soldiers went to investigate. Local residents at the scene of the blast were horrified. They described it: 'Like a nightmare or a scene from a horror film. There was blood and mangled flesh everywhere.' One resident described how

> two soldiers started to carry the first body out and they were nearly hysterical with crying. They were calling out the name of their comrade. I can't remember what it was. I was so sick and shocked. They asked me to help carry the body, so I did. When I got outside I took sick at the thought of what I had seen. I just could not go back in.

Faulkner had apportioned some blame for the attack on the release of the internee. However, Whitelaw pointed out, 'It should therefore be placed on record in order that all the facts should be known that the detainee concerned was released by Mr. Faulkner himself on August 24–15 days after internment was announced and 8 months before direct rule.'[55] The attack clearly shows how sinister the thinking behind the paramilitary campaign had become. The house of a former internee was obviously used because the security forces, having had a report of suspicious activity there, would almost certainly respond in the hope of catching some republican paramilitaries.

Just before Bloody Sunday, the trend of attacking unionist politicians spread to Newry when the OIRA firebombed the home of Major Ivan Neill, Speaker of the House of Commons, in nearby Rostrevor. English maintains the effects of Bloody Sunday and the Widgery Report were that 'northern Catholic confidence that the state would treat them fairly was finally shattered'.[56] It seems possible that this belief that the state was biased added to the increase in support for republican paramilitaries and in the levels of violence.

Undoubtedly, a further escalation of violence occurred in Newry after Bloody Sunday. Republican paramilitary attacks intensified immediately, and, in a short space of time, five bombs exploded in the town. Indeed, as one former PIRA member suggests, 'By 1972 parts of Newry had been reduced to rubble.'[57] However, attacks on certain members of the security forces were still regarded as taboo. As one RUC man was shot and seriously wounded, another, Patrick Rooney, was kidnapped by two armed and masked men but later released. It seems that the fact that he was a Catholic was his saving grace. However, sectarian attacks were taking place in the town. For example, a nineteen-year-old Catholic from Newry, Sean McCorry, was attacked by loyalists and had 'UVF' inscribed on his chest three times. A young Protestant, George Robinson, was also injured in a drive-by shooting. He was one of the few Protestants still living in the Derrybeg estate. At the same time, it was claimed that around fifty families had left Newry because of the Troubles. However, attacks of this nature in Newry were a rare occurrence. As admitted by Eamon Collins, 'Yet for all the violence in Northern Ireland I knew that Newry was not experiencing the agony of the sectarian loyalist murders of Catholics.'[58]

Nevertheless, murderous attacks on the security forces were still taking place. In March, Joseph Jardine (forty-four), a UDR man from Newry, was shot dead at a border post near Middletown, Co. Armagh. He was an ex-B-Special and was married with two sons. Following this, RUC Sergeant Roy Morrow (twenty-eight) was shot dead in Newry. He had been in the RUC since 1966 and was murdered by the OIRA. At the time of his murder he had been investigating a bogus report of a break-in at a local factory. It was at this stage that the security forces stopped releasing the names of members who had been injured in attacks. Despite the feud that had erupted between the PIRA and OIRA, both organisations in Newry still carried out joint operations. In March, a joint attack was carried out on an army patrol. A statement claiming responsibility was issued: 'On Saturday morning last at approximately 10 o'clock am in the Barley Lane, Newry, a unit of the IRA under joint Official/Provisional command attacked a British army armoured patrol.'

In April 1972, four Newry men were among detainees released by Whitelaw. In the same month, Jim Elliott (thirty-three), a UDR corporal and married man with four children, was kidnapped and murdered. He had been taken from his lorry and his body was dumped on a border road. The area around his body was booby-trapped with 600 pounds of explosives. There were, however, allegations that it was his body that had been booby-trapped. There were further accusations that Elliott had also been tortured. Captain L. P. S. Orr, a local unionist politician, claimed, 'Nothing carried out by the Germans or Japanese was ever as low or as filthy as what these inhuman people did to this man.' At the dead man's funeral, an RTÉ film crew was attacked. It was later established, at his inquest, that he had been shot eleven times, but that there had been no torture or mutilation and that his body had not been booby-trapped. The PIRA felt the need to issue a statement on his murder that denied the rumours. They stated, 'He was apprehended by an IRA unit and while being taken to a place of interrogation he drew a revolver and fired on his captors. He was then killed in the ensuing exchange of fire.' A Catholic man, Benny Moane, was murdered in Antrim by loyalists a month later, apparently in revenge for Elliott's murder. In Newry, loyalists carried out a drive-by shooting that injured two Catholics. In May, a car bomb was used in the town for the first time. As a result, severe restrictions were imposed on all traffic entering the town.

Following the PIRA ceasefire, Newry was said to be peaceful. However, just before its introduction, RUC constable David Houston (twenty-two) was murdered in Water Street. His murderers had been attempting to plant a bomb, no doubt to mark the beginning of the ceasefire, when he had intervened. One eyewitness told how 'I saw them and one of them was a young blonde man wearing dark glasses. He shot the constable.'

At the start of 1972, according to army statistics, IRA attacks were falling since the introduction of internment. There had been '262 in June, July – 646, Aug – 1,073, Sept – 999, Oct – 864, and Nov – 694'. The Army was claiming success also because, 'in Dec when the IRA had boasted it would carry out an all-out attack there were only 765 attacks'. However, IRA attacks were still greater in number than they had been prior to internment. Indeed, for all their optimism, the Army's claims of success seem at the very least a little dubious when the situation in Dungannon is examined. In the town, paramilitary operations increased post-internment and continued undiminished up to Bloody Sunday, when they increased further. Following Bloody Sunday, Catholic shops in the town closed for three days, and a protest rally attended by over 300 people was held. The spate of bombings continued when the Imperial Inn Bar was bombed and Catholic man Louis O'Neill (forty-nine) was killed. There were suggestions that the bar had been bombed by the IRA because it had not closed as a mark of respect for Bloody Sunday. However, it is likely that loyalists were responsible for the bombing. It was very clear that loyalists were active in the Dungannon area. A restaurant was also bombed as the SDLP were holding a meeting attended by John Hume, Austin Currie and Paddy Devlin. Loyalists also carried several raids on the homes of UDR men in the Dungannon area, taking guns and uniforms.

Republican violence also continued unabated. In March, Constable William Logan (twenty-three) was murdered while on patrol. He became the 'fifth policeman to be killed in Ulster this year'. A Coalisland man was convicted ten years later of his murder. The IRA shot three UDR men in the Cookstown area, claiming that they had done so 'to teach them a lesson … Let this be a warning to the members of the regiment that if they continue with their "croppies" lie down tactics then worse may be in store for them.' Once again, the inconsistency of republican paramilitary targeting of members of the security forces is obvious. Surely in an area such as Belfast the three UDR men would have unquestionably met a different fate.

In April 1972, a montage of photographs, depicting the destruction caused to Dungannon, appeared in the local press, accompanied by the headline 'Scenes Like This Have Become Commonplace Locally since the Introduction of Internment in August 1971'. However, Austin Currie believed that the will for reconciliation was present on both sides. This was a sentiment clearly ignored by the PIRA when they murdered UDR man Harry Gillespie (thirty-two) who had joined the regiment a year earlier, having previously served with the Irish Guards. The Provisionals were making good their earlier warning, and, in a statement, they proclaimed, 'It must be emphasised that the UDR is a regiment in the British Army.' Then, in May, William Hughes was shot dead by the PIRA. His murder was apparently a case of mistaken identity. In another sinister twist, a pram bomb containing 150 pounds of explosives was discovered outside Coalisland RUC station.

In Fermanagh, the cratering of border roads continued to be a major issue. In January 1972, the destruction of border roads resulted in buses being burned and shots fired. British troops also fired teargas across the border, as civilians were trying to fill in craters, a move which was described as a '[s]erious breach of international law'. Near Roslea, the Army fired teargas and rubber bullets at a crowd of about 800 people. It was reported that locals were angered by the policy and that '[i]t has certainly made people in the border counties doubtful, to put it mildly, of the sincerity of the alleged peace motives of Heath'.

Meanwhile, four young Donegal men were jailed for a total of thirty-two years for a series of explosions in Fermanagh. The financial costs of such actions were mounting, with £144,172 awarded in bomb damages in just under a year. As Aaron Edwards outlines, during 1972, 'The IRA carried out over 1,200 operations ... mainly in rural areas.'[59] Loyalists were also active in the county as a bomb was planted at the Co. Fermanagh GAA annual dinner in the Killyhevlin Hotel. Vanguard held a rally in the town, at which Bill Craig inspected men in military uniform and stated, 'We are going to beat this conspiracy into the ground, and we make no accommodation with the enemies of democracy.' Local nationalist politician John McCarron was appalled by the display: 'When will Britain waken up to the absurdity of allowing these arrogant, overbearing and reckless men, with their thinly hidden gun clubs, and their 107,000 legally held arms, to dictate to the people of Britain and to the majority of the Irish people.'

The situation continued to deteriorate when UDR man Thomas Fletcher (forty-three) from Garrison, a former B-Special, was shot dead near his home. He was taken from his home by four armed men and shot in a shed nearby. Following his murder, 'William Craig called for a "massive mobilisation" of the loyalist community to defeat terrorism.' As a result of his murder, UDR men began leaving their homes in Garrison. Towards the end of March, a substantial gun battle took place at Belleek when 'thirteen IRA men engaged twenty soldiers, 1,000 rounds of ammunition was fired, and a blood-stained car was found near Enniskillen afterwards'. Two soldiers were also killed in a landmine explosion near Roslea. The dead men were Victor Husband (twenty-three), a married man with two sons, and Brian Robinson (twenty-three), married with two children. In another development, it was announced that high-speed patrol boats were to be issued to the UDR in a bid to crack down on arms smuggling. In a new tactical move, republicans planted a huge car bomb in Enniskillen, with a dummy passenger placed in the car, the hope being that the car would not draw as much attention as an unoccupied car might have done. This was an obvious attempt to prevent the detection of the bomb.

From the latter part of 1972 until the end of March 1973, there were fifty bombs and 205 shootings in Co. Armagh, with Lurgan recording the highest number of incidents: fifteen bombs and forty-six shootings.[60] Indeed, during the 1972 PIRA ceasefire, sporadic violence continued in Lurgan with shootings, riots and bombings. Additionally, the end of the ceasefire was marked by an escalation of attacks on the security forces. A military counter-offensive was also conducted, which was praised by the unionist Chief Whip: 'It seems to us sensible that this should be done by combining a firm military response to IRA action backed by political firmness together with conciliatory measures to isolate the gunmen in the community from which it operates.' Meanwhile, loyalists attacked the homes of five RUC men following a confrontation at a loyalist parade. Whitelaw stated, 'I must condemn this incident in Lurgan where members of Tartan gangs actually went to the homes of members of the RUC and stoned the houses.' Loyalists were also involved in setting up roadblocks and the attempted murder of a Catholic.

Following Operation Motorman, the nationalist *Examiner* observed, in August 1972, that 'There was no noticeable British military presence in the Protestant ghettos of Lurgan which harbour large numbers of UDA men and Tartans and from which shots were fired, wounding three Catholics, on Saturday.' During Operation Motorman, the Army took over Tannaghmore Catholic Primary School, where they remained for three weeks. Its location was ideal for conducting operations in the nearby republican estate of Kilwilkie. Army searches in the estate uncovered guns, rifles, ammunition, hand grenades, bombs and explosives. As a result of the raids there was serious rioting in the area. At the same time, it was announced that a new UDR battalion of 650 men was to be formed locally. The *Lurgan Campaigner* called for a collective response from the community:

> On Monday morning the British army rumbled into Kilwilkie, Drumnamoe and North Circular Road without consultation with anyone they occupied Tannaghmore School. Children who turned up for the summer play school were sent home, teachers were ordered to remove their books, ramps were built, sentry posts constructed, hedges cut down all without notice or apology ... This concerns us all, clergy, teachers, parents and children ... massive protests must be made by all groups in their own way to have Tannaghmore returned to the people.[61]

There was no let-up in the continued cycle of violence. In one incident, three men were charged with having guns and ammunition in suspicious circumstances in a nationalist housing estate. All three were Protestants, and one was a member of the UDR. Rachel Breen of Wesley Place, Lurgan, reported that:

> [o]n Saturday 1 July at 9pm a mob of Protestants from Wakehurst estate attacked my house ... There were about 200 of them. They broke all the windows in my front. They broke my front door and the stones damaged some of my furniture. There were three cops standing at the corner. I went to them to ask them for protection. They were talking to the people who attacked me. They laughed at me and as I was going home they clapped. The mob also attacked the car of Gerard Moore who is my son-in-law and was visiting me at the time.[62]

Early in October, the PIRA attempted to murder Bill Craig in the town. He was at his solicitor's office, where the PIRA had planted a 100-pound bomb. It failed to detonate. An advert appeared in the unionist *Lurgan Mail* advising citizens, 'You wouldn't give a gun to a terrorist so don't let them have your car. Remember! All car bombs are left in stolen vehicles.' The Lurgan Anti-internment League was predicting the introduction of special courts: 'The truth is that these courts are needed to hand out sentences to men against whom there is no evidence except that which might be wrested from victims of torture.' The *Lurgan Campaigner* gloated over the murders of members of an undercover SAS unit in Belfast 'OHMS SAS SECTION: Due to promotion of the previous driver to higher things a driver is wanted for a laundry van. Good wages paid. Fringe benefits include a heavy overcoat (oak) eventually.'[63] The increasing viciousness of the conflict was apparent in the sentiments expressed by the news-sheet. The article mocked the deaths of these soldiers and showed that certainly the author, and probably most of the readers, were revelling in their deaths.

In a daring raid in October, fourteen UVF men entered Lurgan Territorial Army camp and stole 104 weapons and 1,300 rounds of ammunition. Indeed, '[t]he raid was the biggest raid on a military arsenal in Northern Ireland since an IRA raid on Gough Barracks in Armagh in 1956.' In a statement, the UVF declared, 'We would stress that these weapons are solely for the defence of loyal Ulster men and women and will not be turned on any of the security forces.'[64] The raiders had told the guards, '"We are the UVF, don't worry we won't harm you, all we want are the weapons which we'll put to better use than you before December".' The authorities clearly believed that it was possible that the guards on duty that night in Lurgan had collaborated with the UVF unit. In the aftermath of the raid, the GOC ordered 'a major review of the protection of all armouries throughout Northern Ireland, to take account of the new factor of <u>possible</u> collusion between individual TA/UDR guards and UDA/UVF raiders.' The Army also noted that 2,298 UDR members had been issued with service pistols.[65] It is apparent that the authorities knew of the activities of loyalist paramilitaries and were worried about possible collaboration with members of the security forces across Northern Ireland. It would be another four months before the first loyalist was interned. In November loyalists also planted a no-warning car bomb at the Glasgow Celtic Supporters Club. In the same month, the IRA claimed another victim when they murdered UDR Lieutenant Irwin Long (twenty-nine). He had been driving past the Kilwilkie estate to collect his child from a relative's house when he was ambushed.

In December, a new dynamic was introduced to violence in the town when the OIRA fired a Russian-made rocket at Kitchen Hill Barracks, injuring seven soldiers. In the subsequent security operation, an unexploded rocket was discovered, which fatally injured Sergeant Roy Hills (twenty-eight) of the Royal Army Ordinance Corps. Amid all the violence, a confidential information line was set up, which offered £50,000 for information leading to the conviction of any persons found guilty of murder or explosions. The year ended with the OIRA murder of RUC Constable George Chambers (forty-four), a married man with six children. In 1974, a local man was sentenced to life for his murder.

During Operation Motorman, twenty men in the Newry area were detained. Shortly afterwards, Colm Murtagh (nineteen), who had been an IRA man since internment, was blown up by his own bomb. August was also to be the month of Newry's worst atrocity since the Troubles began, when nine people were killed by a PIRA bomb that exploded prematurely. The dead included six civilians and three PIRA members.

Among them was the leader of the PIRA in Newry, twenty-two-year-old Oliver Rowntree. The bomb exploded at Newry Customs Office, and the aftermath of the bombing was described as a scene of carnage: 'The bodies of the dead were severely mutilated and firemen and ambulance crew had the gruesome task of picking up limbs and broken skulls.' In a statement condemning the bomb, the local CRA said it would be advocating a national 'say no to the Provos campaign'. Michael Keogh commented, 'The people of Ireland are sick of the PIRA.' The Provisionals countered the criticism by saying that it regretted the loss of life and that the deaths had been an accident. Some senior republicans have tried to excuse such atrocities, maintaining that after internment, because of a massive increase in membership, '[u]nder pressure to increase operations, many IRA units began to take risks with where and when they planted their devices'.[66]

The tragedy did not put a stop the violence as 2nd Lieutenant Stewart Gardiner (twenty-three) was shot dead near the border while investigating a suspect bomb. A UDR man from the town, John Ruddy (fifty), was also murdered. However, paradoxically, an unnamed UDR man, his name withheld for security reasons, was kidnapped but later released. In November, the IRA launched its first ever rocket attack in the area on Crossmaglen police station.

In September 1972, in the Dungannon area, three soldiers were killed in an explosion in Eglish and four others were injured. A massive landmine of 300–500 pounds had been used. It was biggest ever used in Northern Ireland to date. Fr Denis Faul condemned the murders: 'the death of the soldiers must be deplored by all who valued the sanctity of human life'. The security forces were making efforts to win the 'hearts and minds' of the community. For example, soldiers in Coalisland fixed an elderly woman's wall, and she rewarded them by making them cups of tea. An advert was published that asked the public to 'Help protect your town: join the RUC Reserve and help your community'. Despite the violence, the local press noted that normal life carried on: 'Killings, bombings, internment – in the midst of all this, life continues on a pattern of normality that is surprising. Couples get married, babies are born and people die in tragic though accepted circumstances.'

In October, a UDR major was wounded in Coalisland, and two OIRA men were shot dead by the Army. They were Patrick Mullen (thirty-four) and Hugh Herron (thirty-eight); both men were stopped in a stolen car. The republican clubs issued a statement, saying, 'Heron was shot at point blank range and Mullen was shot in the back as he tried to escape.' Shots were fired over Herron's coffin as it passed through Coalisland.

Loyalists were also active and had attempted to murder local civil-rights leader, Plunkett O'Donnell, in Dungannon. Austin Currie's home was attacked once again, and the attackers, when they discovered he was not at home, had beaten up his wife. The Tyrone civil-resistance committee commented, 'The attack is clear evidence of the existence in East Tyrone of an organised murder gang. Armed attacks have been made on the homes of at least six anti-unionists. How many of these people must be killed before action is taken by the Whitelaw regime to end these attacks?'

In December 1972, the PIRA also introduced rocket attacks to the Dungannon area. They issued a defiant statement:

> We can only smile at Whitelaw's claims that the British are winning. We have succeeded in closing down all the towns in the six counties ... something which would have been undreamt off some years ago. Our campaign has resulted in deserted shopping centres, barricades ... The British army, by sealing off town centres, have achieved our objective for us. Only the Provos can open the towns again.

Indeed, the authorities had assessed as early as October 1971 that '[i]n brief while the terrorists clearly have no hope of defeating the British Army in purely military terms, they are now dangerously close to their prime objective of destroying the economic and social life of this community.' Additionally, it was admitted 'that Northern Ireland ... is rapidly approaching the condition of disaster area. Economic collapse and social chaos ... are looming realities ... they are now dangerously close to their prime objective of destroying the economic and social life of this community.'[67]

In another development, a new style of robbery, the 'Tiger kidnap', occurred in Dungannon. A local bank manager's family was held hostage while he and another employee were taken to his branch and threatened with kneecapping if they did not open the safe. The term 'Tiger kidnap' comes from the fact 'that the criminals mimic the predators by stalking their victims before pouncing'.[68] The year ended with the nationalist *Dungannon Observer* proclaiming that the 'Shadow of the gunman hangs over Tyrone at Christmas'. There were to be two more victims before the year ended. Alphonsus McGeown (nineteen) from Dungannon was shot by the UVF as he walked home from work; his companion was also injured in the attack. In nearby Armagh, a UDR man was also shot dead; he was Eric Greeves who was murdered going to his car after work.

In Fermanagh, the impending PIRA ceasefire resulted in an outbreak of violence. A member of the UDR was shot while returning from duty in Newtownbutler, and Belleek police station came under heavy gunfire. The financial cost of the violence was also being calculated; £300,000 had been awarded in damages in Fermanagh for explosions in the year from mid-1971.

Any hopes of peace were shattered with the renewal of the PIRA campaign, in July 1972, which brought a spate of bombings. The implementation of Operation Motorman appeared to have a negative effect in Fermanagh: 'As activity grows less in the northern cities of Derry and Belfast, it becomes increased somewhat in volume in the border areas like Fermanagh, now resembling the campaign of the fifties.' Indeed, in March 1972, the British realised that, 'The army's progress had been considerable, particularly in Belfast, but the facts are that the situation outside of Belfast and Londonderry is still very serious.'[69] Additionally, Lord Carrington had suggested in March 1972 that successes against the IRA in Belfast 'had led to an intensification of IRA activity in Border areas, where terrorists could find a ready refuge in the republic'.[70] The increase in activity included the murder of two soldiers in a huge blast near Lisnaskea. The dead men were Lance Corporal David Wynne (twenty-one) and Gunner Errol Leroy Corden (twenty-two), a married man from Jamaica. Also murdered was UDR man William Creighton (twenty-seven), who was shot dead near his home a month before his marriage was due to take place. The situation continued to deteriorate as two Enniskillen UDR men were blown to bits by a car bomb just outside Enniskillen; thirteen soldiers were also injured in the attack. The dead men were Lance Corporal Alfred Johnston (thirty-two), a married man with four children, and Private Edward Eames (thirty-three). They had been investigating a suspicious car when it exploded, killing them instantly. A Newtownbutler farmer, William Trotter (fifty-seven), was also blown up by a booby-trap bomb. At his inquest, the coroner stated that a 'concerted effort to drive families from their homes' was being undertaken. The nationalist *Fermanagh Herald* commented on the escalation of violence, 'Fermanagh is suffering from some of the worst of the bombing that has now developed along the border areas, since the takeover by the British of the former no-go areas in Belfast and Derry.'

The image of the security forces portrayed by republicans was undermined by the Army's treatment of Brian Maguire, a Catholic from Clones, who was arrested on the border. He stated, 'I thought I was in for a rough time when they took me with them but it wasn't bad at all … What I heard about other people who were taken in I just couldn't believe it.' Gun battles on the border continued between the Army and republican paramilitaries. The murders of a husband and wife in their own home brought scathing condemnation. The murdered couple were part-time UDR man, Thomas Bullock, and his wife, Emily.

A loyalist parade took place in Enniskillen in October 1972, attended by 900 masked men in paramilitary uniform. Craig stated at the rally, 'We seek no confrontation with the British army but if the British politicians put the army in a false position that is just too bad, for we shall not be deprived of our rights ... We are in a war situation and I ask people to come out and join us in winning it.'

A series of tit-for-tat killings now occurred. First, John Bell (twenty-two), a UDR man from Newtownbutler, was shot dead. His brother, Richard, who was also in the UDR, had fired back at the attackers. In the same month, the gruesome murders of two Catholics from Newtownbutler, Michael Naan (thirty-one) and Andrew Murray (twenty-four), took place. They were stabbed to death one mile from Bell's farm. The murders became known as 'the pitchfork killings'. Local people were convinced that the murders were sectarian and had been carried out by loyalists. There was a huge outcry after the murders, and it was believed 'that both men were struck on the head with some instruments to render them only partly conscious before the gang set about their murderous work'. It was also suspected that four men had carried out the murders using long knives or bayonets. It was to emerge some years later that the men were actually murdered by Scottish soldiers from the Argyll and Sutherland Highlanders. It appears that the murders were carried out in reprisal for the murder of UDR man John Bell. In their tour of duty, four members of the same Scottish regiment had already been murdered and at least a dozen injured. Naan was a prominent civil-rights activist and had been mentioned as a paramilitary suspect in an intelligence briefing just before the killings. He was stabbed nineteen times and Murray was stabbed thirteen times. It seems that Murray was murdered solely because he had witnessed the first murder. One of the soldiers involved told the RUC some years later, 'I killed them. Oh my God. Yes, I did it. They would not stop screaming.'

In his recent study, Tim Wilson believes that the violence in Upper Silesia, in the period 1918–22, was more violent than in Northern Ireland because the demarcation lines between the two sides in the conflict were less obvious. He maintains that '[r]eligious difference between communities in Ulster constituted a far clearer line of demarcation than linguistic practice did between the "national sides" in Upper Silesia.' Wilson's contention is that more grotesque violence occurred in Upper Silesia because the boundaries between the two opposing sides were not as well established as in Northern Ireland. Indeed, he maintains that the only noticeable difference between the Polish nationalists and German unionists was language, and, as a consequence, the violence was more vicious because it was about 'boundary creation'.[71]

However, it is very clear that some appalling murders did take place in the early 1970s in Northern Ireland. Murders such as the 'pitchfork killings' were obviously very grotesque, and, although these types of murders were not widespread during the early Troubles, other such killings did take place. For example, in July 1972, a fourteen-year-old boy from Belfast with learning difficulties, David McClenaghan, was murdered by loyalist paramilitaries who also raped his mother during the attack. The attackers proceeded to shoot his mother in both arms and legs and to crush her fingers.[72] In another incident, in August 1972, a nineteen-year-old Catholic, Eamon McMahon from Portadown, was found floating in the river Bann with a rope around his neck. Republican paramilitaries were also quite capable of carrying out extreme violence, as is demonstrated by the murder of the UDR man and his wife Emily Bullock, near Derrylin, in September 1972. She was 'shot in the chest at the front porch and the gunmen then stepped over her dead body and went inside where they shot her husband several times in the head'.[73] So it is obvious that terrible crimes did occur, at this time, in a conflict with already well-established boundaries. As fictional IRA man Jack Gallagher, a character in Eugene McCabe's 1979 novel about hostage-taking in Co. Fermanagh, outlines, 'this war is not merry ... it's ugly, very very ugly'.[74] Perhaps these horrific attacks are examples of what Frank Wright has termed 'representative violence'. In Naan's case, he had been identified as a possible republican paramilitary, and the soldiers were determined on revenge. As Frank Wright outlines 'victims of violence ... are attacked because they are identified as representing groups of people'.[75]

In November, a series of rocket-launcher attacks, probably carried out by the OIRA, resulted in one RUC officer being killed in Belleek.[76] Rockets had now been used in all four provincial towns. The use of Russian rockets in particular drew a typical response from the British tabloid press. The *News of the World* led with the headline 'Russia in IRA Plot Sensation'; alongside a picture of a submarine, the article stated, 'camera catches red submarine off the Irish coast. Intelligence agents have discovered that the Russian government is directly involved in the supply of rocket launchers and other arms to the IRA.'[77] In fact, the Soviet Chargé d'Affaires, Ivan Ippolitov, had rejected British requests for help in establishing how Russian-made rockets had been acquired by the IRA.[78]

The year ended with more murders. RUC man Joseph Calvin (forty-two) was killed in a booby-trap bomb during a twenty-minute gun battle in Belleek. Eleven days later, a reserve constable, Robert Keys (fifty-five), was killed in a rocket attack on the same police station. Loyalist paramilitaries were not to be outdone. In December 1972, Louis Leonard (twenty-five),[79] a Catholic from Derrylin, was murdered in a butcher's shop; he was shot six times in the back. The *Fermanagh Herald* despaired: 'The sadistic revenge killers have struck again savagely in Fermanagh.'

Overview

Following the introduction of internment, local politics developed a new dynamic. Immediately, all shades of nationalism joined forces in their hostility to the measure, and a campaign of civil disobedience was launched. The deployment against internment included republicans, constitutional nationalists, sporting organisations such as the GAA and even the Catholic Church. As Ó Dochartaigh outlines, 'The development of a marginal conspiratorial movement into a mainstream part of Catholic politics was made possible only by the responses of the British government and army in July and August 1971 which signalled that Catholic dissent would be repressed, not addressed.'[80]

Unquestionably, there was an increase in support for the IRA. Indeed, many republicans would agree with Gerry Adams's analysis that 'Thousands of people who had never been republicans now gave their active support to the IRA; others who never had any time for physical force now accepted it as a practical necessity.'[81] Additionally, a widespread disapproval of the security forces, the unionist Stormont administration and its decision to introduce internment had developed. 'Many Catholics … saw internment as a punitive measure directed against their entire community.'[82] Republicans and left-wing activists also established local anti-internment leagues, which were irredentist in their outlook. Unionists were as forceful in their endorsement of internment and stricter security measures. This was evident with the formation of the DUP in late 1971 and Vanguard in early 1972.

The dynamics of the security situation in Lurgan, Newry, Dungannon and Enniskillen changed dramatically after the introduction of internment. Prior to internment there had been relatively low levels of violence in the four towns, but now the tensions that had been simmering were brought to boiling point. Just as the Falls Road Curfew in Belfast and the killings of Cusack and Beattie in Derry brought the conflict in those two cities onto a new plane, it was after the introduction of internment that similar levels of violence were to occur in the four provincial towns. A sustained IRA campaign was under way. As Tommy

Mckearney maintains, 'PIRA only emerged as a national phenomenon post-internment'.[83]

The sociologist Randall Collins maintains that the real nature of violence is 'that it is hard to perform' and that 'most people are not good at it'.[84] Collins concentrates on a micro-theory based on fear and confrontational tension as obstacles to violence, but it is also certain that macro-factors come into play. Furthermore, it is explicit in Collins's analysis that most people dislike violent acts and are not bloodthirsty murderers. So, what had persuaded many nationalists in the four towns that armed resistance was the only alternative? It is important to remember that the introduction of internment was the first repressive measure applied across the whole of Northern Ireland by both Westminster and Stormont since the onset of the Troubles. This was the first time that people had first-hand experience of formal state repression in the nationalist communities of Lurgan, Newry, Dungannon and Enniskillen. This geographical application of repression across the four towns, where levels of violence remained relatively low, led to a familiar pattern in the history of conflict: violence → state repression → increased levels of violence. It maybe that, in the final analysis, the decision to join the IRA that nationalists made came down to simple cost-and-benefits judgement. Before the introduction of internment, many nationalists did not support the IRA, and the cost for those who did join a republican paramilitary organisation was either lengthy imprisonment or maybe even death. The way that internment had been introduced gave it an appearance of an indiscriminate attack on the nationalist community, and, as a result, the perception was that even if you were innocent you could be sent to jail. Faced with weighing up the costs and benefits of doing nothing or joining the IRA, many made the judgement that there was more benefit in taking action. This decision was also influenced by the perceived injustice that was being perpetrated on the whole nationalist community across Northern Ireland by the introduction of internment, taken in context with the situation that had existed since the start of the civil-rights campaign. The violence of the IRA had brought repression, which, in turn, had brought increased IRA support and more violence which led loyalists also to escalate their campaign, an ever-deteriorating situation.

Murders, deaths, bombs, shootings and rocket attacks all now became part of the conflict in the four towns. In fact, there was an increase of 400 per cent in Troubles-related incidents after the introduction of internment. Attacks on local members of the security forces, as well as members of the British Army, along with sectarian murders now became commonplace. The security forces also contributed to the escalation of the conflict.[85]

Between 1970 and 1972, a total of seventy-seven people lost their lives across the four towns as a result of the Troubles. Republicans were responsible for fifty-eight of these fatalities, killing thirty-four soldiers, fifteen of whom were members of the UDR, three being ex-B-Specials. They also killed eight RUC men and sixteen civilians. Loyalists were responsible for the murder of four civilians, and the security forces killed six people, two of whom were republican paramilitaries.

The precise definition of when a dispute becomes a conflict is always problematic. It is also debatable whether or not the Troubles can be considered, in its true sense, a civil war. However, Prince and Warner use Kalyvas's definition for civil war: 'Civil war is defined as armed combat within the boundaries of a recognised sovereign entity between parties subject to a common authority at the outset of hostilities.'[86] Then they identify their respective positions regarding their starting points for conflict in Belfast and Derry. Their interpretation is based upon the premise that conflict commences as soon as the first significant confrontations take place. However, Ó Dochartaigh provides a more nuanced interpretation of how the conflict developed in Derry when he argues that it did not truly commence until July 1971. He uses a localised study of Derry to provide us with a more illuminated version of events. Similarly, Chapters 4 and 5 have conducted a localised study of four key urban centres in the four counties outside Counties Antrim and Derry. This study also sheds light on events in the immediate hinterlands of these key towns. As a result, this study enhances our understanding of how the Troubles developed across the whole of Northern Ireland.

The University of Uppsala and the Peace Research Institute are institutions that collect data on conflicts across the globe. They define conflict to be 'a contested incompatibility that concerns government and/ or territory where the use of armed force between two parties, of which at least one is the government of a state, results in at least twenty-five battle-related deaths'.[87] If we take this formula and apply it to the four provincial towns, then conflict did not occur until early January 1972, almost four months after the introduction of internment. From Stormont's perspective, by July 1971 'the IRA had committed itself to total war against the state, and was demonstrating a capacity to carry it out on a more widespread and organised scale than ever before'.[88] However, it has been demonstrated that this perspective was centred on events in Belfast and, to a lesser extent, Derry. It seems apparent that all-out conflict did not commence across the whole of Northern Ireland until after the introduction of internment in August 1971.

Notes

1 For local references in this section, see the *Dungannon Observer,* the *Fermanagh Herald,* the *Fermanagh News,* the *Lurgan Mail,* the *Lurgan and Portadown Examiner,* the *Newry Reporter* and the *Tyrone Courier,* 1 August 1971–31 December 1971.

2 Dermot Keogh, *Jack Lynch: A biography* (Dublin, 2008), p. 309.

3 McGuffin, *Internment*, p. 109.

4 McGuffin, *Internment*, p. 109.

5 Interview with McKearney.

6 'A chronology of the conflict 1971'.

7 Bew and Gillespie, *A Chronology of the Troubles*, p. 40.

8 McGuffin, *Internment*, p. 109.

9 Memo from Minister for Development, 13 September 1971, PRONI, CAB/4/1615/6.

10 Interview with Brian Tipping, prominent member of the Official Republican movement in the 1970s, 16 March 2010.

11 *Northern Ireland House of Commons Debates*, 6 October 1971, vol. 82, col. 903–4.

12 'Award for act of valour amid internment turmoil' (n.d.) *Newry Memoirs*, available online at www.newrymemoirs.com/stories_pages/internmentandvalour_1.html (accessed 28 February 2012).

13 'A chronology of the conflict 1971'.

14 McGuffin, *Internment*, p. 109.

15 Kelley, *The Longest War*, p. 158.

16 'A chronology of the conflict 1971'.

17 Bew and Gillespie, *A Chronology of the Troubles*, p. 39.

18 McGuffin, *Internment*, p. 109.

19 For local references in this section, see the *Dungannon Observer,* the *Fermanagh Herald,* the *Fermanagh News,* the *Lurgan Mail,* the *Lurgan and Portadown Examiner,* the *Newry Reporter* and the *Tyrone Courier,* 1 January 1972–31 December 1972.

20 'A chronology of the conflict 1971'.

21 *Lurgan Campaigner*, vol. 2 no. 15, no date.

22 'A chronology of the conflict 1971'.

23 Craig, *Crisis of Confidence*, p. 110.

24 Hanley and Millar, *The Lost Revolution,* p. 176.

25 Ian S. Wood, *Crimes of Loyalty: A History of the UDA* (Edinburgh, 2006), p. 5.

26 Michael Kerr, *The Destructors: the Story of the Northern Ireland Peace Process* (Dublin, 2011), p. 34.

27 *Concerned*, 13 June 1972.

28 'A chronology of the conflict 1971'.

29 *Irish Times*, 6 April 1972.

30 Kerr, *The Destructors*, p. 74.

31 *Concerned,* 19 August 1972.

32 Cabinet conclusions, 15 June 1972, TNA PRO, CAB/128/48.
33 *Concerned,* 7 October 1972.
34 For this section, see the *Dungannon Observer,* the *Fermanagh Herald,* the *Fermanagh News,* the *Lurgan Mail,* the *Lurgan and Portadown Examiner,* the *Newry Reporter* and the *Tyrone Courier*, 1 August 1971–31 December 1971; and McKittrick et al., *Lost Lives.*
35 Award for act of valour, available at www.newrymemoirs.com.
36 Collins, *Killing Rage*, p. 44.
37 *Irish News*, 29 November 2011.
38 Hennessey, *Evolution of the Troubles,* p. 222.
39 Quoted in Bean and Hayes, *Republican Voices*, p. 38.
40 Ó Dochartaigh, *From Civil Rights to Armalites*, p.16.
41 Hennessey, *Evolution of the Troubles*, p. 241.
42 Heath, *The Course of My Life*, p. 429.
43 Kelley, *The Longest War,* p. 161.
44 Notes of a meeting held at Chequers, 9 August 1971, PRONI, CAB/4/1607/19.
45 Moloney, *A Secret History,* p. 102.
46 Rosita Sweetman, '*On Our Knees': Ireland 1972* (London, 1972), pp. 231–32.
47 Notes on security information/Assessment of operations in Northern Ireland, 1 May 1971–1 November 1971, PRONI, HA/32/2/51.
48 For this section, see *Dungannon Observer, Fermanagh Herald, Fermanagh News, Lurgan Mail, Lurgan and Portadown Examiner, Newry Reporter* and *Tyrone Courier*, 1 January 1972–31 December 1972; McKittrick et al., *Lost Lives.*
49 Amnesty International, *Report on Torture* (London, 1973), p. 112.
50 Hennessey, *Evolution of the Troubles*, pp. 224–26.
51 *Lurgan Campaigner,* 7 May 1972.
52 *Lurgan Campaigner,* 7 May 1972.
53 *Lurgan Campaigner,* vol. 2 no.15, no date.
54 *Lurgan Campaigner,* 14 May 1972.
55 Disturbances in Northern Ireland: Press release, 16 June 1972, PRONI, CAB/9/B/312/4.
56 English, *Armed Struggle*, p. 153.
57 Collins, *Killing Rage*, pp. 46–47.
58 Collins, *Killing Rage*, pp. 46–47.
59 Aaron Edwards, *The Northern Ireland Troubles: Operation Banner, 1969–2007* (Oxford, 2011), p. 65.
60 *Hansard*, 10 April 1973, vol. 854, col. 272.
61 *Lurgan Campaigner,* 4 August 1972.
62 *Lurgan Campaigner,* 10 September 1972.
63 *Lurgan Campaigner,* 8 October 1972.
64 Cusack, *UVF*, pp. 104–5.
65 Loose minute from H. S. L. Dalzell-Payne (Colonel General Staff) re: raid on TAVR Centre Lurgan, 23 October 1972, TNA: PRO DEFE/24/832.

66 McKearney, *From Insurrection to Parliament*, p. 114.
67 Meetings of Permanent Heads of Northern Ireland Departments containing economic and social implications of the present security situation in NI: A paper by the permanent secretaries, 4 October 1971, PRONI, CAB 9/J/83/1.
68 Chris Summers, 'Can "tiger kidnappings" be prevented?' (n.d.) *BBC News*, available online at www.news.bbc.co.uk/1/hi/uk/7154374.stm (accessed on 5 April 2012).
69 Memo from Home Secretary, 2 March 1972, TNA: PRO CAB 129/162(26).
70 Smith, *From Violence to Power-Sharing*, p. 187.
71 Tim Wilson, *Frontiers of Violence: Conflict and Identity in Ulster and Upper Silesia, 1918–22* (Oxford, 2010), pp. 213–14.
72 *Irish News*, 12 July 1972.
73 Ryder, *The UDR*, p. 56.
74 Eugene McCabe, *Victims* (Dublin, 1979), p. 69.
75 Frank Wright, *Northern Ireland: A Comparative Analysis* (Dublin, 1987), p. 11.
76 *Hansard*, 20 November 1972, vol. 847, col. 419.
77 *News of the World*, 10 December 1972.
78 News Department Foreign and Commonwealth Office News Department, 20 December 1972, TNA: PRO FCO/87/135.
79 Leonard's name appears on the IRA's roll of honour.
80 Ó Dochartaigh, *From Civil Rights to Armalites*, p. 285.
81 Adams, *Before the Dawn*, p. 142.
82 Smith, *From Violence to Power Sharing*, p. 166.
83 Interview with McKearney.
84 Randall Collins, *Violence: A Micro-Sociological Theory* (Oxford, 2008), p. 24.
85 Troubles-related incidents for the period: Lurgan, 164; Newry, 150; Dungannon, 114; Enniskillen, 114; Total: 542.
86 S. N. Kalyvas, *The Logic of Violence in Civil War* (Cambridge, 2006), p. 5.
87 'Armed Conflict Database', *Department of Peace and Conflict Research*, available online at www.pcr.uu.se/digitalAssets/63/63658UCDPActorDatas etCodebook2011.pdf (accessed 19 November 2011).
88 Faulkner, *Memoirs*, p. 115.

6

Conclusion

The central premise of this book has been that the use of internment without trial in Northern Ireland in the early 1970s has not been given proper academic consideration. This study has sought to demonstrate this point by examining the high politics and intelligence that surrounded the introduction of the measure. The repercussions of the use of internment, which have not been adequately identified previously, have been highlighted. Additionally, the evolution of the conflict outside of Belfast and Derry before and after the introduction of internment has been examined.

Chapter 2 had three main research questions: What were the respective positions of the Stormont and Westminster administrations in relation to internment? What was the true nature of the initial arrest operation? What was the level of intelligence on both republican and loyalist paramilitaries? The positions of Westminster and Stormont administrations regarding the use of internment without trial to combat the activities of paramilitaries were examined. It seems apparent that, in the face of much provocation, both governments had been planning for internment for some time. By August 1971, the Conservative government gave a much greater emphasis on a security solution to the conflict, but they had not abandoned seeking a political settlement. They adopted this stance in the hope of sustaining the Stormont administration and combating the IRA. It is also clear that both governments realised, before the introduction of internment, that if it failed then direct rule would be the only option left open to them. Faulkner never wavered in his defence of internment; however, his claim that the measure was introduced purely for security reasons is certainly questionable. The pressure he was under from hard-line unionists, for tougher security measures, clearly had an impact in his decision. Furthermore, there can be no doubt that both governments actively supported Operation Demetrius.

This study has also challenged the two main narratives regarding Operation Demetrius by arguing that a more nuanced interpretation of events is required. The operation was not an indiscriminate attack on the nationalist community, neither was it based on poor intelligence. It would be closer to the truth to say that it was based on limited intelligence, which was, nevertheless, of a reasonable standard. It seems unlikely that Faulkner would not have appreciated the pitfalls of any such indiscriminate arrest operation. Indeed, as already noted, just prior to the introduction of internment he had attempted to get the SDLP involved in his administration. If his intention was to introduce an indiscriminate arrest operation, there would have been no point in contemplating such a move. It is likely that the initial arrest operation had been undertaken to placate hard-line unionism, to intimidate nationalists and to provide intelligence. However, the augmentation of the arrest lists, coupled with the Army's operational instructions, only served to exacerbate the problem. As a result, many innocent individuals were detained, and some were interned; therefore, the arrest operation was easily portrayed as indiscriminate. This only served to alienate further the nationalist community from the authorities. As a consequence, support for and membership of the IRA increased. Moreover, the effort to improve intelligence was one of the biggest weaknesses of Operation Demetrius. Any such security operation should be intelligence-led and not intelligence-driven. As English outlines, '*intelligence is the most vital element in successful counter-terrorism*' (italics author's own emphasis). He continues, 'In short, intelligence-based strategies are absolutely key to the success of counter-terrorism.'[1] It may have been in the best interests of the authorities to base their arrest operation solely on the intelligence available to them at the time.

It is also obvious that both the Stormont administration and the British government had intelligence on loyalist paramilitaries which was not acted on until February 1973. The main reason loyalists were not detained was because of the fear of a Protestant backlash, a policy that took no real account of how the nationalist community would react. It cannot be said either that the authorities had no intelligence on republican paramilitaries. It seems apparent that they had a reasonable level of intelligence on republicans and that they did have information on the 'main players' within the republican movement. The truth is that the initial arrest operation had been badly planned and badly implemented.

Chapter 3 advanced the contention that internment has not received proper academic attention. It demonstrated that the timing of the introduction of the measure may also have had an effect on the reaction of the nationalist community to its imposition. A number of clear research questions were established, such as how does the use of a flawed repressive measure by a liberal state impact on the targeted community? What were the major effects of internment in the wider context? How did internment change the IRA, especially the PIRA, and what was the main long-term legacy of internment for the conflict? It was outlined how formal and informal state repression combined with an institutional denial of any wrongdoing in the shape of events such as the brutality of the initial arrest operation, the Ballymurphy killings, the use of SD, Bloody Sunday and the Compton and Widgery Reports all contributed to the increase in support received by the IRA. The fact that a number of campaigns for justice are still ongoing more than forty years after some of these events is testament to the impact they must have had at the time.

The increase in republican activity after the introduction of internment also led to a hardening of unionist attitudes and increased paramilitary activities by loyalists. This study has also demonstrated that, after the introduction of internment, the position of the SDLP on negotiations with the authorities changed. It is also true that British policy changed after direct rule, and they gradually phased out internment until it was finally ended in 1975. This was part of their steady change of policy, which gave a political settlement priority over a security solution to the conflict exemplified by their willingness to enter negotiations with the PIRA. However, during this period, they did also find internment still useful both politically and as a security measure.

Undoubtedly, the use of internment resulted in an increase in support for the IRA, which gave the organisation an increased capacity to carry out operations. Counterfactually, this period was also to see a decrease in support for the PIRA, especially after Bloody Friday. However, they still retained enough support and membership to carry on their campaign until the hunger strike of 1981, when they once again received a boost in membership and support. Repression, brutality, mistakes and the denial of those mistakes by the state all contributed to the increase in support for the IRA. Consequently, the PIRA was boosted, despite its own mistakes, by support, particularly from youths eager to confront the authorities; as a result, it retained enough support to carry on its armed campaign, and it was therefore axiomatic that the conflict would not be over quickly.

Chapters 4 and 5 examined the period immediately before and after the introduction of internment in four towns: Lurgan, Newry, Dungannon and Enniskillen. The main thrust of this research has been to see if any changes occurred in the political and security situations in the four provincial towns after the introduction of internment. It is obvious that the situation in these four urban centres and their environs was quite different from Belfast and, to a lesser extent, Derry before August 1971. Conventional political issues dominated the debates at the local level, although other traditional differences between unionists and nationalists did still figure in the political landscape. As 1971 progressed, the prospect of the introduction of internment did begin to become a greater issue. Equally, the security situation in the four provincial towns had not deteriorated to the extent it had in the country's two main cities. Therefore, the deterioration of local politics and regional security was more gradual and possibly less inevitable than has been previously identified.

This was to change after the introduction of internment, and the Troubles were to develop on a new level in the four provincial towns. Both the political and security situation now entered a new phase. As had happened earlier in Belfast and Derry, the tensions that had been simmering were now brought to boiling point. All the forces within the Catholic community united in their opposition to the use of internment in a civil-disobedience campaign. It was at this stage that almost complete opposition to the Stormont administration emerged. The unionist community became equally belligerent in defence of its political position. The dynamics of the violence in these towns also changed dramatically and were now on the same scale as Belfast and Derry. As had happened in Belfast following the Falls Road Curfew and in Derry following the shootings of Cusack and Beattie, many nationalists in the four provincial towns now felt that they had no other choice but to turn to the IRA to combat the actions of the state. It is obvious that rational humans are not prone to, and in fact dislike, violence, but the flawed way in which internment had been introduced led many in the nationalist community to believe that the benefits of resisting the state outweighed the potential costs. It was at this point that the dimensions of the conflict became uniform across the whole of Northern Ireland. Perhaps as MI5 had been contemplating in March 1971, internment might have been applied differently. In areas such as Lurgan, Newry, Dungannon and Enniskillen, where levels of violence remained relatively low before August 1971, a more targeted arrest operation may have proved more successful. Admittedly, opposition to the measure would probably still have been widespread, but perhaps not as many nationalists would have been convinced of the need to join paramilitary organisations. The minute reconstruction of events from local newspapers shows clearly how the momentum of the political and security situation changed dramatically after the introduction of internment. The intimacy of the violence that occurred is also very apparent. In Lurgan, all the violence happened within a five-mile radius; in Newry, within a twenty-mile radius; in Enniskillen, within twenty-five miles; and in Dungannon within forty miles. Local knowledge and intelligence were clearly of great importance to all sides in the conflict. As Kalyvas maintains, 'Intimacy is essential rather than incidental to civil war: it defines "civil war in its most basic sense"'.[2]

Dickson shows how opinions differ on whether the use of internment between 1971 and 1975 increased or reduced levels of violence. He outlines how some commentators believe that internment was gradually proving more successful and actually restricted the levels of violence while others adhere to the perceived wisdom that the use of the measure increased the scale of the violence. He himself suggests that it is possible that the increase in violence may well have taken place even if the measure had not been introduced. Despite this, he does admit that the conflict escalated in 1971 and in the following five years. However, he believes that 'proving cause and effect in this context is well nigh impossible'.[3] Nevertheless what is undeniable is that the catalyst for the evolution of the early Troubles was the use of internment.

Notes

1 Richard English, *Terrorism: How to Respond* (Oxford, 2009), pp. 131–33.
2 Kalyvas, *The Logic of Violence in Civil War*, p. 330.
3 Dickson, *The European Convention on Human Rights and the Conflict in Northern Ireland*, pp. 59–60.

Bibliography

State archives

National Archives of the United Kingdom: Public Record Office
Cabinet Records
Foreign and Commonwealth Office
Home Office
Ministry of Defence
Prime Minister's Office
War Office

Public Record Office Northern Ireland
Cabinet records
Security files
Other archives

Linenhall Library Political Collection
Members' brief on internment, Unionist Research Department, UUC.
Memo on British military assessment of internment in 1971, from the
    Commander Land Forces to the CGS on British military assessment of
    internment.

Government publications and papers

Public Order Act (NI) Amendment 1970.
The Civil Authorities Act Northern Ireland, 1922–43.
House of Commons Parliamentary Debates (*Hansard*).
Northern Ireland House of Commons Parliamentary Debates (*Hansard*).
*Great Britain Committee of Privy Counsellors to Consider Authorised
    Procedures for the Interrogation of Persons Suspected of Terrorism.* Cmnd;
    4901. (London, HMSO, 1972). [Parker Report].
*Northern Ireland Committee to Consider, in Context of Civil Liberties and
    Human Rights, Measures to Deal with Terrorism in Northern Ireland.* Cmnd;
    5847. (London, HMSO, 1975). [Gardiner Report].

Report of the Bloody Sunday Inquiry/The Bloody Sunday Inquiry: Lord Saville of Newdigate (Chairman), William Hooyt, John Toohey. HC. 2010–11; 29. [Saville Report].

Report of the Commission to Consider Legal Procedures to Deal with Terrorist Activities in Northern Ireland. Cmnd. 5186. (Belfast HMSO). [Diplock Report].

Report of the Enquiry into Allegations Against the Security Forces of Physical Brutality in Northern Ireland Arising Out of Events of 9th August 1971. Cmnd; 4823. (London, HMSO, 1971). [Compton Report].

Report of the Tribunal Appointed to Inquire into the Events on Sunday 30th January 1972, Which Led to Loss of Life in Connection with the Procession in Londonderry on That Day. 1971/72 HC 220/ 1971/72 HL 101. (London, HMSO, 1972). [Widgery Report].

Newspapers

Belfast Telegraph
Concerned (Enniskillen Anti-Internment League Newsletter)
Dungannon Observer
Fermanagh Herald
Fermanagh News and West Ulster Observer
Guardian
Irish News
Irish Press
Irish Times
Lurgan Campaigner (Lurgan Anti-Internment League Newsletter)
Lurgan Mail
Lurgan and Portadown Examiner
Newry Reporter
Newsletter
News of the World
Protestant Telegraph
Republican News
Sunday Times
Tyrone Courier

Interviews

Interview with Brian Tipping, prominent member of the Official Republican movement in the 1970s, 16 March 2010.
Interview with Gerard McDonnell, former member of the Provisional Republican movement, 24 March 2010.
Interview with Jim Auld, Former PIRA member, 21 July 2010.
Skype interview with Tommy McKearney, former PIRA member, 10 February 2012.

References

Adams, Gerry, *Before the Dawn: An Autobiography* (Kerry, 2001).

Amnesty International, *Report on Torture* (London, 1973).

Anderson, Brendan, *Joe Cahill: A Life in the IRA* (Dublin, 2002).

Anderson, David, *Histories of the Hanged* (London, 2005).

Andrew, Christopher, *The Defence of the Realm: The Authorised History of MI5* (London, 2009).

Aretxaga, Begona, *Shattering Silence: Women, Nationalism, and Political Subjectivity in Northern Ireland* (Princeton, NJ, 1997).

'Armed Conflict Database' (n.d.), Department of Peace and Conflict Research, available online at www.pcr.uu.se/digitalAssets/63/63658_UCDP_Actor_Dataset_Codebook_2011.pdf (accessed 19 November 2011).

Arthur, Max, *Northern Ireland Soldiers Talking* (London, 1987).

'Award for act of valour amid internment turmoil' (n.d.) *Newry Memoirs*, available online at www.newrymemoirs.com/stories_pages/internmentandvalour1.html (accessed 28 February 2012).

Bardon, Jonathan, *A History of Ulster*, 2nd edn (Belfast, 2001).

Bean, K. and M. Hayes (eds), *Republican Voices* (Monaghan, 2001).

Bew, Paul, *Ireland: The Politics of Enmity, 1789–2006* (Oxford, 2007).

Bew, Paul and Gordon Gillespie, *Northern Ireland: A Chronology of the Troubles, 1968–1999* (Dublin, 1999).

Bishop, Patrick and Eamon Mallie, *The Provisional IRA* (London, 1987).

'Bloody Sunday: PM David Cameron's full statement' (2010), *BBC News*, available online at www.bbc.co.uk/news/10322295 (accessed 21 October 2014).

Bloomfield, Ken, *Stormont in Crisis: A Memoir* (Belfast, 1994).

Bradley, Gerry and Brian Feeney, *Insider: Gerry Bradley's Life in the IRA* (Dublin, 2009).

Brady, Brian J., Denis Faul and Raymond Murray, *Internment, 1971–75* (Dungannon, 1975).

Callaghan, James, *A House Divided: The Dilemma of Northern Ireland* (London, 1973).

'The campaign' (n.d.), *Ballymurphy Massacre*, available online at www.ballymurphymassacre.com/campaign2.htm (accessed 4 May 2011).

Carver, Michael, *Out of Step: The Memoirs of Field Marshal Lord Carver* (London, 1989).

'A chronology of the conflict' (n.d.), *Cain*, available online at www.cain.ulster.ac.uk/othelem/conflict/chron.htm (accessed 8 November 2010).

Collins, Eamon, *Killing Rage* (London, 1997).

Collins, Randall, *Violence: A Micro-Sociological Theory* (Oxford, 2008).

Collins, S. J. D., 'British security policy in Northern Ireland since 1969', PPE FHS thesis, Exeter College, Oxford, 1991.

Conroy, John, *Belfast Diary: War as a Way of Life* (Boston, Mass., 1987).

Craig, Anthony, *Crisis of Confidence: Anglo-Irish Relations in the Early Troubles* (Dublin, 2010).

Craig, Tony, 'Sabotage! The origins, development and impact of the IRA's infra-structural bombing campaigns, 1939–97', *Intelligence and National Security*, 25 (3) (2010): 309–26.

Crossman, R. H. S., *The Diaries of a Cabinet Minister, vol. III* (London, 1977).

Cunningham, Michael, *British Government Policy in Northern Ireland, 1969–2000* (Manchester, 2001).

Cusack, Jim, and Henry McDonald, *UVF: The End Game* (Dublin, 2008).

De Baroid, Ciaran, *Ballymurphy and the Irish War*, 2nd edn (London, 2000).

'Desmond Boal biography' (n.d.) *Cain*, available online at www.cain.ulstr.ac.uk/othelem/people/biography/bpeople.htm (accessed 2 June 2011).

Dickerson, James L., *Inside America's Concentration Camps: Two Centuries of Internment and Torture* (Chicago, Ill., 2010).

Dickson, Brice, *The European Convention on Human Rights and the Conflict in Northern Ireland* (Oxford, 2012).

Dixon, Paul and Eamonn O'Kane, *Northern Ireland since 1969* (Harrow, 2011).

Dixon, Paul, *Northern Ireland: The Politics of War and Peace* (New York, 2001).

——'Contemporary unionism and the tactics of resistance', in Maurice J. Bric and John Coakley (eds), *From Political Violence to Negotiated Settlement: The Winding Path to Peace in Twentieth-Century Ireland* (Dublin, 2004).

Edwards, Aaron, *The Northern Ireland Troubles: Operation Banner, 1969–2007* (Oxford, 2011).

English, Richard, *Armed Struggle: The History of the IRA* (London, 2004).

——*Terrorism: How to Respond* (Oxford, 2009).

Farrell, Michael, *Northern Ireland and the Orange State* (London, 1976).

Faulkner, Brian, *Memoirs of a Statesman* (London, 1977).

Fields, Rona M., *A Society on the Run* (Harmondsworth, 1973).

'Forums' (n.d.) *Military Images*, available online at www.militaryimages.net/forums/archive/index.php/t-1640.html (accessed 5/04/2012.

Guelke, A., 'Political comparisons: from Johannesburg to Jerusalem', in M. Cox, A. Guelke and F. Stephen (eds), *A Farewell to Arms? Beyond the Good Friday Agreement*, 2nd edn (Manchester, 2006).

Hanley, Brian and Scott Millar, *The Lost Revolution: The Story of the Official IRA and the Worker's Party* (Dublin, 2009).

Heath, Edward, *The Course of My Life: My Autobiography* (London, 1998).

Hennessey, Thomas, *The Evolution of the Troubles, 1970–72* (Dublin, 2007).

Hillyard, Paddy, *'Law and Order' in Northern Ireland: Background to the Conflict* (Belfast, 1983).

——'The normalisation of special powers: From Northern Ireland to Britain', in Philip Scraton (ed.), *Law, Order and the Authoritarian State* (Milton Keynes, 1987).

Hogan, Gerard and Clive Walker, *Political Violence and Law in Ireland* (Manchester, 1989).

Jackson, Alvin, *Home Rule* (London, 2004).

Kalyvas, S. N., *The Logic of Violence in Civil War* (Cambridge, 2006).

Kelley, Kevin, *The Longest War: Northern Ireland and the IRA* (Dingle, 1983).

Keenan-Thompson, Tara, *Irish Women and Street Politics, 1956–73* (Dublin, 2010).

Kennedy-Pipe, Caroline, *The Origins of the Present Troubles in Northern Ireland* (London, 1997)

Keogh, Dermot, *Jack Lynch: A Biography* (Dublin, 2008).

Kerr, Michael, *The Destructors: The Story of the Northern Ireland Peace Process* (Dublin, 2011).

Livingstone, Ken, *Livingstone's Labour: A Programme for the Nineties* (London, 1989).

MacAllister, Ian, *The Northern Ireland Social Democratic and Labour Party: Political Opposition* (London, 1977).

MacStíofáin, Seán, *Memoirs of a Revolutionary* (London, 1975).

Mansfield, Michael, *Memoirs of a Radical Lawyer* (London, 2010).

Maudling, Reginald, *Memoirs* (London, 1978).

McCabe, Eugene, *Victims* (Dublin, 1979).

McCann, Eamon, *War and an Irish Town* (London, 1980).

McCleery, Martin J., 'The creation of the "New City" of Craigavon: A case study of politics, planning and modernisation in Northern Ireland in the early 1960s', *Irish Political Studies*, 27 (1) (2012): 89–109.

——'Debunking the myths of Operation Demetrius: The introduction of internment in Northern Ireland in 1971', *Irish Political Studies* 27 (3) (2012b): 411–30.

McElroy, Gerald, *The Catholic Church and the Northern Ireland Crisis* (Dublin, 1983).

McEvoy, Kieran, *Paramilitary Imprisonment in Northern Ireland* (Oxford, 2001).

McGrattan, Cillian, *The Politics of Entrenchment* (London, 2010).

McGuffin, John, *Internment* (Tralee, 1973).

——*The Guineapigs* (Harmondsworth, 1974).

——*The Guineapigs*, 2nd edn (San Francisco, Calif., 1981).

McKearney, Tommy, *The Provisional IRA: From Insurrection to Parliament* (London, 2011).

McKeown, Laurence, *Out of Time: Irish Republican Prisoners, Long Kesh, 1972–2000* (Belfast, 2001).

McKittrick, David and David McVeigh, *Making Sense of the Troubles: The Story of the Conflict in Northern Ireland* (Chicago, Ill., 2002).

McKittrick, David, Seamus Kelters, Brian Feeney, Chris Thornton and David McVea, *Lost Lives: The Stories of the Men, Women and Children Who Died as a Result of the Northern Ireland Troubles*, 2nd edn (Edinburgh, 2007).

McLoughlin, P. J., 'John Hume and the revision of Irish nationalism, 1964–79', Ph.D. thesis, Queen's University Belfast, 2004.

——'"… it's a united Ireland or nothing"? John Hume and the idea of Irish unity, 1964–72', *Irish Political Studies*, 21 (2) (2006): 157–80.

Moloney, Ed, *A Secret History of the IRA* (London, 2002).

——*Voices from the Grave* (London, 2010).

Mulholland, Marc, *Northern Ireland at the Crossroads: Ulster Unionism in the O'Neill Years, 1960–9* (Basingstoke, 2000).

Murray, Gerard and Jonathan Tonge, *Sinn Fein and the SDLP* (Dublin, 2005).

Ó Dochartaigh, Niall, *From Civil Rights to Armalites: Derry and the Birth of the Irish Troubles* (Cork, 1997).

O'Donnell, C., 'Pragmatism versus unity: The Stormont government and the 1966 Easter Commemoration', in M. Daly and M. O'Callaghan (eds), *1916 in 1966: Commemorating the Easter Rising* (Dublin, 2007).

O'Halpin, Eunan, 'A poor thing but our own: The Joint Intelligence Committee in Ireland, 1965–72', *Intelligence and National Security*, 23 (5) (2008): 658–80.

O'Malley, Padraig, *The Uncivil Wars: Ireland Today* (Belfast, 1983).

Patterson, H. and K. Kaufmann, *Unionism and Orangeism in Northern Ireland since 1945: The Decline of the Loyal Family* (Manchester, 2007).

People's Democracy, *Internment '71–H Block '81: The Same Struggle* (Belfast, 1981).

Prince, Simon and Geoffrey Warner, *Belfast and Derry in Revolt* (Dublin, 2011).

Public statement by the Police Ombudsman under Section 62 of the Police (Northern Ireland) Act 1998: Relating to the complaint by relatives and victims of McGurk's Bar, Belfast on 4 December 1971(n.d.), *Police Ombudsman*, available online at www.policeombudsman.org/Publicationsuploads/McGurk's–finalreport.pdf (accessed 7 April 2011).

Quinn, Raymond, *A Rebel Voice: A History of Belfast Republicanism, 1925–72* (Belfast, 1999).

Ramsey, Robert, *Ringside Seats: An Insider's View of the Crisis in Northern Ireland* (Dublin, 2009).

Regan, Patrick M., *Sixteen Million One* (London, 2009).

'Religion and Politics' (2010), *Irish Press Releases*, available online at www.irishpressreleases.ie/2011/04/04/fr.sean-mcmanus.

'Research' (n.d.), *McGurk's Bar*, available online at http://mcgurksbar.com/research (accessed 23 October 2014).

Ruane, Joseph, 'Contemporary republicanism and the strategy of armed struggle', in Maurice J. Bric and John Coakley (eds), *From Political Violence to Negotiated Settlement: The Winding Path to Peace in Twentieth-Century Ireland* (Dublin, 2004).

Ryder, Chris, *The Ulster Defence Regiment* (London, 1991).

Shanahan, Timothy, *The PIRA and the Morality of Terrorism* (Edinburgh, 2009).

Shields, Jeremy (n.d.), 'Northern Ireland's civic festival that was overshadowed by turmoil', *BBC News*, available online at www.bbc.co.uk/news/uk-norhern-ireland-13839746 (accessed 5 April 2012).

Smith, M. L. R., *Fighting for Ireland* (London, 1995).

Smith, M. L. R. and P. R. Neuman, 'Motorman's long journey: Changing the strategic setting in Northern Ireland', *Contemporary British History*, 19 (4) (2005): 413–35.

Smith, William Beattie, *The British State and the Northern Ireland Crisis, 1969–73: From Violence to Power Sharing* (Washington, 2011).

Snedden, S. E. (n.d.), 'Defence research paper', *Ministry of Defence*, available online at www.da.mod.uk/defac/colleges/jscsc/jscsc-publications/drp/Lt.Col .Snedden.pdf (accessed 16 July 2012).

Spjut, R., 'Executive detention in Northern Ireland: The Gardiner report and the Northern Ireland (Emergency Provisions) (Amendment) Act 1975', *The Irish Jurist*, 10 (new series) (1975): 272–99.

——'Internment and detention without trial in Northern Ireland (1971–75)', *Modern Law Review*, 49 (1986): 712–39.

Summers, Chris (n.d.), 'Can "tiger kidnappings" be prevented?', *BBC News*, available online at www.news.bbc.co.uk/1/hi/uk/7154374.stm (accessed 5 April 2012).

Sweetman, Rosita, '*On Our Knees*': *Ireland, 1972* (London, 1972).

Taylor, Peter, *Brits: The War against the IRA* (London, 2002).

'Torture Files', RTÉ Investigations Unit, *RTÉ 2*, 4 June 2014.

Walker, Graham, 'The Ulster Unionist Party and the Bannside by-election of 1970', *Irish Political Studies*, 19 (2004): 59–73.

Warner, Geoffrey, 'The Falls Road Curfew revisited', *Irish Studies Review*, 24 (3) (2006): 325–42.

Wharton, Ken, *Bloody Belfast: An Oral History of the British War against the IRA* (Stroud, 2010).

Wheatley, Michael, *Nationalism and the Irish Party: Provincial Ireland, 1910–16* (Oxford, 2005).

White, Robert W., *Ruairí Ó Brádaigh: The Life and Politics of an Irish Revolutionary* (Bloomington, Ind., 2006).

White, R. W. and White, T. F., 'Repression and the liberal state: The case of Northern Ireland', *Journal of Conflict Resolution*, 39 (2) (1995): 330–52.

Whitelaw, William, *The Whitelaw Memoirs* (London, 1989).

Whyte, John, *Interpreting Northern Ireland* (Oxford, 1990).

Wilson, Tim, *Frontiers of Violence: Conflict and Identity in Ulster and Upper Silesia, 1918–22* (Oxford, 2010).

Wood, Ian S., *Crimes of Loyalty: A History of the UDA* (Edinburgh, 2006).

Wright, Frank, *Northern Ireland: A Comparative Analysis* (Dublin, 1987).

Index

Lightning Source UK Ltd.
Milton Keynes UK
UKHW022107070520
362944UK00004B/275

9 781526 150264